My Dear Governess

New York.

March 21st
1880

My dear Louis

There is a sort of
friendship which makes itself felt less by personal
intercourse, than by those
shocks of intellectual
sympathy which seem to
bridge over silence and
space and make two
minds as one — and it
is for that reason that
in certain moments I
feel as strongly "die ver-
bunden" as if you were
in the room and talking
to me — Can you guess

My Dear Governess

The Letters *of*
Edith Wharton
to Anna Bahlmann

Edited by

IRENE GOLDMAN-PRICE

Yale

UNIVERSITY PRESS

New Haven and London

Frontispiece: Edith Jones to Anna Bahlmann, March 21, 1880.

Yale University Press books may be purchased in quantity for educational, business,
or promotional use. For information, please e-mail sales.press@yale.edu (U.S. office) or
sales@yaleup.co.uk (U.K. office).

Designed by Sonia Shannon.
Set in Adobe Garamond type by Tseng Information Systems, Inc.
Printed in the United States of America.

Library of Congress Cataloging-in-Publication Data
Wharton, Edith, 1862–1937.
[Correspondence. Selections]
My dear governess : the letters of Edith Wharton to Anna Bahlmann /
edited by Irene Goldman-Price.
pages   cm
Includes bibliographical references and index.
ISBN 978-0-300-16989-8
1. Wharton, Edith, 1862–1937—Correspondence. 2. Authors, American—20th century—
Correspondence. 3. Authors, American—19th century—Correspondence. 4. Bahlmann,
Anna Catherine, 1849–1916—Correspondence. I. Bahlmann, Anna Catherine, 1849–1916,
addressee. II. Goldman-Price, Irene C., editor. III. Title.
PS3545.H16Z48 2012
813'.52—dc23
[B]
2011048136

A catalogue record for this book is available from the British Library.

This paper meets the requirements of
ANSI/NISO Z39.48-1992 (Permanence of Paper).

10 9 8 7 6 5 4 3 2 1

To all my teachers
and, as always,
for Alan.

Behold my gifts, the sunset none but I
Remembered, or the book none other read;
The picture that I treasured for your eye
—Edith Wharton, "Gifts"

CONTENTS

ILLUSTRATIONS FOLLOW PAGE 142

PREFACE

The arrival at auction in 2009 of the personal papers of Anna Catherine Bahlmann (1849–1916) caused a stir in the literary community because Anna Bahlmann had been a lifelong companion to the American writer Edith Wharton. First in the capacity of tutor in the German language, then as governess and chaperone, as companion, and finally as personal secretary, Anna Bahlmann served Edith Wharton for more than forty years, and she was in a position to know her as well as any of Wharton's more noted friends did, perhaps better.

Wharton scholars were unaware of the existence of this correspondence. The letters and records have remained in the custody of the Bahlmann family, passing at Anna Bahlmann's death to her niece, Anna Louise Bahlmann Parker, in whose home she died, then on down until they came into the possession of Anna's second great grandniece, a teacher herself, who took great care to preserve all of the documents in the order in which the letters had been kept by Anna Bahlmann.

The most important contents of the archive, acquired by the Beinecke Library at Yale University, which already owned sixty-seven boxes of Edith Wharton's records, are 135 autograph letters from Edith Wharton to Anna Bahlmann, spanning the years 1874 until Bahlmann's death in 1916. Of these letters, some forty were written before 1893, a period for which we have had until now only three letters; many more were written during the 1890s, when we have had little primary documentation of Edith Wharton's life. The early letters offer an unprecedented view of young Edith Jones's emotional and intellectual development as well as her family life; they demonstrate her growing vocation as a woman of letters practicing in virtually every genre, and they suggest a close intellectual and personal relationship with her governess. Later letters include many travel descriptions, conversation about Wharton's reading and her study of paintings and architecture, and news of family and household. There is much to be learned about Edith Wharton that might alter and enhance our understanding of her. Included in this collection are all but one of the letters—a brief note inviting Bahlmann to lunch—and several postcards.

Edith Wharton is not the only object of interest in this archive. Letters and postcards from Anna Bahlmann to her family, letters to her from other former pupils, photographs she cherished, lecture notes from courses she gave, and careful expense records create a detailed portrait of an American governess, someone who spent her life among—if never as a part of—the wealthiest and most socially prominent families in America during the late nineteenth century into the twentieth. In the course of introducing the Wharton letters, I have also sketched Anna Bahlmann's life, her occupations and preoccupations, the many ways she made herself useful to the families she served and yet maintained a life of her own.

My primary goal in publishing this collection of letters was to make available to subsequent scholars an accurate transcription of the Wharton correspondence, along with thorough annotations to the many books, works of art, and people mentioned in the letters. I also wanted to reveal the life of this hitherto obscure governess and companion and to tell the story of her service to Edith Wharton.

Editorial Methods

Edith Wharton preferred the English spelling of most words (including such English archaisms as "shew" for "show" and "Shakespere" for

"Shakespeare"), and I have retained her spellings. She also punctuated her letters by placing periods and commas outside of quotation marks, but I have emended those to conform to present-day American usage. I have retained her use of abbreviations, for example "wh." for "which," "yr." for "your," "affte." for "affectionately," and her use of the ampersand, and I have retained the frequent words and phrases from other languages, translating when necessary. Where I could not make out words, I have placed a question mark in square brackets; I have also provided some context and translation within the text in square brackets. Where significant words were crossed out, I have retained these words with lines through them. I have regularized presentation of letterheads, headings, dates, and complimentary closings.

Particularly in the early letters, when Edith Jones was conscious of using up every bit of space on the paper, she did not separate paragraphs by creating a new line and indenting. Frequently she ended a sentence with a long dash, and in the course of my reading I began to intuit that those dashes came at a place where we might expect a paragraph break. With that in mind, and for the sake of making the long letters easier to read, I have chosen at times to introduce paragraph breaks where these longer dashes occurred. In the very rare occasions of her misspelling words or writing a word twice, I silently emended the errors.

The dating of the letters was perhaps the most significant challenge I faced in editing this volume. Because we have so little documentation of the first thirty-five years of Edith Wharton's life, the letters from this period were the most difficult to date. I relied significantly on three major biographies of Wharton, by R. W. B. Lewis, Shari Benstock, and Hermione Lee, and on the extremely helpful *Edith Wharton Chronology* prepared by Edgar F. Harden. Nevertheless, without much primary documentation of Wharton's first thirty-five years, more research was necessary. Clues I used to assign years included a perpetual calendar that matched dates with days of the week; internal evidence such as exhibitions that Wharton attended, magazine articles to which she referred, the publication dates of her own works that she mentioned in her letters; external events such as an earthquake she experienced in Venice;

and the inscriptions in books she received as gifts and mentioned in the letters. Dates that I assigned appear in square brackets. Where there are no brackets, the dates were written by Edith Wharton herself, or in one case, by Anna Bahlmann. For those letters that were particularly problematic and of which I cannot be reasonably sure, I added a question mark after the year.

All of the transcriptions of the letters are my own, from original documents, with the exception of two letters by Anna Bahlmann, transcribed by her second great grandniece, Laura Shoffner, and marked accordingly.

The choice of how to refer to the correspondents was a difficult one, partly because their relationship began before Edith Jones was Edith Wharton, and partly because of the intimacy of the correspondents, who called each other by first names and nicknames. There is also the problem of sorting out the various people with the last name Wharton. I have solved this dilemma, imperfectly, by referring to Wharton as "Edith" until the moment in 1890 when she ceased signing her letters "Herz," or heart, and began using her initials, E.W. At that point I switch to "Wharton." I refer to Anna Bahlmann most frequently as simply "Bahlmann," but in moments of particular closeness between the women, I revert to first names.

ABBREVIATIONS

BG	Wharton, *A Backward Glance*
DH	Wharton, *The Decoration of Houses*
EWAB	Lewis, *Edith Wharton: A Biography*
EWAZ	Wright, *Edith Wharton A to Z*
F&L	Wharton, *Fast and Loose*
FF	Wharton, *Fighting France*
LEW	Wharton, *Letters of Edith Wharton*
L&I	Wharton, *Life and I*
MF	Wharton, *A Motor Flight through France*
NGC	Benstock, *No Gifts from Chance*
NYHS	New-York Historical Society
NYT	*New York Times*
YCAL Bahlmann	The Anna Catherine Bahlmann Papers relating to Edith Wharton. Yale Collection of American Literature, Beinecke Library, Yale University
YCAL Wharton	Edith Wharton Collection. Yale Collection of American Literature. Beinecke Library, Yale University

My Dear Governess

INTRODUCTION

Anna Catherine Bahlmann was twenty-four years old when young Edith Jones, called Pussy, joined her list of pupils. She was to instruct the child in the German language. Discovering an eager, flexible mind hungering for the beauty of words and images, Bahlmann quickly added German poetry and folk tales to the girl's curriculum. By the end of their first term together, in the spring of 1874, it was clear that teacher and pupil were mutually delighted. Edith Jones was twelve years old, and Anna Bahlmann may have been the first to sense the extent of her talent and potential. She was certainly the only one to preserve Edith's early letters.

Little has been written about Anna Bahlmann and her role in Edith Wharton's development. As a matter of propriety, Bahlmann stayed in the background of Wharton's life, a comfortable position suited both to her reserved personality and to her recognition of her place as part of the Wharton household rather than as friend or social peer. The paucity of commentary about Bahlmann in Wharton scholarship, which probably results from Wharton's failure to make much mention of Bahlmann in her memoir, *A Backward Glance,* reflects the social dynamic of their positions. And yet Anna Bahlmann, an erudite, refined person in her own right, remained in close contact with Edith Wharton, frequently traveling and living with her, serving as teacher, companion, and secretary, for forty-two years. The recently recovered letters from Edith Jones Wharton to Anna Bahlmann provide an occasion for a closer examination of the relationship between these women and its significance in Wharton's life and work.

Thanks to *A Backward Glance* and Wharton's other memoirs (the unfinished *Life and I* and "A Little Girl's New York"), as well as to a number of excellent biographies, we know quite a lot about Edith Wharton's long life of writing, travel, socializing, creating homes and gardens, and wartime relief work. We also know something of her more private life with her family: her distant mother, her unsuitable husband, her unfortunate choice of a lover, and her inner circle of friends, mostly men. Some of what we have surmised about her, however, will warrant reconsideration with the addition of new evidence discovered in these letters, particularly the ones written during her childhood and early years of marriage. The cold, uncaring mother, the disastrous marriage—these may be exaggerations, and the myth of self-making that Edith Wharton created in *A Backward Glance* will bear scrutiny in light of what we learn from her correspondence with Anna Bahlmann.

"How I learned, no one ever knew"

At twelve, Edith Jones had never been to school. Like many of the girls of her social class, she was taught privately at home by a series of governesses. Several of her contemporaries dwell happily—or less so—on their own memories of governesses and teachers and their experiences at school. Edith's friend Margaret (Daisy) Terry Chanler, for instance, who was raised in Rome, seems to have been comprehensively educated, studying Latin, the sciences, and history as well as the usual modern languages, art, and literature. When she got a little older, Daisy had a tutor with whom, over the course of three years, she read the entire *Divine Comedy*. Edith's sister-in-law, Mary (Minnie) Cadwalader Jones, raised in Philadelphia, read daily with her parents and received two governesses a day, one in English, the other in French. After her mother died, she had a tutor whom she described as "useless" to her education, and then she was enrolled in school for a while, but was sent home because the headmistress thought she was too advanced in English and history, yet inadequately prepared in arithmetic and geography (*Lantern Slides*, 99–100). The education of girls at this social level was sporadic and often haphazard; parents moved from place to place and the governesses in these households were hired and dismissed frequently.

Some girls of Edith Jones's social class did attend school, either day schools in New York or finishing schools in Europe. Her neighbors Margaret and Louisa Rutherfurd—at one time pupils of Anna Bahlmann—spent several years at a boarding school on the Isle of Wight, for instance; and her social peer, Emily Price—the future Emily Post— attended the Misses Graham's School in lower Manhattan. Perhaps in 1872, when the Joneses returned with their ten-year-old daughter from a long stay in Europe, they chose not to send her to school because she had been so desperately ill with typhoid that they feared for her health, or perhaps simply because they enjoyed her company at home. If the Misses Graham's School was too strict—certainly Mabel Dodge Luhan found it so—or too Presbyterian, Edith's parents may not have been able to find another school in New York that suited their gifted child. Coincidentally, Edith needed a school during the 1870s, just the years between the closing of one famous school for the daughters of wealthy society members and the opening of two others. For fifty years Madame Heloise Chegaray had maintained a school in New York where many girls of high social standing and some intellectual talent had been educated and "finished," but her school closed in the 1860s. In the early 1880s—a bit too late for Edith Jones—the Brearley School, for a long time a marker of upper-class status, opened its classrooms. One of its early graduates became a successful professional woman: Elsie Clews Parsons, an acquaintance of Edith Wharton's, would graduate from Brearley, then, despite strong parental objections, earn an A.B. from Barnard College and a Ph.D. in sociology from Columbia College and become a noted anthropologist. In the late 1890s another little girl from a famous family— Eleanor Roosevelt—was found by her aunts to be unable to read, and she was tutored by Frederic Roser. When Roser completed his service in the Roosevelt family, he opened a successful school for children of privilege, but by then Edith Jones was already married.

Schooling, however, might not be the proper measure of learning for these girls. In response to my inquiry about educating the women in her family, the granddaughter of Wharton's friend Daisy Chanler said: "Looking back at my own education, I have realized that the point was to be cultivated, rather than educated: French and German, and Italian if possible, and companions of your own class and speech patterns, widely read, much poetry by heart, and an overall familiarity with European history, literature, and art" (Jay). Her mother—Daisy's daughter Laura—had thought of higher education, but the idea of college—even Smith College—for a daughter of Mr. and Mrs. Winthrop Chanler was equally as horrifying to her family as it had been to Elsie Clews's parents, who gave in only upon the strong insistence of their daughter. Rather than training the mind to think, cultivating good manners and one's talents and sensibilities was the objective for a young woman.

According to *A Backward Glance,* written when she was in her early seventies, Edith was not taught much when she was a child: the modern languages, deportment, and proper English usage. Teachers did not figure prominently in her recollections. Her father taught her the alphabet, and somehow she made the leap from letters to words on her own, or so she says: "One day I was found under a table, absorbed in a volume which I did not appear to be using for improvisation. My immobility attracted attention, and when asked what I was doing, I replied: 'Reading.' This was received with incredulity, but on being called upon to read a few lines aloud I appear to have responded to the challenge." (*BG,* 35–36). Wharton goes on to describe how she taught herself literature, art, and history by reading freely in her father's library, with little discipline or direction, except for being forbidden by her mother to read novels. This undirected reading, deprived of rigorous, disciplined study, resulted, she gently complains, in her developing "a restless curiosity which prevented my fixing my thoughts for long" (*BG,* 47–48). In *Life and I* she writes, coyly: "How I learned, no one ever knew" (*L&I,* 1074). Nevertheless, by twelve she already read and spoke French, Italian, and

German, a result of having lived abroad for most of the first ten years of her life with playmates and nursery governesses of various nationalities.

Anna Bahlmann, who taught Edith from the time she was eleven, is the only teacher mentioned in *A Backward Glance*. She appears in the memoir four times, though just once by name: "But for the wisdom of Fräulein Bahlmann, my beloved German teacher, who saw which way my fancy turned, and fed it with all the wealth of German literature, from the Minnesingers to Heine—but for this, and the leave to range in my father's library, my mind would have starved at the age when the mental muscles are most in need of feeding" (*BG,* 48). Later Bahlmann, "my dear governess," is credited with attempting to alleviate her pupil's "perplexity over the structure of English verse" by giving her Quackenbos's *Rhetoric,* a book the aspiring writer needed at the time, but which as an adult she satirized as narrow and confining (*BG,* 74).[1] And finally Bahlmann is noted, without being named, as the companion of what was perhaps Edith's most foundational journey abroad, when she was seventeen and eighteen, an eighteen-month trip during which the two toured historical and architectural sites, haunted galleries and museums, inspected churches, castles, and stately homes, and meandered through the countryside on long, leisurely walks. Beyond that, Anna Bahlmann does not receive any attention in Wharton's writing as a defining factor in her life, certainly not the equivalent quality or frequency of mention as most of the people Wharton called friends, people of her own social class: Henry James, Egerton Winthrop, Walter Berry, and others.

Yet "Tonnie" (from the German *Tante,* or aunt), as Edith called Bahlmann for most of her life, was much more than a German teacher. She read German literature and mythology in the original with her pupil, and also, in translation, Norse, Greek, and Roman mythology and Arthurian legend, as well as English and American literature. She critiqued Edith's early poetry and assigned, and assisted with, her translations of Goethe and other German poets (it is mistaken to suggest, as some biographers do, that Anna Bahlmann forbade the reading of Goethe, who was the governess's favorite author).[2] The two of them shared their reading about history, art, architecture, poetry, and literature in English, French, and Italian as well as in German. Together they improved their intellects, and if the mind of the pupil soon surpassed that of the teacher, the affection between the two remained strong.

Why, then, would Wharton nearly omit Bahlmann from her memoir? Did she simply forget all the ways in which her teacher had been involved in her early encounters with literature, art, and culture? Was she prey to an unconscious, class-dictated blindness, an inability to recognize the necessary sustenance that a governess and secretary could have given to her genius? Perhaps Wharton's conviction about her intellectual and artistic isolation, a feeling that persisted throughout her life, compelled her to deny her closeness to her teacher. All these explanations may apply. Primarily, however, Edith Wharton's self-portrait seems to have been a deliberate attempt to present herself as a literary orphan, a solitary child with a head full of stories and no one from whom to learn or with whom to share her thoughts. The persona she wished the world to see was that of a woman alone in her "secret garden," the source of her literary imagination. It made for a better story.

The reality, however, was that the child Edith Jones was well supported in her quest for knowledge and her efforts as a writer. Early letters to her teacher chronicle a fervent exchange on a range of literary subjects and a steady stream of Edith's poetry being sent for Bahlmann's critique. These letters, along with other evidence, also suggest that, despite her depiction of her family's indifference, her parents and her brother Harry took an active interest in her intellectual and artistic development. In *A Backward Glance,* Wharton credits her mother, Lucretia Jones, with recording some of her poems; in the letters we find that her father involved himself too, frequently copying out her poems to show to others when Edith herself was too lazy to do so. Edith's beloved brother Harry Jones, twelve years older than she, made the contact with his friend, Allen Thorndike Rice, editor and owner of the *North American Review,* that eventually resulted in Edith having five poems published in the *Atlantic Monthly.* And Edith evidently had unlimited credit at booksellers in Newport and in New York City, as she knew the booksellers by name, frequently visited them, and seemed to order from them at her pleasure.

Additionally, one can find evidence of the many books that her friends and family bought for her in what remains of her library at The Mount, her elegant home in Lenox, Massachusetts, which contains well over sixty books inscribed by or to Edith Jones.[3] For Christmas 1874, a month before her thirteenth birthday, Edith's father bought her a nine-volume set of Maria Edgeworth's *Tales and Novels*—so much for Wharton's famous claim that her mother forbade her reading novels—and Harry bought her a dictionary of Latin and Greek quotations. Two years earlier, when she was but eleven, Harry had given her *Goethe's Correspondence with a Child*. Her sister-in-law, Frederic's wife Minnie, gave Edith *The Golden Treasury of the Best Songs and Lyrical Poems in the English Language* in the summer of 1875 and a book of Scottish poetry the following year, and over the years her close friend Emelyn Washburn gave her more than a dozen books of German, Italian, and French poetry as well as the German epic the *Nibelungenlied*. The two girls read many of these works together. Even the Jones's neighbor, Mrs. Rutherfurd, not particularly known for her erudition, must have noticed her little neighbor's passion for stories and literature and offered a gift of the *Dictionary of the Noted Names of Fiction*. A single book inscribed by Anna Bahlmann to Edith Jones remains in the library: the Goethe-Schiller correspondence, given in May of 1879, when Edith was seventeen. Still, we know from their letters that Bahlmann gave Edith many books over the course of their friendship. In fact, despite Edith's inner sense of isolation, virtually everyone surrounding young Edith Jones knew of her love of literature and gave her opportunities to indulge her passion. The romantic notion that Edith Wharton was a solitary autodidact is one of her most successful fictions.

A Backward Glance credits Egerton Winthrop and Walter Berry as mentors to the young wife and aspiring author, paying tribute to them perhaps because they were, aside from being her friends, well-known names in her society and in world affairs. Clearly Winthrop, a longtime friend of the Jones family who was a direct descendant of John Winthrop and a prominent member of the highest New York society, had an important role in her early years of marriage. He traveled with Edith and

Teddy Wharton and showed them how to appreciate Italy. He hosted and visited them, and perhaps most important, he offered Edith some skills for studying and retaining what she read. Similarly Walter Berry, a deeply cultivated lawyer and diplomat whom Edith met the same summer she was courted by Teddy, remained an important part of her life until his death in 1927. His letters to Edith in the late 1890s through the early 1900s demonstrate that he was her constant intellectual companion, reading and critiquing everything she wrote, often writing to her several times a week. These relationships have been broadly explored and deserve to be explored further. But now we know that Edith's earlier, more modest companion, her teacher Anna Bahlmann, also provided important literary and moral support.

"Miss Anna"

Thirteen years older than Edith Jones, Anna Catherine Bahlmann was born in New York City in 1849, the sole daughter among the four surviving children of Alois and Amelia Rasche Bahlmann, immigrants from Westphalia and Bremen who had met and married in New York. Alois was a machinist with a business successful enough to enable his family to retain servants to help with the household chores. But by 1851, when Anna was just two years old and her eldest brother William fifteen, both of their parents had died. Who raised Anna? How did she endure the Civil War? And how did she get an education sufficient to make her a suitable governess to daughters of the first families of New York? These are questions for which we do not yet have sufficient answers.

When Anna was born, her family was living on Cortlandt Street in lower Manhattan just on the edges of Kleindeutschland, which in the 1850s was the largest German-speaking community outside of Berlin and Vienna. Her parents were married at Saint Matthew's German Lutheran

Church on Broome Street, and the children were baptized there. A huge church with several pastors, Saint Matthew's was the social and religious center of the German Lutheran community. The congregation was split during the mid-nineteenth century between those who wished to conduct worship and Sunday school in German and those who preferred English. Anna's family belonged to the latter contingent. Her father, Alois, went into partnership with three men—an Irishman, an American, and another German—making gold and silver pencil cases. When the parents died, Amelia of rheumatism in 1850 and Alois of an undisclosed cause the following year, the family was broken up. The two middle boys, Alois and Charles, were sent to a German-American boarding school, while William, living with a guardian, was prepared by tutors for college. William was the brother with whom Anna would become close later in her life. He attended the University of the City of New York (now New York University), taught for a few years in Virginia, then in 1858 went abroad to study at the Academy of Münster and then the University of Munich. Returning to America, he fought for the Confederacy and married Lydia Abbot of West Virginia. They settled in Missouri, and it is through his descendants that we have the records of Anna's life and her correspondence with Edith Wharton (W. F. Bahlmann; Conant, 866–67).

According to William's autobiography, written in old age, little Anna was sent to her mother's sister, Charlotte Paul, in New Bedford, Massachusetts, when her parents died. Yet no census records connect Anna with her Aunt Charlotte, nor does she ever mention her aunt in subsequent letters, so it may be that they were together for only a brief time. The 1860 census records a ten-year-old Anna Bahlmann as one of nine students, aged eight through fifteen, residing in North Bergen, New Jersey, with four adults, including two German men in their fifties described as teachers, one a doctor of philosophy. It is likely that this was our Anna Bahlmann. The German community established schools as promptly as they established churches, and there were many small boarding schools in New York and New Jersey at the time. This one was a short ferry ride from lower Manhattan, where at least one of Anna's brothers, Alois, was working in the cigar industry, and where her older brother William briefly practiced law.

Who, if anyone, loved the little girl, acknowledged her talents, and nurtured them? This we don't know. Anna Bahlmann was fortunate to possess intelligence and diligence—without them she might have gone the way of many unmarried girls in Kleindeutschland and spent her life as a domestic servant rather than a governess, in which case she would have been housed, clothed, and fed, and perhaps not much more. Most unmarried women in the German community were seamstresses or laundresses. Often these jobs failed to pay the girls' expenses, and if no marriage materialized and no family member intervened, many girls spiraled downward into prostitution (Nadel, 25–26). Anna Bahlmann was indeed both hardworking and lucky.

She did not see much of her eldest brother William, who was living in Missouri by the time Anna came of age, but they kept up a correspondence. An 1874 letter from Anna to her sister-in-law, Lydia Abbot Bahlmann, suggests that while they were in contact by mail, perhaps she had not yet met her nephew Alois, born in 1866, or her niece Anna Louise, born in 1870. Another letter dated July 1875 tells us that she had recently seen William, perhaps for the first time in many years: "I wish I could tell you how much I enjoyed making William's acquaintance, for it really amounted to that, as I cannot say I knew him before" (25 July 1875). William, whom Anna always addressed as either "Captain" or "Professor," went on to become a distinguished educator in Missouri, and he and his family kept in close touch with Anna all of her life.

Fortunately, wherever Bahlmann spent her childhood, she was being well educated, so that by 1871 she was employed by the family of Lewis Morris Rutherfurd, lawyer, astronomer, and head of one of the Old New York families which traced its ancestors back to Signers of the Declaration of Independence. The Rutherfurds had five surviving children (two daughters had died in infancy): the eldest, whose name had been legally reversed in order to inherit from the wealthy and influential Peter G. Stuyvesant (direct descendant of Governor Peter Stuyvesant), was Rutherfurd Stuyvesant, born in 1842 and thus seven years older than

My Dear Governess

Anna Bahlmann. The next living child was Margaret (Daisy), born in 1854, then Louisa (Poodle), Lewis, and finally Winthrop, born in 1862, the same year as Edith Jones. Rutherfurd Stuyvesant was married in 1863 to Mary Pierrepont, who was evidently quite fond of Anna Bahlmann, as several letters between them attest. In exactly what capacity Anna Bahlmann first came to work for the Rutherfurds is unclear.

It is possible that she began as a finishing governess to the two girls, Margaret and Louisa, who in 1871 would have been fifteen and seventeen. And she was governess to the two younger boys, Lewis and Winthrop, preparing them for boarding school. When the family was away from home, Bahlmann served as household manager and personal secretary to Mrs. Rutherfurd. An eighteen-page letter written from Paris by Mrs. Rutherfurd to Bahlmann at the Rutherfurd home in New York City, dated July 1873, instructs Bahlmann in great detail about household arrangements: "It is absolutely necessary for me to have the exact shade of the dining room plush. . . . Could you not take the sofa cushion to Stewarts [a fashionable department store] and get the color on something and send it to me *immediately.*" "Mr. R. dictates the following questions and begs an answer as soon as possible. 1. What is the height between floor & ceiling in each of the three stories? 2. What is the depth of cornice and height of [?] in parlors, halls, in *each* story and dining room?" And so on. Mrs. Rutherfurd charges Bahlmann to look out for a good cook and to engage a laundress who will also sew; she conveys orders for a groom and several servants; and she dictates which rooms are to be aired and dusted and which should have their windows washed regularly. Care of the bedding, flooring, and carpets, even proper care of the lawn is detailed minutely, and everything, she stresses, must be finished exactly as she wishes "*in every respect.*" It is no wonder that when the family returned from a European trip in October 1874, Bahlmann could write to her sister-in-law:

> The R. family arrived on Friday, & I leave you to imagine
> the hubbub we are all in. What with all the trunks, etc. the
> house looks more than ever like a hotel. Well, they are all well

& safe & more one cannot ask. I have been up to my ears in work which accounts for my letters being few & far between.

When the young people were in the house, Bahlmann taught them the German language and literature and continued tutoring the boys in grammar and supervising their reading. She also served as companion to the elderly Mrs. Peter G. Stuyvesant—Mrs. Rutherfurd's aunt—and was in attendance when Mrs. Stuyvesant died. Mary Pierrepont Stuyvesant wrote to her mother-in-law: "We all ought to be more than thankful that she [Mrs. Stuyvesant] had such a person as Anna to be with her. She . . . cared for her all winter & waited on her as she never had allowed before" (to Margaret S. C. Rutherfurd, 30 August 1873). Mary's husband, Rutherfurd Stuyvesant, wrote similarly to his mother: "Miss Anna is devoted and thoughtful and I don't know what I should do without her" (19, 29 August 1873). Bahlmann was twenty-four years old.

Anna Bahlmann was a diminutive person of five feet, one inch, with, by her own description, a high forehead, gray eyes, an ordinary nose and mouth, and a round chin. Only one known photograph of her as a young woman exists. Taken when she was living in Havana as governess to a girl called Lita, possibly de las Bañas, it shows Bahlmann *en famille,* winsomely attractive with wisps of curls escaping from her pinned-up hair. She was by then thirty, her aspect distinctly sad. One wonders what she had been hoping for, with what dreams and desires had she, at age twenty-eight, sent off a page of her handwriting to be analyzed, to have her character delineated by a reader called Mirage? Or, later, to visit a reader of palms? Had a young Anna gone to dances— there were many in the German settlements in New York and New Jersey—dreaming of meeting her future in the form of a serious young man, perhaps a scholar? Did she continue to wish for such an outcome as she moved from one wealthy family to another? It was not unheard of for a young man, even an older widower, to fall in love with his sister's or daughter's governess; he might even marry her. But Anna Bahlmann never married.

Living sometimes in Mrs. Kirchner's boarding house in lower

Manhattan from November to June, sometimes with the families by whom she was employed, renting rooms in the watering holes where her pupils and their families summered, Bahlmann had no home of her own except for a few years in the 1890s, when she took a small apartment on East 95th Street in Manhattan, just outside of the German neighborhood of Yorkville. Her belongings were frequently in storage. When she died in Missouri, her possessions beyond her wardrobe consisted of a trunk with Mrs. Wharton in Paris and two boxes of books stored at the home of Wharton's sister-in-law Minnie Jones, for whom she had been a companion, secretary, and governess to her daughter Beatrix. Bahlmann's estate amounted to eight hundred dollars, enough to pay her executors and leave her family a few months' salary.

After Edith Jones's marriage to Edward (Teddy) Robbins Wharton in 1885, Bahlmann probably could have lived permanently in the employ of the family in one capacity or another. The Jones family tended to share servants; for example, when Edith's mother left New York City, Edith's mother-in-law inherited her cook. When Edith's sister-in-law Nannie Wharton needed a companion while traveling in Europe, Anna Bahlmann filled the job, just as she had served as Lucretia's companion earlier. In this way the family always had familiar people about, and the servants had a measure of job security. Anna Bahlmann would have been considered a "treasure" worth retaining.

But Bahlmann relished teaching, and she had her pride. Rather than allow herself to be supported solely by Edith and her family, she continually looked for work, and because she was good at her job, she had great success. Among her pupils were Van Rensselaers, Jays, Robinsons, Frelinghuysens, Stokeses, and other children of Old New York families, as well as a few Vanderbilt grandchildren, a reflection of the successful infiltration by newer-monied families into the highest New York society. During winters in New York, Bahlmann would travel between well-appointed schoolrooms and personal libraries to read German with her students, or English poetry, or to engage them with stories from the *Nibelungenlied,* the foundational German mythology, or from Greek and Roman mythology. Perhaps if her pupils were left in the care of servants, as were Pauline and Anna Robinson when their parents traveled to Europe and their brothers were at boarding school, Miss Bahlmann would join the children and their nursery governess for dinner, regaling them with stories of faraway places. Anna Bahlmann loved children—one can see that from her letters and cards to her nieces and nephews. "Dear little Charlie," she wrote to one great nephew, "what fun to ride the donkey! When I come to see you I'll sing you a song about the donkey and the cuckoo—oo—oo" (to Charles Parker, Jr., undated).

Bahlmann was both strict and tender with her pupils. On a report card Pauline Robinson's little sister Anna brought home in 1897, Anna Bahlmann wrote, in addition to the weekly record of the girl's progress in several subjects: "Anna lost her story because she was so untidy about her things" (report card, 5 February 1897). When the Robinson boys proudly sent Miss Bahlmann their own report from the Cutler School (from which Theodore Roosevelt had been the first of many prominent graduates), which indicated that both of them had received honors, she wrote to them:

> I want to express to both of you my very real pleasure in the result of your winter's work. I know how hard & earnest that has been, & I know your best reward is the opportunity now given you of continuing your work. . . . I am delighted at the prospect opening before you, & I am sure your parents must be proud of such a beginning. . . . I thank you both for recognizing my claim to an interest in your development & welfare. (21 August 1894)

She prepared young boys for Saint Paul's or Andover or other private preparatory schools, she taught German language and literature to slightly older girls, and she also served as a finishing governess, shepherding girls through the awkward adolescent years, preparing them to come out into polite society, grammar and languages intact, secure in the knowledge of how to behave and converse at a dinner party and how to write a graceful letter for any occasion. Her favorite task would have been sharing with them the ability to speak intelligently about paintings, sculpture, architecture, and music, all the things they might encounter in a privileged life of travel and elite acquaintance. Long after she began secretarial work for Edith Wharton, when she was well into her fifties, Anna Bahlmann continued to teach.

As much as Bahlmann enjoyed her work, she also needed the income. Her well-kept records indicate that remaining decently housed and dressed, traveling, and giving gifts to her pupils all required careful attention to income and expenditure. We know that Edith Wharton subsidized Bahlmann's rent quietly in several instances, particularly when Bahlmann spent summers in Lenox and served as her secretary. She also purchased Bahlmann's firewood each winter in New York, and when Bahlmann traveled in Europe on vacation, the Whartons helped pay for nicer hotel rooms and extra taxis and, when Bahlmann allowed it, supplemented her passage as well, to enable Bahlmann to get a better accommodation. Wharton made gifts of clothing, sometimes her own little-used clothes for Bahlmann to have made over. Wharton's letters demonstrate her cleverness and discretion in finding ways to help Bahlmann financially without embarrassing her.

Bahlmann's clothing ledger is a fascinating account of a woman's attempt to dress modestly, frugally. Beginning in 1898, it details every purchase through 1909 (when she moved to Paris with the Whartons), including corset covers, boots, slippers, jackets, summer and winter outfits, trimmings, underclothing, hats, ribbons, gloves, and lace. In 1898 her clothing expense totaled $290.24; of this, the three largest expenses were in dresses and other ready-made clothing, $78.23; underclothing, $51.25; and "making," dressmaker's fees, of $58.60. We don't know what her salary from Wharton was at that time, nor do we know what she was able to charge for lessons, or how many pupils she had. But fifteen years later Wharton paid Bahlmann $150 per month, thus her yearly income as secretary would have been $1,800; clothing could have cost up to a quarter of that amount. Later, when they were living in France, Wharton paid Bahlmann a salary of 125 French francs—not quite $25 at the prevailing rate of conversion, reflecting the economic disparity between New York and Paris, where the cost of living was much lower.[4]

This was the only income Bahlmann received, having left her other employers back in New York. Her expense records indicate that, despite not having to pay for rent or food, she just managed month to month on this income. In December 1913, for instance, her monthly income of 125 francs did not come close to covering her expenses of 340.55 francs, and she was forced to draw on her modest savings in an American bank account to make up the difference. Back in the United States in 1914, her salary from Wharton increased again to $150 per month. Buying gifts for friends and former pupils, making the charitable donations which was her habit whenever she saw need, even just the cost of transport around the city, all required careful managing. Several times she needed to borrow small sums from Edith or her brother William to tide her over at the end of the month.

As widely different as their social and financial status was, Anna and Edith were both autodidacts who shared a love of reading and learning. Both relished the effort of understanding historical context and articulating the defining characteristics of a style of art, a period of history, or, indeed, a civilization. Bahlmann's careful preparations for a series of lectures on architecture that she gave in Lenox one summer in the early 1900s indicate that she drew her lecture materials from several sources and fit them into a framework that would allow her to compare architecture from all over Europe and America. The lectures were well organized and carefully illustrated with postcards she had collected during her years of European travel, as well as pictures from a variety of books, each meticulously noted in the lecture script.

And, like her employer, Bahlmann had a knack for telling stories. A series of letters written by a young Pauline Robinson to her parents in 1895 and 1896 includes many references to Miss Bahlmann, ostensibly Pauline's German teacher, but really so much more. "Miss Bahlmann came to dinner and told many amusing stories about the Queen and the etiquette of the English Court" (15 May 1895). "Yesterday night Miss Bahlmann came to dinner. . . . We talked about Hypnotism the whole evening" (28 April 1896). Later that week Pauline reported attending, at Miss Bahlmann's recommendation, Ellen Terry's performance in *Mac-*

beth, and a few weeks later she reports: "Miss Bahlmann came to dinner and told just fine ghost stories" (19 May 1896). To her brother Beverley, a former pupil of Bahlmann's then away at boarding school, she wrote that she had just finished studying Schiller's *Die Jungfrau von Orleans* with Miss Bahlmann. "Miss Bahlmann is so cultivated and well read that every evening she dines here I always learn something new" (May 1896). A highlight of one week was an electrical exhibition to which Bahlmann took Pauline. There they learned about X-ray technology, cooking with electricity, and the new gramophone, which Pauline promptly recommended that her mother buy, as it was far superior to the phonograph. She reported seeing an X-ray photograph of a foot with a bullet in it and another of a woman whose bones could be seen through the sleeves of her dress. Bahlmann took pleasure in providing a variety of experiences for this lonely child.

At about the same time, Edith Wharton's mother, Lucretia Jones, who corresponded with the fourteen-year-old Pauline, wrote to the child from her home outside Paris, "I have often wished that you and Miss Bahlmann could have been here with me this summer. I know how much you would have enjoyed it—and she is so fond of you and of giving you pleasure in your life, and teaching you to see charm and beauty in all country life and things, that her softening and gentle influence is sure to do you good." Lucretia adds her gratitude for the letters that Miss Bahlmann writes to her: "Her letters always do me good, for she remembers all that she knows most interests me and tells me all the pleasant things that are happening about her" (13 January 1897).[5] Margaret Rutherfurd, mother of the Rutherfurd children, had written almost exactly the same words about Bahlmann's letters a quarter century earlier.

It is a pity that so few of Anna Bahlmann's letters remain. Not only did Edith Wharton not save her letters, but neither did any of the Rutherfurd children or the Robinson children or their parents, with the exception of Bahlmann's letter of congratulation to the Robinson boys on their schoolwork and, later, a condolence letter on the death of Herman Robinson. By contrast, both families saved hundreds of family letters. Even Pauline Robinson, who remained close to Anna Bahlmann all of her teacher's life, retained only the last two letters sent to her before Bahlmann's death. There are no pictures of Anna Bahlmann in either the Robinson family archives or in any of Edith Wharton's. Dear as she might have been to her pupils and their families, Bahlmann was not a family member.

Nevertheless, her employers did appreciate and reward her service. At some point, perhaps on the occasion of Bahlmann's sixtieth birthday, her pupils and their mothers got together and gave her a gift totaling $1,175. Among the donors were Mrs. Charles B. Alexander (the former Hattie Crocker), daughter of a railway magnate and wife of a prominent lawyer and businessman; Mrs. Robert Winthrop, wife and daughter of immensely wealthy bankers, and Mrs. Winthrop's daughter, Mrs. Hamilton Kean.[6] The other donors, equally prominent, included Emily Vanderbilt (Mrs. W. D.) Sloane and her sister, Florence Vanderbilt (Mrs. Hamilton McKeon) Twombly, as well as Edith Wharton and her sister-in-law and niece, Minnie Cadwalader Jones and Beatrix Jones. Miss Lucy Frelinghuysen (daughter of Secretary of State Frederick Frelinghuysen), Louise Van Rensselaer Baylies (descendant of the original patroon of upstate New York and wife of a Wall Street attorney), and Mrs. Beverley Robinson and Mrs. William Jay, both from equally prominent New York families, were also donors.

Bahlmann was not without friends of her own social class. Augustus and Louise Schultz were lifelong friends. Bahlmann must have known them in New York when Herr Schultz was inventing an important process for tanning leather, which brought him some fame and a comfortable income. The Schultzes had a second home in Manassas, Virginia, where Bahlmann was a frequent guest, and when Louise Schultz was widowed and dying, Bahlmann left Paris and traveled to see her friend through her final illness. Another Virginia family that she visited was the Tuckers, whose son Douglas was nominated Bahlmann's residual legatee in the event that her family did not survive her. Other friends included professional women like herself: Ella Denison, draughtswoman for the architectural firm of Hoppin & Koen (which designed the Whartons' Lenox, Massachusetts, home, The Mount), and Frances (Fanny) Thayer and Anna Whelan, both of whom were typists for Edith Wharton. Bahlmann traveled with these women and attended them when they were in need. She also made friends as an active member of the Women's Association of German Teachers, for which she served on the Relief Committee.

Only one sustained description of Anna Bahlmann remains, but it is a good one by Percy Lubbock, author of *Portrait of Edith Wharton*. By the time he observed her Bahlmann was in her fifties and living in Paris with Edith. Lubbock and Wharton, he writes,

> were alone when we talked about books; but there was another inmate in the house, who had slipped noiselessly out of the room when we fell to our discussion. This was Anna Bahlmann, her good governess of old days, now installed in the Rue de Varenne as secretary, treasurer, companion—I don't know what, but the title was of no consequence. She was American, of German parentage, and she was very small and unobtrusive, but quite a little personage too, with a droll little humour behind her spectacles, a wild little bravery beneath her gentility—a trifle astray in her surroundings, yet mistress of them in her degree. Only one anxiety confessedly tormented her: what could Edith give her to do, couldn't she give her more to do, to justify her position? Edith was full of understanding of such scruples. It mattered not at all to her what Anna did or didn't do, so that Anna was happy and provided for in her years; but she quite knew that it mattered much to Anna, and she was ingenious and imaginative in protecting her feelings. One good way would be to place her in control of the household expenditure; but this was soon defeated by Anna herself. "When I see, my dear," said she desperately, "what your expenses are, and the many calls on you, it is quite impossible for me to add to them by taking a salary." It mattered little to Edith, I dare say, what Anna took

or didn't take; but things must be adjusted to suit her compunction, so I suppose she was relieved of the eye-opening, breath-taking accounts. Perhaps she found her peace in typing the morning chapters. It was altogether a charming and amusing relation: Edith protective, indulgent, considerate, the ardent young pupil become the bountiful guardian-angel; and Anna the governess, proud of the transfiguration of her young charge, tenderly attached and devoted, but preserving her upright little independence in the midst of all this exotic glory. She slipped in and out of the company as she chose, with perfect discretion, for a few years, till she slipped out of the world. (Lubbock, 82–83)

Two Lives in Letters

In Edith Wharton's world, discretion and privacy were established values. The subjects Wharton chose not to address in her letters were often the ones uppermost in her mind. This reticence applied particularly, curiously, to her writing, which she occasionally even downplayed, calling it "littery" work, as if it belonged in the dustbin rather than on the short list for a Pulitzer Prize. In *A Backward Glance,* she wrote of the world of her imagination as her "secret garden," and secret she kept it, sharing it with only a select few of her closest friends. Yet Wharton lived with—indeed, considered herself possessed by—a soaring imagination that had a life of its own. "Wild wingèd thing," she called it, "mirthfullest mate of all my mortal games," "sister, my comrade" ("La Folle du Logis"). Most mornings Wharton would remain in bed with a light breakfast and a small dog or two beside her, writing, on blue stationery, long stories and short about the characters who inhabited her mind. Anna Bahlmann collected these pages—or was handed them by Wharton's maid—and saw to it that they became manuscripts. Only glimpses of this work appear in Wharton's letters.

Neither does Wharton speak of her lover, Morton Fullerton, in any but the blandest of references, nor of family trauma, disappointments, or disillusionment. One can see her reaching for interesting, unique experiences with which to entertain Bahlmann, and good news of the family to share. Nevertheless, one can read the darker things in tiny outbursts of frustration, short asides, and in the silences, as first Lucretia, then Teddy, then Harry disappear from her correspondence.

As Wharton knew, lives contain many stories, and reading letters written over a long period reveals these stories unfolding with an immediacy lost to retrospective narrations like memoir and biography. Edith Wharton's letters tell several stories along with the sympathy and mutual regard of the two women. Here is hinted the story of a relatively close family, the Joneses, which collapses under the strain of sexual desire and greed. Likewise the marriage of Edith Jones to Edward Wharton, reasonably happy at first, cannot withstand the emotional corrosion that inevitably ensues when one partner is mentally ill and loses the ability to control himself.

Happily, the clearest and strongest story that emerges from these letters is the ripening of a young girl's powers of observation and expression, the maturation of her talent and ambition, and the strengthening of her will. Her letters reveal Edith Wharton snatching at every bit of learning and experience she can reach, embracing the life she was determined to live. By the time she reached fifty-four, when the correspondence ended, Wharton was at the height of her literary and executive powers, a woman of prodigious achievement and admirable character.

Inherent in Wharton's individual history we can read the story of Edith and Anna, two women of different social classes who lived in relation to each other, tied in a bond of loyalty and affinity that outlasted most of Edith Wharton's own family ties. Anna Bahlmann was ever loyal to Edith Wharton, traveling to her side whenever she was needed, several times crossing the Atlantic to do so. Edith, in turn, was a kind employer and benefactor to Anna. When illness struck, in the form of severe headaches or painful rheumatism, Edith sent Anna for cures and once even accompanied her so that Anna could take the baths at La Motte les Baines, a thermal spring in the southeast of France, near Grenoble. She saw to it that Anna had vacations and enough money to enjoy them; that she was nicely clothed, and that when Anna worried over a friend in trouble, she had some spare money to give. They were not, in Edith's definition of the word, "friends," because they were not on the same social plane. Anna was a part of her household, a member of what Edith referred to as "the gang," which included housekeeper Catherine Gross, butler Alfred White, the other servants, and the dogs. And as Edith's circle of acquaintance and opportunities continued to expand, offering her companions such as the novelist Henry James, the art historian Bernard Berenson, and numerous English and European writers and members of the aristocracy, Anna naturally inhabited a smaller part of her imaginative and emotional life.

Yet Anna clearly offered Edith critical support throughout their years together. When Edith was a child, hungry for words and images and ideas, Anna fed her. As the child grew older and felt more strongly the expectations of society, the teacher remained her touchstone for the life of the mind and the beauty of words, pictures, and the natural world. Anna was a rare visitor in Edith's secret garden of the imagination who watered the fruits and flowers until others with more talent and influence — editors, friends, writers — could assist with the harvest. Perhaps a few of Anna's experiences — living in other people's houses, being secretary to frazzled and disorganized women, negotiating public transportation to visit poor friends in distant suburbs, knowing the inside tales of fathers who mistreated their daughters — perhaps some of these experiences made it into what Mrs. Wharton called her *données,* the germs of stories that turned into tales and novels.

Certainly Anna Bahlmann's work enabled Edith Wharton to do her own. By answering mail, typing manuscripts, helping to run the elaborate households and the business of being a famous author, she freed Edith to write and to live her very social life. By looking after first the widowed Lucretia Jones and then the mentally unstable Teddy

My Dear Governess

Wharton—not to mention all the times she took care of the Wharton dogs—Anna took much of the weight of family obligations from Edith, who could rest secure in the knowledge that her loved ones were being carefully tended. Anna's work during the war may not have come up to Edith's high standards, but her dedication and long hours, her handwork and fund-raising, made her a worthy partner up to the end.

For Anna, life with Edith Wharton was far more than a job, albeit a fulfilling job that provided her with physical comforts, travel, and the chance to touch greatness. Anna Bahlmann clearly cherished her relationship with Edith Wharton from their earliest acquaintance, preserving her childhood letters, keeping detailed scrapbooks of Edith's every achievement, working beyond her own capacity to support Edith's projects. If Edith's investment in Anna was not as deep as Anna's in her, we must not fail to understand that Anna's in Edith was complete. As she once told Edith's friend Mary Berenson: "For years the only object I have had in life has been to help Edith and spare her trouble and fatigue."[7] This she did, always.

NOTES

1. George Payn Quackenbos (1826–81) wrote numerous educational texts on history, arithmetic, grammar, rhetoric, and natural philosophy. His *Advanced Course of Composition and Rhetoric* was probably the one to which Anna referred her pupil.

2. The misconception that Anna Bahlmann forbade Edith's reading Goethe arises from a letter (3 September 1938) written in old age by Edith's childhood friend Emelyn Washburn to Elisina Tyler.

3. At Wharton's death, her library of approximately four thousand books was divided in two, with books on art, archaeology, and history going in trust to William Tyler, son of her friends Royall and Elisina Tyler, and the literary books being given in trust to Colin Clark, the young son of her friend Sir Kenneth Clark. The books belonging to William Tyler, which were stored in London, were destroyed by German bombs in 1940. The other portion of the library survived, not completely intact, and was recently purchased by the Edith Wharton Restoration at The Mount. An excellent description and catalogue of these books has been made by George Ramsden, who at one time owned them.

4. The question of Bahlmann's salary is complicated by frequent fluctuations in the French franc and by adjustments made depending on her living arrangements. Her salary of $150 per month in 1914 reflected the fact that she lived in a New York hotel, and so had to pay for lodging and board, whereas in Paris she lived with Wharton and these expenses were covered.

5. Of interest to Wharton scholars, this letter indicates that Lucretia, rather than moving to Paris of her own volition, seems to believe—or to want others to believe—that she was settled there by the decision of her family, presumably her sons.

6. Anna's teaching may have had far-reaching effects; among the descendants of her pupils are several legislators, a governor of Puerto Rico, several ambassadors, and other prominent people, including former governor of New Jersey and chairman of the 9/11 Commission Thomas Kean, grandson of Katherine Taylor Winthrop Kean.

7. Mary Berenson to Bernard Berenson 23 July 1915.

I

"Herz" and "Tonnie"

MAY 1874 TO MARCH 1885

When Anna Bahlmann first met her in 1873, Edith, called "Pussy" Jones, was a well-mannered, much-petted child of twelve, indulged the more by her parents for being the baby of the family, the only girl, and for having recently survived a near-fatal attack of typhoid fever. Not conventionally pretty, she had a strong, somewhat plain face with melting brown eyes and a torrent of auburn hair. She was possessed of a natural courtesy and an enchanting facility with words. In her imagination, the grasses in the wild spoke to her, and she understood, she later wrote, what animals said to one another. This prodigious imagination had compelled her, before she could read, to pace the floor, upside-down book in hand, passionately making up stories. Pussy Jones was already on her way to becoming one of America's most gifted and respected women of letters, Edith Wharton.

Edith's family consisted of her parents, Lucretia Rhinelander Jones (1825–1901) and George Frederic Jones (1821–82), and two older brothers. Harry (Henry Stevens) Jones (1852–1922) was unmarried and frequently traveled and lived with the family; Edith later described him as "the dearest of brothers to all my youth" (to Bernard Berenson, 23 Aug 1922, *LEW*, 453). Her oldest brother Freddy (Frederic Rhinelander) Jones (1846–1918) was married to Minnie (Mary) Cadwalader Rawle

Jones (1850–1935), and they had a young daughter, Beatrix, called Trix (1872–1959).

Edith was tutored in German by Anna Bahlmann in the fall and winter of 1873–74. Her letters to her teacher began when they parted in May 1874: the Jones family going to Newport, Rhode Island, and Anna remaining in New York for a short time before traveling to Newport herself to prepare Edgerston, the summer home of her employers, the Rutherfurds, for the family's arrival. Anna's travel was not as convenient as that of her employers, who would have had an elegant stateroom in which they could sleep until their carriage met them at the Newport dock. Anna's description to her sister-in law of her own trip displays a nice humor and self-irony: "I managed to put myself on board the New-port boat before the gang-plank was drawn up & arrived here at 3 o'clock last Sunday morning. You see what an advantage a plain face is—a pretty young woman could never have arrived at that hour unmolested, taken a cab & driven along the solitary roads by moonlight. It *might* have been romantic but I found it only chilly, & was not sorry to stretch & rest my weary limbs in a comfortable bed" (to Lydia Abbot Bahlmann, 25 July 1875).

Edgerston was next door to Pen craig, the Jones home, and Edith played with the two Rutherfurd boys, Lewis and Winthrop, the latter of whom was just Edith's age.[1] She enjoyed Sunday walks led by their father, the amateur astronomer Lewis Morris Rutherfurd (1816–92). She looked up to the Rutherfurd daughters, Margaret (Daisy) and Louisa (Poodle), who served as inspiration to her both in becoming a young lady herself and in her writing, as she said many years later: "The young gods and goddesses I used to watch strolling across the Edgerston lawn were the prototypes of my first novels" (*BG,* 47).

These earliest letters, written over several summers, chronicle Edith's family life and her activities. Along with tennis and archery, Edith read avidly and widely, critiqued what she read, and wrote poetry with a dedication she would retain for the rest of her writing career. Anna was her touchstone for all literary endeavor, offering a cultivated mind against which Edith could test her literary judgments. We can observe

Edith's command of the language broaden even as her tone takes on a growing sense of privilege and expectancy of having her desires gratified. We also see the deepening of her fondness for her teacher: "My dear Miss Anna" becomes "My dearest Miss Anna" and soon "Dearest Tonnie" (derived from *Tante,* aunt); "Ever your very affectionate E. N. Jones" intensifies to "Most lovingly yrs, E. N. Jones," then "Your devoted 'Herz,'" or heart.

Edith was twelve years and four months old when she composed this first invitation to "Miss Anna."

1. In *A Backward Glance,* Wharton spells her childhood home as one word, Pencraig, and biographers and critics have followed suit. However, in her letters the young Edith spells it as two words, Pen craig, and the house letterhead is the same. I have retained the two-word spelling throughout the text. Pen craig is Welsh for top of the rock.

Pen craig, Newport
May 31st, 1874

My dear Miss Anna,

Mamma has commissioned me to write and tell you that, when you come up to put the house in order we shall have a room ready for you and be very, very glad indeed to see you. Newport is delightful and we are ready for you whenever you may come, if you could let us know on what day to expect you. Besides, if I don't see you until next winter—Ich wurde [*sic*] mein Deutsch ganz und gar vergessen! [I would completely forget my German!]

So you really must come and pray be a long time putting the house in order—
Ever your very affectionate,

E. N. Jones

At nearly fifteen, Edith has expanded her vocabulary and developed decided literary opinions.

Pen craig, Newport
Nov. 13th, 1875

My dearest Miss Anna,

How kind you are to your stupid "Hertz" in sending her such a long, charming letter in the midst of your busiest days! If you knew how much I enjoyed it & how overwhelmed I am by the honour of being allowed to do a commission for you, you would realize my thanks better than I can write them. Just fancy it's trusting me to do anything for you! It is the greatest pleasure that you could give me, & I will do my best for you when I go into town this morning—taking it for granted, however, that you don't want a medallion of Tasso, who, apparently, was by no means as handsome as he was unfortunate, & which Hammett shewed me the last time I was there—[1]

Today is what the poets call "halcyon" weather; a word which always brings to "my mind's eye, Horatio" a vision of becalmed ships in blue seas, with white birds swooping overhead—but we have not been without storms since you left.[2] Now, dear Miss Anna, pray don't tire yourself, & leave my books alone until I go to town & I will get them myself. You will have enough to do without going to Christern's for them—[3]

Yesterday I got Longfellow's new book, "The Masque of Pandora & other poems."[4] I like "Pandora" quite well. It is a dramatic poem in blank verse, with Greek choruses, but it is too short—it has not substance enough, & it wants, as I think all Longfellow's poems do, fire & passion & reality. His poetry always reminds me of a chilly sculpture, it is so lifeless. I think his characters want vigour. They are passionless & collected as if they were walking in a trance, or beneath the influence of a calming spell. Such at least is the impression that he gives me, but I judge merely from my own feelings. Some parts, however, of "Pandora" are very beautiful, & I think these two lines run very smoothly.

"Who would not love, if loving she might be
Changed like Callisto to a star in Heaven?"[5]

My Dear Governess

I don't want to fill my letter with a review, but I must send you the last three lines spoken by Pandora, for I think them very fine & I want to know if you agree with me. She says:

> "Only through punishment of our evil deeds,
> Only through suffering are we reconciled to the Immortal
>   Gods & to ourselves"—

I hope that I have not bothered you with all this, but when I get on one of my pet subjects, I never feel inclined to leave it off, & I do like occasionally to have a discussion about poetry—

I hope that your arrival has made both Mr. & Mrs. Rutherfurd feel better, as I am sure it ought to—And you yourself—how are you?—

Sit down quietly by the fire in a comfortable chair when I come to visit you in the shape of this letter, and don't run away after your house-keeping, but rest yourself while you are listening to my chatter. When we last heard from my brother, my sister was in Philadelphia, but I daresay she will have returned by the time you find leisure to go & see her, & at all events lonely little Beatrix will be glad of a visit from "Anna"—Fred's address is 34 East 23rd. I think that we shall go to New York next week. I have packed up all my china ornaments & today I think I must pick out my books to take to town—which is a horrid task because I cannot bear to leave one behind me & yet cannot take them all along. The best way would be to have one copy of each book here & one in New York.

Mamma is much better, & Doyle thanks you very much for your remembrance of her.[6] I am very sorry to say that she has a bad, *croaking* cold, which has been hanging about her for some days. The green-house looks very nicely & I water there every day. I saw Daisy [Margaret Rutherfurd] the day before yesterday, to my great surprise. I make my best dancing-school curtsey to Mr. & Mrs. Rutherfurd & to "Francis Beaumont" my co-author, & remain, with much love, yours in a very small space[7]

E.N.J.

1. The Italian poet Torquato Tasso (1544–95) is noted, among other work, for having composed his poem "Rinaldo" before reaching the age of twenty. Edith owned a copy of Tasso's *Le Gerusalemme Liberata.* Additionally, Anna's favorite author, Wolfgang von Goethe, wrote a play called *Torquato Tasso,* and one might speculate that Anna has given the play to Edith and has used the model of Tasso to encourage Edith's aspirations as a young poet. Charles E. Hammett, Jr., was a Newport bookseller, publisher, and mapmaker.

2. Edith's quoted allusion is to Shakespeare's *Hamlet,* which shows that she had already studied the play.

3. F. W. Christern was a New York bookseller who specialized in foreign books. Edith's familiarity with him and with Charles Hammett suggests frequent commerce in books.

4. Henry Wadsworth Longfellow (1807–82) was at the time America's most widely read and admired poet.

5. In Greek mythology, Callisto was seduced by Zeus, then changed into a star in the Ursa Major constellation.

6. Hannah Doyle, Edith's much-loved Irish nursemaid, remained in the Jones household as seamstress.

7. She has written herself into a tiny corner. For many years Edith will write on every bit of space of the paper, even writing across an earlier page. This may be the reason she uses so few new paragraphs. "Francis Beaumont" may refer to Anna herself, who, as we see in later letters, assists Edith in her translations and probably her writing, too. Francis Beaumont (1584–1616) famously collaborated with John Fletcher (1579–1625) in writing plays. That Edith knows this suggests that, at age thirteen, she is already familiar with a variety of Renaissance plays.

Pen craig, Newport
August 1876

My dearest Tonnie—

It is a double pleasure to receive a letter from you. The present pleasure of reading it, combined with the prospect of answering it—which, you see, I do not leave long to the future, for it is not an hour since Trix came rapping at my door with "Here's a letter, Aunt Eduff." I am so terribly shy of shewing to any one whom I know to be a fair judge, any of my writings, that after I sent Mignon I was half-frightened; but I have been more than rewarded by your frank criticism, which is so much more of compliment to me than the polite, unmeaning, "Oh, it's lovely," which I so often get when I beg for an honest opinion.[1] And now I wish that you would help me to correct it. "Still stands the myrtle & the laurel high" bothers me because it is so absurdly literal—but "calm grows the myrtle" is just as bad, & as I can only use a word of one syllable, I am at a loss how to correct it. Then—"O thou poor child, what hath man done to thee?" does not satisfy me. Yet what can I put in the place of "man"? "The cloud-ridged mountain" is a difficult line, for Wolkensteg is not very easily translated. Then again, "The mule *ascends* with care" is not a literal rendering of what, correctly, would be "The mule seeks his way through the fog." Please, if it be not troubling you too much, tell me which lines you do not like, in your next letter. "So laßt mich scheinen, bis ich werde" is much more difficult, & consequently my translation is much worse. Is "so let me seem until I be" good English, or would "am" be better? But I will not bewilder you with any more questions lest you should find your encouragement rash. I have half in mind to send you something that I wrote about Friederike this Spring when you were dictating that sketch of Goethe[2]—It is very poor & too spun out, but if I decide to send it please find its chief virtue in the fact that it is associated with some very pleasant hours—

I was delighted to get that account of the "Trilogie" which I have not yet had time to read entirely, but which will of course be interesting.[3] I thought that it was to be called "Ragnarok." Is it not taken from the original version of the Nibelungen in the Edda? It seems to me a mixture of the two, for we have Valhalla & the giants (Fafner, whom Fafnisbane slew) & the scene is laid on the Rhine. I do not understand how Herr Wagner can blend the two poems, for the later one has a sort of barbarous Christian veil thrown over its heathenism, a mixture of murder & high mass which is very amusing.

I agree with you in thinking that "music hath something or other to soothe the savage ear," for I, who am in that respect a South Sea Islander, am often fascinated by a soft, old-fashioned air or a stirring song[4]—"Robin Adair" has really bewitched me, it is so exquisitely simple & pathetic. Over & over again I beg M. Bininger, who is staying with us & who sings it charmingly, to let me hear it. How can anyone sing opera music & foreign trash, when there are so many sad, beautiful English ballads & songs?

I have just been reading some of Lowell's blank verse, his Prometheus, Rhoecus, Columbus, etc., & I find them very beautiful indeed. The opening of Rhoecus is admirable. I think you said you had not read "The Vision of Sir Launful"; I am sure that you will be as much pleased as I was with it.[5]

We expect the Dickeys here at Newport a week from yesterday, & it will be a great & delightful change to have my dear Ella back again.[6] (I should have accounted long ago for my very bad writing by telling you that I have only my very short-sighted eye to guide me, the other being tied with a wet cloth, because it is inflamed. I am weeping tears of alcohol & water from my dripping bandage as I write.)

Do not crow over us any longer. The rain withholds itself but the weather is cool & breezy. As for the family, M. & Trix came last week & Fred comes up for his "Sunday out" not being wholly free, poor boy. The great rose-tree in the greenhouse is blooming prosperously & the "farm" flourishes to one's heart's desire, from the bull to the ferns & geraniums. As much cannot be said for one horseflesh, the new chestnut pair having been ill for a long time—but Poney is blooming & beautiful. Mr. Rutherfurd is away & the boys are off on the Palmer [the Rutherfurd yacht]. So that Edgerston is an establishment like that in Tennyson's "Princess," but not so rigidly guarded against the other sex, who go there to play lawn tennis almost every afternoon.[7] It is a most fascinating game; difficult, tiresome, & destructive to pretty dresses, & to the complexion, but nevertheless delightful. Pin your skirts up high (it is well to have nice boots, still better & rarer to have small feet), put on a small hat & "go it!" Once begin & you will never care to stop chasing the magnetic balls hither & thither, throwing them back with your bats, etc.

For two or three days my eyes have been ailing, & reading & writing forbidden pleasures, but now they are well again & I have got a new pen and I am quite comfortable. The Palmer came back yesterday afternoon with the other yachts & I must call on Mr. Rutherfurd today. I

My Dear Governess

have been asked to join an archery club & the first meeting is to be held this afternoon.

But I dare not write any more, not even to answer your questions. I will send Friederike another time.

Your affectionate

E N Jones

Ella may arrive today or tomorrow.

1. Edith was translating two of the "Mignon" poems from Goethe's *Wilhelm Meisters Lehrjahre.*

2. Goethe immortalized his love affair with Friederike Brion in his poems "Welcome and Farewell" and "May Song," which Edith read with Anna. Unfortunately, whatever Edith wrote about Friederike has not been found.

3. Richard Wagner's (1813–83) *Der Ring des Nibelungen* is a four-opera cycle, considered by some a trilogy, with *Das Rheingold* as the prelude. Although all the poetry was written by 1852, composing the music was a work of decades, and the final opera of the series, *Götterdämmerung,* was performed for the first time the month that this letter was written.

4. She is paraphrasing William Congreve, "Music has charms to soothe a savage breast."

5. James Russell Lowell (1819–91), "Prometheus" (1843); "Rhoecus" (1843); "Columbus" (1844); "The Vision of Sir Launful" (1849).

6. I have been unable to identify Ella Dickey definitively. An Ella Dickey served as bridesmaid to Miss Mary Mason Jones at her April 1884 wedding to Louis Hassell. This was not Edith Wharton's more famous great-aunt Mary Mason Jones, but it suggests that the Dickeys were a part of the same Old New York society as the Joneses.

7. "Princess" is an 1847 poem by Alfred, Lord Tennyson (1809–92) about a princess who founds a school for women that is eventually infiltrated by her suitor.

Pen craig, Newport
Sept. 17th, 1876

My dearest Tonni,

When I sent off that very laconic note to North William Street the other day, I durst not even trespass as far as to thank you for your letter—but my eyes are much better now, & I hasten to do so on regaining my privilege of using them. I was so sorry that you were not well—but I hope it has not prevented your coming on to New York, for I wanted you to get that note about next Winter's lessons as soon as possible, that you might not miss the chance it offers should you care to avail yourself of it. Mrs. Van Rensselaer would like your time from a quarter before two till a quarter before five every afternoon. Loulie Van R. is a very clever child, very fond of studying & trained in excellent habits, I fancy, by Maggie Wingate, who has given her a good start & improved her very much. She was one of Maggie's favourite pupils.[1] But I have something else to propose in this letter much nearer to me (I will confess my self-ishness frankly) than this matter. Namely, a special message from Papa & Mama in which I join, to beg that you will give us the pleasure of a visit not later than the first of Oct—Later, our plans are indefinite. We may go to the Centennial & prolong our trip—or we may go to town early—but before that time, nothing could make us happier, dear Miss Anna, than to see you here again at Pen craig.[2] Do be tempted—by the rocks & the Sunday wanderings & the greenhouse, if by nothing else— do be persuaded. I am sure the Autumn air here would do you good, & pray remember that we have not seen you since last Spring, & that we can't spare you any longer. We can read German together, & collect Autumn leaves & do a thousand things which are nothing to me now, but so much with you. I can but repeat, do come.

Trix sends this kiss to you & also a note which I took down from her rather rambling dictation. [Encircled here are the words "Kiss for Miss Anna from Trix."][3] She has pervaded my apartment today & it is rather distracting, as I have given up my morning to letter-writing, which is not easy under the circumstances. We are all well, & Mama sends much love in which I unite, remaining always
Most lovingly yrs

E. N. Jones

1. Louise Van Rensselaer, later Mrs. Edmund Baylies (1865–1946), was to re-main a lifetime friend of both Edith and Anna, and Anna would also teach her

My Dear Governess

younger sister Mabel. Maggie Wingate, like Anna, gave lessons to numerous society children.

2. The Centennial International Exhibition of 1876, held in Philadelphia to commemorate the signing of the Declaration of Independence, was the first World's Fair. It is not known whether the family attended.

3. Trix's dictation is indeed rambling—she was only four—so I have omitted it.

Edith's "Bravo!" here refers to her teacher's suggestions for translating the two "Mignon" poems of Goethe that Edith was working on in her letter dated August 1876. It matters greatly to Edith that she render the translation accurately, elegantly, and with felicitous sound and rhythm. Castalia, to whom Edith likens Anna, was a mythical nymph from the spring at Delphi; all who drank from her waters were said to draw inspiration. The relationship between pupil and teacher deepens as Edith recognizes the gifts Anna brings her.

Newport

Sept. 23 1876

My dearest Tonni—Bravo! "O thou poor child, what has befallen thee?" Perfect! I know now where my Castalia must be—whence I can draw inspiration for the proper rendering of the immortal Wolfgang—O nine muses in one! I congratulate you on your successful hit. My poem is made. In short, a thousand thanks from a grateful poetaster for your assistance, encouragement & criticism. Let us fly at once to Mignon. In the second line I do not like the "no" you suggest as an alteration. Would not "and golden fruits athwart the foliage grow" be better? There each syllable retains its natural emphasis etc., & of course it is more musical. "*Still stands* the myrtle" is my bête noire. Do you think "*Calm blooms* etc., would be an improvement?—I think now Mignon is disposed of; I am more frightened about "So let me seem" which is much harder, but I will pluck up heart & send it where I know it will get its dues, and yet be leniently read. The rhymes are very difficult to get, especially in the third stanza, where I would not spoil the last line, & so had to make the first three rather unsatisfactory. The last stanza is flat—cramped—horrid—excepting, again, in the last line—which couldn't help itself. With this preface of apologies (my translation cannot travel safely without such a body-guard) I commend it to your tenderest mercies. Papa has made an angel (like Mignon) of himself & copied it—for rewriting my eloquent effusion is horrible to me—so here it is. As for Friederike, she is very long, & I should expire before I had copied her. I will shew her to you in N.Y.

And now the poetess subsides & the naughty girl, Miss Pussy, makes her appearance—heart-broken that the Fates have forbidden your coming to Newport. Seriously, rebellious nature says "it is too bad" & will not be comforted. Isn't necessity the mother of Invention? Then do feel the necessity of coming (as we of having you) & get out a patent for coming to Pen craig when you ought to be somewhere else. That is the only prayer I can offer. I am by no means content not to have you, & I don't think "Must" is a nice person at all. Come—think of the sea, dancing into silver where the sun strikes it, of the rocks that have put on their royal cloak of purple & gold blossoms, blazing along the roadside, of the cool, delicious air, & the lawns freshened at last by rain. "Here is the apple, Eve. Look at it on the rosy side & bite it." I really sympathize with that wicked, wriggling serpent who insinuated himself into Eden.

I delivered your letter solemnly to Beatrix, who, I have no doubt, fully appreciated such an unexpected compliment, & will redouble her hugs in consequence when she gets to N.Y. Beatrix her aunt is also waiting to hug someone in N.Y.

As for the inmates of Edgerston, since the boys are off at conquered, as they pronounce Concord, & Mr. Rutherfurd is here only by fits & starts, I have very little to tell—& can communicate no later news than that probably familiar to you—the arrival of several infant Topseys [puppies], who, Bessie Chanler solemnly asserts, "Are all going to be bull-dogs." Not on the principle of degeneration of the races, then? What dreams of glory Topsey must cherish for her giant family!

I always get a good fit (that departs, alas! Like my other diseases) in the Autumn, & I feel really beatific tonight, having received a letter from Brooklyn, practiced violently one of Beethoven's waltzes, (a species of funereal hymn) made two rosettes for a new pair of slippers & generally behaved myself—a sensation still having the charm of novelty. (To make fun of myself is a healthy outlet for my venomous little vein of sarcasm.) About such prosaic things as business matters, what can the immortal translator of Goethe have to say? I leave that to Mama, who is going to write to you on rational subjects—As for me, I must return to literature & ask you if you have yet read Daniel Deronda—a question which just now is probably being written in millions of letters.[1] I have nearly finished the first vol., & though I am not disposed to judge it has [sic] harshly as at first, I cannot think it compares to my beloved Romola. The story is nothing, & I do not care for the style, but the thoughts with which it overflows are wonderfully clever—& I don't think as ill of the hero as most people do. To be sure, he is a parcel of theories, loosely tied up, a puppet so badly stuffed that the sawdust shews—but the contents of the parcel & the doll—the theories, or sawdust—are good. Gwendolen is interesting, but I don't care for your pieces of faultlessness, like the good girls of such extravagant saintliness in Sunday school books—& Mirah is of that type—Like diluted rosewater. There! Daniel has nearly used up my last page & barely allowed me space to say again & again how much I, and we all, regret your not coming, & to thank you properly for your dear letter in answer to which this is written by

Your ever affectionate

E.N.J.

1. *Daniel Deronda,* which had just been published, and *Romola* (1862–63) are novels by George Eliot (Mary Ann Evans, 1819–80). Edith's sophisticated critique of Eliot's characterizations prefigures her own attention to creating characters who seem to come alive. Her critique of the plot—"the story is nothing"—is curious, given that there are two complicated plots about women in trouble, each of whom relies on the gallantry of young Daniel Deronda to rescue her.

Shortly after Edith wrote the letter above she began a novel, Fast and Loose, *which she finished in January of 1877, sharing it only with a friend. The story, written under the pseudonym David Olivieri, traces its origins from such English classics as* Jane Eyre, *from which her heroine's name is derived, and* Daniel Deronda, *from which we can discern elements of the plot. While she cannot yet get deeply into her characters and tends to explain their motivation rather than dramatize it, her attention to language and her taste for satire are already manifest. The novel comes complete with the author's own scathing reviews of it— "If Madeline be Mr. Olivieri's conception of innocence, we no longer have any difficulty in understanding the motives which prompted Herod to the Massacre of the Innocents" (F&L, 114)—giving proof to Edith's earlier observation that "To make fun of myself is a healthy outlet for my venomous little vein of sarcasm."*

Two years pass between letters, years during which Edith continues to study with Anna in New York in winter and spend summers in Newport. And she continues to write poetry, which her parents will gather and have published as Verses *later in 1878. Despite the self-criticism, her literary judgments and self-approval could occasionally be breathtakingly audacious, as here when she compares her own writing to Shakespeare.*

Pen craig

Sept. 2nd [1878]

My dear Tons,

I know nothing nicer than to have a letter really *answered,* as you have answered my last critical effusion. It has inspired me at once to write again, so if you please you will "change your plate & take a little more of the same."

I have finished Julius [Caesar] since I last wrote & I cannot say that it left a very glowing impression on me. It was too much like my own earliest attempts at tragedy to move me in the least. I am now reading your most charming present, Goethe's & Schiller's Correspondence than which I could not have a more delightful reminder (if any were needed) of my dear Tonni. I know nothing nobler in its way than that letter of Schiller's which Roquette quotes you remember, analyzing Goethe's character to Goethe himself.[1] I hope you did not think I was too hard on Miss Mitford. I took her up at an unfortunate moment, I suppose. But literary merit there is none in her letters, beyond a good plain style, & social & historical interest is lacking as well, for she "twaddles" as you call it, of mere nobodies. One only wishes that she & her correspondence had remained as obscure as her friends![2]

You ask if I remember a certain part in Klytemnestra (you see, I am trying to answer *your* letter.) No! I confess I remember nothing but the plagiarisms. One from Marlowe's Faustus & one or more from Shakespere. But how can one look for high tragedy in a vers au société writer? "Aux Italiens" & "Chess" will survive Klytemnestra I imagine.[3]

By the way I have discovered a new poem in Browning & even in that wretchedest of books "Dramatis Personae." It is called "May & Death." Do you know it? There is not a single quote-able (what a word!) line in it but the whole is "round and perfect as a star."[4] You were so very flattering in your commendation of "I met my love" that I send you some more serious lines which I think are worth a great deal more. Tell me how they strike you.

As for Middlemarch, we must return to it & continue our discussion. I always have a sweet faiblesse for Rosamond which I suppose denotes a sympathetic flaw in my own moral structure.[5]

As for Dorothea, what most jars upon me is her want of artistic feeling,—a wonderful touch of character drawing, but so well drawn that it continually ~~jars~~ provokes me. There was no aesthetic side to her nature. And indeed your enthusiasts are all narrow-minded. Will Ladislaw is charming, but somehow although a great deal is *said* of the passion between him & Dorothea one fails all through to feel its power. When it was so dangerous to love at all, they ought to have loved a little more! A continual desire on my part to throttle Mr. Brooke, Mrs. Cadwallader & Cecilia & Sir James only shows how wonderfully life-like they all are. Well, goodbye to literature for the present.

I ought to put a good deal of gossip in this letter but I have got a chronique scandaleuse to send to Minnie [Jones] so you must excuse any for the present.

What I still have to say is this—When do you propose to make us happy by your annual Autumn visit? Not a short one, mind you, like last year's, which was a mere peep, but a genuine *stay* with us. Can you come this month? The sooner the better, but never too late to be welcome. We have asked Lewis [Rutherfurd, Anna's former pupil] to come some time & I hope he means to. It would be all the nicer if we could have you together. Name your own time for we are alone & have plenty of room & a welcome always ready, as you know. Say you will come, dear Tonni! How we can talk & read & make up for the Summer's separation. Mama & Papa join with me in begging you most heartily to agree to our plan. Your devoted

Herz

1. Wharton's copy of this book, now in her library at The Mount, is inscribed "To E. N. Jones from Anna Bahlmann May 29, 1878." Otto Roquette (1824–96) was a poet, novelist, and professor of literature in Germany. His 1878 two-volume book about German literature is probably the source of the quotation mentioned here.

2. The letters of Mary Russell Mitford (1787–1855), British author of *Our Village* and other novels, were published in 1872.

3. Works by Edward Robert Bulwer-Lytton (1831–91), son of the novelist Edward George Bulwer-Lytton. "Aux Italiens" and "The Chess Board" are sentimental ballads of lost love. Lord Lytton's first collection of poetry, published under the name Owen Meredith, included a long verse play, *Clytemnestra*. Edith had used his novel in verse, *Lucile,* for the title and many of the epigraphs in *Fast and Loose.*

4. Robert Browning (1812–89), *Dramatis Personae* (1864). Alexander Smith (1830–67), *A Life Drama* (1852), "a poem round and perfect as a star." Smith was a Scottish poet whose work was at first acclaimed but later satirized as representative of the "Spasmatic School."

5. The 1871–72 novel by George Eliot. The next paragraph also pertains to this novel. It is interesting to compare her early critiques of Eliot with her 1902 review of Leslie Stephen's book about Eliot, wherein she refines her objections to certain aspects of the novelist's work and offers appreciation of others, including her "power of characterisation" (*George Eliot,* 77).

My Dear Governess

Pen craig
Sept. 11th [1878]

My dear Tonnie,

I wrote you a long letter of eight pages about ten days ago and as it contained a question which I think you would have been likely to answer before this, I fear it may not have reached its destination. The question was, cannot you come this month to make us your yearly Autumn visit? — & as the month is fast escaping into October, I hasten to repeat my demand at once. Mama and Papa are as anxious as I am to have you, & we all beg that you will come very soon & make us a much longer visit than that miserable little glimpse we got of you last Fall. Will you write at once & let us know when we may expect you? The sooner the better, as far as we are concerned, but any time this month will suit us & you must consult your own convenience without hesitation.

Newport offers its usual Autumn attractions which I think you know how to appreciate of old. The season, indeed, is over & I am sorry you will not see the English men of war wh. departed yesterday after spending a gay fortnight in the harbour. But we are having splendid weather, & the rocks, the sea, the goldenrod & the *stewed pears* are here to welcome you as usual. I will devote my fourth page to my last effusion which, if it reminds you of anything, ought to suggest "Violet Fane."[1]

Ever yours, E.N.J.

Counting the Stars

Have you forgotten, Love, the night
We sat & counted the stars together?
The Autumn moon o'erhead was bright
And ~~calm~~ soft the blue September weather.

The stars came peeping, faint & pale,
Thro' drifts of cloud fleece torn & riven,
That swept, like a thin & tattered veil,
Across the violet vault of Heaven.

And as we counted, one by one,
The mystic nine in the sky a-quiver,
I breathed a wish to the silent stars, —
A wish my heart will hold forever.[2]

Ah, half in jest, & half in love,
We sat & counted the stars together.
The Autumn moon was bright above
And soft the blue September weather.

1. Violet Fane was the literary pseudonym of Lady Mary Montgomerie Lamb Singleton Currie (1843–1905), a British baroness who was a novelist, poet, and essayist. She published four slim volumes of poetry between 1872 and 1878, and her work was well received. A number of the poems concern mutability and regret.

2. The "mystic nine" is probably the constellation Pleiades, said to be the seven sisters of Greek mythology and their parents. The constellation is linked with loss and mourning.

Pen craig
Oct. 17th [1878]

My dear Tons,

Thanks many times for your kind criticism which has encouraged me very much. I got your letter of Oct. 14th yesterday & was so glad that you were really pleased with Phantoms & June & December.[1] As for the latter it has not appeared yet — & I don't know when it will as I have heard nothing from Little Raymond Belmont about it.[2] I send you some other verses, but I don't know whether they are very bad or quite good. I think they will admit of both constructions, so you may choose. You are my Supreme critic in these matters & I look upon your verdict with infinite faith & respect.

I am very glad that June & Dec. pleased you especially & that you liked that last stanza. I have been reading lately the most bewitching book — Mrs. Brassey's "Around the World in the Yacht Sunbeam." It is simply absorbing — written in the form of a private journal, in a simple, graphic style that is quite irresistible.[3] I never knew so much geography in my life as I have learned from it. Why my dear Tons, do you know that the Andes are in South America, & that Terra [*sic*] del Fuego is divided from Patagonia by the Straits of Magellan? But I will not dazzle you by exhibiting all at once too much of my newly acquired knowledge. It shall dawn upon you gently in the course of the Winter—if I have not forgotten it. I have also been reading Aldrich's poems, with some of which of course I had long been familiar. There is one "The Lady of Castelnoire" which is exquisite.

I must give you the last stanza entire—it is so perfect.

"And they called her cold. God knows . . .
Underneath the Winter snows
The invisible hearts of flowers grew ripe for blossoming!
And the lives that look so cold, if their stories could be told
Would seem cast in gentler mould, would seem full of love &
   Spring!"[4]

Do you know, I have been trying to read "What will he do with it?" but I happened to open the book at the place where the Marchioness of Montfort finds Guy Darrell reclining under a tree with a doe at his feet, & he addresses her as "Ha! Caroline, Marchioness of Montfort," & tells her that he is not "an airy gallant but a *Man*." The sublime & beautiful sentiments in that scene were quite too much for my prosaic nature, & I gave up the book as a bad job—I never did take to Bulwer.[5]

Well, I believe I must end now as I want to post this note this afternoon—& I had almost forgotten to copy my "pome" for you. I was not at all vexed at your having shewn the "Sensuchtsroman" [*sic*] to Mr. Schultz but pleased on the contrary that you thought it worthy to be read by a German.[6]

Ever your

[Edith has drawn a heart with an arrow through it, but has also dropped an ink blot.]

That would have been "high *art*" if it hadn't been for the blot.

1. "June and December" appeared in Edith's volume *Verses*. Similar to "Counting the Stars," its subject is two lovers, late in life, recalling earlier moments of love. "Phantoms" has not survived.

2. Raymond Belmont, son of banker August Belmont and Newport neighbor of the Joneses, was a year younger than Edith. It is hard to believe that at fifteen he could have been responsible for publishing something, but he may have edited a local magazine in Newport or may have been working for a publisher. We have no record of "June and December" being published anywhere besides *Verses*.

3. Anna Brassey (1839–87) chronicled her 1876 eleven-month voyage from England to South America, around the Cape, and on around the world in this 1878 book. Edith's delight in the tale tells us that from a young age she loved the thought of extensive and exotic travel. She quotes another of Brassey's books, *Sunshine and Storm in the East* (1880), in her diary of her cruise on the *Vanadis*.

4. Thomas Bailey Aldrich (1836–1907) was a poet, novelist, editor, and critic. The book from which Edith was reading (*Poems*, 1865) is at The Mount, inscribed to Edith Jones, October 11, 1878, and has a light pencil mark at this stanza.

5. *What Will He Do with It*, an 1864 novel by Edward Bulwer-Lytton (1803–73), a prolific and popular novelist now frequently ridiculed for his overblown prose.

6. Augustus and Louise Schultz were lifelong friends of Anna Bahlmann. "Sehnsuchtsroman" does not survive.

In quoting the stanza above from Aldrich's "The Lady of Castelnoire," and in some of her own poems written in this period, Edith manifested interest in a theme she would explore throughout her career: the disjunction between an outward appearance of calm and an inner life of passion or turmoil. As an adolescent girl she must have been struggling with her society's mandate to ignore, or at least mask, strong or "inappropriate" emotions.

We have in the following letter the first account of Edith, at seventeen, publishing her poetry. Allen Thorndike Rice (1851–89), then owner and editor of the North American Review, *was a neighbor of the Jones family in Newport and the nephew of two of Lucretia's friends, sisters who each married a count, the Countess Bañuelos and the Countess Sartiges. Rice had purchased the periodical in 1876 and was making his name publishing articles with diverse and contrary viewpoints. According to R. W. B. Lewis, Rice sent Edith's*

My Dear Governess

poems to Henry Wadsworth Longfellow, who passed them along to William Dean Howells at the Atlantic (EWAB, 32).[1] Howells published five poems: "A Parting Day" was published in the February 1880 issue of The Atlantic, "Areopagus" in March, "A Failure" and "Patience" in April, and "Wants" in May.

Along with her regimen of study and writing, Edith clearly had time to socialize. Some of her early poems (see, for example, "What We Shall Say Fifty Years Hence, of Our Fancy-Dress Quadrille," which bears the epigraph "Danced at Swanhurst, August 1878"), suggest that she has engaged in flirtations with young men, and here we see evidence of her pleasure in being courted. In December 1879 she "came out," that social ritual in which a girl is presented to the world as an adult, available for marriage. Of this event Edith wrote: "That evening was a pink blur of emotion—but after it was over my mother had no fears for me! For the rest of the winter, I don't think I missed a ball; & wherever I went I had all the dancers I wanted" (L&I, 1093). Biographers have made much of her shyness, but there was also gaiety and exuberance.

In the year between the previous letter and this one, Anna moved to Cuba as governess to Lita, daughter of Osuna and Marietta (possibly de las Bañas), an experience she has evidently described expressively in a letter to Edith and her mother. Perhaps the letter was in German, as Edith mentions translating it for her mother.

1. William Dean Howells (1837–1920), editor and novelist, was a friend and mentor to most of the American writers of the late nineteenth and early twentieth centuries.

Pen craig

Oct. 16th, 1879

My dear Tonni,

I have spent a very interesting half hour in reading and translating to Mamma your long and delightful letter. The only unnecessary part was the postscript at the end, for as "good wine needs no bush" a good letter certainly needs no apology.[1] We enjoyed every word, groaned over the cockroaches, and your various other melancholy adventures, and see the "Pathe" before us to the life. Well, you have dropped into a queer region and I hope you won't fail to go on giving me as many "ausführliche" [detailed] descriptions of all fresh wonders as you have begun by doing.

Quand à nous—we are civilized but dull! However, I have better news to give than when I last wrote. Mama has been steadily [here the word is smeared] if slowly improving (that blot is occasioned by Tiny's having just walked over the page) and she now comes down to dinner, walks about the grounds and goes out driving. I am very well indeed and weigh 123 pounds. Just think of that, my dear!

Ever since you have left we have had the most heavenly weather, almost without interruption, and we have now settled into a sort of Indian Summer as breathless and warm as August, the thermometer Heaven knows how high! white dresses, umbrellas—lemonade—don't think to overwhelm us by a description of Cuban heat for we have got a sample of it here—perhaps to remind us of you. As for me, what shall I tell you? I have written two sonnets and a long piece (196 lines, and *finished*) all of which I should like you to see, but I am too lazy to copy them. By the way, did I or did I not tell you that I have four things coming out in the "Atlantic"? They are respectively A Failure—Patience—Wants—and A Parting Day—Here is what Howells, the editor, says about them: "If I can think of any good name I will print them in a little group. They strike me as having a fresh, delicate and authentic quality. It is something very uncommon to find so young a writer reminding you so very little of other writers." So much for Mr. Howells. It is undoubtedly a very good opening to get into the Atlantic at seventeen—but I owe it all to Mr. Rice and his unfailing kindness.

I think it was after you left that the *Doppeladler* made a formal apology for his rudeness, and returned in full force to his former allegiance. It was a great advantage to have him come back at the end of the Season! Well, joking apart, he made himself very agreeable, and I have three compliments, which I look upon as for *you* not for *me,* and have saved up accordingly for exportation to Cuba. He said that I knew more of German literature than he does (And he sets up to be rather well-read) that "my knowledge of the language was wonderful" and that he had never quoted anything (and he is very quote-y) which I had not recognized. There! "Lay that flattering unction to your soul, good Tonni."[2] Think of my turning out to be a credit to you after all! Well, you taught me German to such good purpose that the Sécrètaire de la Majesté Imp. & Royale &c sent me two splendid bouquets within a week before he left, and I am engaged to dance the Cotillion with him at the "Patriarch" ball in December, when he comes on to New York.

I think that is all the personal gossip I have to give, for everything is dead quiet here, nothing going on, everybody gone, as usual at this season — and the combination makes it delightful to us.

Have you heard of poor Rob Dickey's death, last Sunday morning? They were at Morristown. We have heard no particulars as yet — but, although we expected it, it came with a start after all.[3]

I must bid you goodbye now, for I have another letter to write, and it is *so* hot that my eloquence very quickly runs dry.

I am looking forward to your next letter which will come very soon I hope.

Meanwhile, I am always

Affectionately yours,

E.N.J.

Mama sends her love and says "we miss you awfully" in which I join.

1. From Rosalind's Epilogue (l. 4) to *As You Like It:* "If it be true that good wine needs no bush, 'tis true that a good play needs no epilogue."

2. *Hamlet* III.iv.145. Hamlet tells his mother "Lay *not* that flattering unction to your soul" — that is, she should not attribute to his madness, rather than her wrongdoing, the unrest of the ghost of his father. I am unable to identify the "Doppeladler," except to speculate by the term *doppeladler,* or double eagle, the symbol of Austria, that he is an Austrian of an upper-class or even an aristocratic family, and that he had paid attentions to Edith before. I also speculate that her copy of C. M. Wieland's *Oberon* was a gift from him, whose initials may have been A.L.B.

3. Rob Dickey (not from the Dickey family mentioned earlier) was a classmate

of Teddy Wharton's at Harvard and attended law school at Columbia University when Edith's brother Harry was an undergraduate there. It is unclear how Edith knew him, but he may be the link that introduced Teddy Wharton to Harry, and, eventually, to Edith. Dickey died of pneumonia.

New York
March 21st, 1880

My Dear Tonni,

There is a sort of friendship which makes itself felt less by personal intercourse, than by those shocks of intellectual sympathy which seem to bridge over silence and space and make two minds as one—and it is for that reason that in certain moments I feel as strongly "dir verbinden" [united with you] as if you were in the room and talking to me. Can you guess what has inspired me to write this? I heard Faust sung on Friday night at the Academy and somehow you got mixed with the lyric rapture, and you were with me hearing it, and drinking your fill of those

> "Divine ideas below
> That always find us young
> And always keep us so"[1]

Ah, Tons, there is a sort of Olympian youthfulness about that story and that music that ought to turn the dullest proser into a poet, and it is wonderful how the German mind of the poet and the French mind of the composer could have been so attuned to each other. It was beautifully sung, except Gretchen, who was a conventional doll, such as one too often sees. The divine simplicity of the part is an excuse for making it a piece of affected *simplesse* (vide Matthew Arnold for the difference between "simplicité" and "simplesse") and the purity of Gretchen's character has come to be generally symbolized by a white gown and pigtails, just as her subsequent condition is represented by a dark dress and disheveled hair.[2] It is a pity that all great rôles are so easily conventionalized and that after a time it requires the touch of a great genius to lift them again to their original height.—

I have given up "Consuelo" in despair.[3] All the clap-trap and folde-rol and mysticism were too much for me after one volume, in spite of the fine style. As if there wasn't beauty and mystery and charm enough in real life without going over to the supernatural for your great effects. It must be the vulgarest kind of mind which has to resort to blue lights and tinsel and pantomime to produce any impression. I believe that I have never sent you the Atlantic yet—mea maxima culpa![4] If I can find a copy you shall have it promptly—

We are going to hear the Stabat Mater again on Good Friday evening, and I wish, dear Tons, you could hear that.[5]

March 23rd

I have just appeared in the Atlantic for April wh I will forward you at once.[6] Better news is that I have had a charming photograph done at Mora's, whose only fault is in being too pretty for the original, and you shall have one sent to you as soon as I get them, probably next week.[7] Maggie W[ingate] comes on Thursday to stop with us—Think what a pleasure for all concerned. I want to post this before it runs on into such a frightful yarn as the last, so I think that in spite of my elaborate beginning I will finish abruptly. I hope that you will think me "grandement en beauté" when you see my picture—*I* should never recognize it, it is so pretty, but they tell me it is very like. Do be pleased with it, meine liebe, beate Alte—I have written a so-so pretty ballad, wh I will copy for you "at my leisure" (Pinafore) Meanwhile, Liebste at-chieu! atchieu!! Auf wiedersehn!

Your devoted

Herz

1. Ralph Waldo Emerson (1803–82), "Ode to Beauty."

2. In "On Translating Homer," Arnold (1822–88) discusses the French distinction between *simplicité,* which is true simplicity, and *simplesse,* which is merely the appearance of simplicity. Edith's volume of Arnold's *Essays in Criticism,* acquired a month earlier, is well annotated.

3. A novel by George Sand (Amandine-Aurore Lucille Dupin, Baronne Dudevant, 1804–76), a writer Edith was to admire later in life, more for her unconventional life than for her novels.

4. She is speaking of the February issue of the *Atlantic,* in which her poem "A Parting Day" was published.

5. Mapleson's company, which performed *Faust,* also performed Gioacchino Rossini's (1792–1868) setting of the thirteenth-century hymn to Mary in the fall of 1879; it is likely that they kept it in their repertoire for the season.

6. Two more poems, "A Failure" and "Patience," were published by editor William Dean Howells.

7. The Cuban-born José Mora was one of the most successful photographers in New York City, catering to society patrons, and known for having numerous backgrounds and props to enhance his photos. His studio was at 707 Broadway. The picture to which Edith refers is probably the one of her appearing to be outside in the snow.

The warmth of Edith's response to the opera Faust *and the way she linked it to her feelings for Anna tell us much about Anna's centrality to Edith's emotional, as well as intellectual, development. Gounod's* Faust, *based on the Goethe play which she had read with Anna, would remain a touchstone for Edith all her life. She would immortalize a performance of the opera in the opening scene of her novel* The Age of Innocence *(1920), in which she describes Christina Nilsson singing the role of Gretchen/Margherita. And in her last completed novel,* The Gods Arrive *(1932), she portrays Vance Weston drawing inspiration from the Mothers, Faust's mythical figures for the source of knowing. The performance at the Academy of Music that Edith attended was by the company of British impresario Colonel John Henry Mapleson, who produced and toured with* Faust *for fifteen years ("Record of Amusements"). Although Christina Nilsson had sung in the past with Mapleson's company, the cast this night featured Alwina Valleria in the role of Margherita.*

According to the Wharton biographer R. W. B. Lewis, the Jones family was in Bar Harbor, Maine, early in the summer of 1880, and Henry Leyden (Harry) Stevens, to whom Edith would later become engaged, was "in close attendance" (EWAB, 39). Nevertheless, in August, Edith was concentrating, at least in her letters to Anna, more on her writing and on the thrilling possibility of a family trip to Europe. The Jones family had invited Anna to come along as companion and chaperone, but she was in Cuba, and Edith was impatiently waiting for the adults to settle their arrangements. In this letter and the next we see Edith preparing intellectually for the trip, and perhaps more important, we see her capacity to imagine the settings of the Romantic poetry she loves.

Edith was also celebrating another publication and contemplating a proposal by Allen Rice to write a long narrative poem as was currently popular, based on a myth of her own choosing. For Anna's part, her Cuban employers were reluctant to let her go, and it would be some time before the relationship between teacher and employer was mended. To retain her reputation as a reliable governess was crucial to Anna's employment opportunities.

Pen craig
August 26th 1880

Dear Tonni,

My fingers have been aching to get hold of a pen again and enlarge upon the subject broached in my last letter. That was written in a hurry and in my most business-like style; now I am going to sit down and gossip about it. It is very hard to bear in mind the possibility that we may not go after all, but there is certainly a very good chance of it our going, and I am already poring over maps and have [?] over Harrison's "Spain in Profile," Warner's "Saunterings," Green's "Sketches in England and Italy" & Howells's "Italian Journeys"—the only available books of travel here.[1] I am going to "*cram*" before we start, for you know it is impossible to take many books with one and I want to know as much as possible about what we *may* be going to see. That question of not taking my books is certainly a very trying one—of course I may take some, but which shall I take? And how hard it will be to leave the rest—Milton, Shelley and Browning must certainly go—and Wordsworth of course. Think of reading Shelley's "Evening" at Pisa where it was written—think of seeing the Campo Santo, and the pine woods where Byron rode near Ravenna, and Tintoretto's fresco in the Council Chamber (isn't it?) at Venice. The first place where I shall go in Florence will be the church of Santa Maria Novella, for I shall never forget the impression made upon me years ago by its black and white façade and the silver lamps hanging in all its side chapels. You cannot think how the prospect of seeing it all again has revived my faded recollections—I am sure I could shew you about Florence like a guide-book, from the shop where they sell gingersnaps to the Via Tornabuoni to the Venus in the Tribunal.[2] "Dahin, dahin! Möcht ich mit Dir, Du alte Tonni, geh'u."[3] And perhaps we *shall!!*—

I must stop "enthusing" for a minute and tell you about my literary affairs. Scribner has accepted my sonnet "St. Martin's Summer" & sent me a cheque for $7. Which is doing very well for 14 lines.[4] The others are going to be offered to Harpers. Mr. Rice was here today and his last proposition is that I should take, and turn into rhymed narrations, some of the old German Volkssagen, or for instance one of the early poems such as one of Wolfram von Eschenbach's or von der Aue's—and the others whose names I have forgotten. I am very much pleased with the idea, for I remember there was one beautiful poem, was it "Parcival"?, which Roquette tells about—Will you bring Roquette when you come? I think he will be very useful. I am going through the book you gave me—Schwab's "Deutsche Volksbücher" for my material and then I think I shall read "Sintram" [Tristan?] and "Undine" and "Aslauga" for "colour" and part of "Ihr Earthly Paradies" for a good story-telling style. Don't you wish I may succeed? Glück auf!—[5]

I wish you were here, you dear old Tonni—I am continually on the verge of explosion now, but I don't say much for I don't want to be able to reproach myself, if any thing should go wrong, with the idea that I urged them to leave home—and if we don't go, I promise you I shan't say a word—except "Ach weh!" in German which they won't understand. But "For this I nurse my myrtle-tree, My golden chain I keep
Today I smile; but *then,* ah weh,
For gladness I may weep!" My dear little Tons! How I am waiting for your letter to come saying yes, I will go with you, Herz—Remember, dear Tonni, your promise to come whenever we called you. I shall feel when we have heard that you are coming, that I can gush to really sympathetic ears and that we can be preparing our minds in communion for all the new sights and wonders to be poured into them. Having given

My Dear Governess

you my impressions in prose, I think I will send you at the same time a copy of some verses inspired the other day by my present frame of mind. Poor Mamma has been *quite* poorly, but is better today. For my part I have gained three pounds I am happy to say. Write soon and take care of yourself and be very well for October.

Affectionately your

Herz

1. James A. Harrison (1848–1911), *Spain in Profile* (1879); Charles Dudley Warner (1829–1900), *Saunterings* (1872); John Richard Green, *Stray Studies from England and Italy* (1876); William Dean Howells, *Italian Journeys* (1867); the kinds of anecdotal travel books in which George Frederic Jones delighted.

2. The Venus de Medici in the Uffizi Museum, which was originally built as offices, a tribunal, and state archives.

3. Edith has adapted these lines from Goethe's "Mignon." Roughly translated, it means "away, away with you, dear old Tonni, would I go."

4. This poem has not before been attributed to Edith Wharton. The text can be found in Goldman-Price, "Young Edith Jones: Sources and Texts of Early Poems by Edith Wharton." Her pleasure at receiving seven dollars for the sonnet calls into question Emelyn Washburn's assertion that Edith had earned fifty dollars for a translation several years earlier (Lee, 43).

5. Hartmann von Aue (c. 1160–c. 1210), a German poet known for his long narrative works, wrote two Arthurian poems, but he did not address the story of Parcival in either. Wolfram von Eschenbach (1170–1220), a contemporary of von Aue's, is author of Parzival. The Roquette she refers to is probably *Geschichte der deutschen Dichtung* (1862–63), a two-volume history of German literature. Gustav Schwab's (1792–1850) *Die deutschen Volksbücher* (1843) is a collection of German folk stories. Edith's handwriting is not clear here. She is certainly talking about Friedrich de la Motte Fouqué's (1777–1843) romance about the nymph Undine and her unfaithful husband Huldbrand. She might also be referring to de la Motte Fouqué's *Sintram and his Companions,* or perhaps Gottfried von Strassburg's (d. c. 1210) Tristan. "Aslauga's Knight," by de la Motte Fouqué, and William Morris's (1834–96) *The Earthly Paradise* (1868–70), a copy of which she owned.

Pen craig
Sept 23rd 80

My dearest Tonni,

I feel as if we had touched bottom at last. Your dear and altogether satisfactory letter of Sept 17th has just reached me and I write this at once on the chance of its reaching you before you start for home. After the everlasting confusion and uncertainty of your plans (as far as we were concerned) you can't tell the relief it was to hand your letter to Mamma and to hear her exclamation "It's perfect! I *knew* it was just what she would do!" Of course your last letter reassured us but I now feel for the first time that you are really coming and that D.V. [Deo Volente, God willing] we shall be standing together on the deck of the Britannic a month from today—Doesn't it seem strange? Dahin! Dahin! Can it be you are really going *dahin?* We are beginning to pull things to pieces here and it was with the saddest feelings that I saw my books taken away to be packed. I have only kept out Dante, Milton and Shelley besides a grammar and dictionary, and I advise you to take as few as possible as one can buy them over there for next to nothing and they are inconvenient and liable to duties if taken with one. Such is Fred's advice and I have followed it. Poor Mamma has been quite poorly again lately with her chest and the doctor says that the sooner she goes to town the better so we are making all our preparations to sta leave here within the next week or two. I wrote you in such haste in answer to your letter of Sept. 11th that I forgot to acknowledge your advice about the Rheinsagen. I agree with you in the choice you have suggested, but unfortunately so many have been before me. Morris has written a "Gudrun," Matthew Arnold a "Tristan," and Owen Meredith I think "Tannhäuser," Wagner "Lohengrin"! It is for that reason that I pitched on "Parzival." I think von Aue is too repulsive and too dull also.[1] But I have no time now for such occupations and shall probably wait until we get to the other side before I make my attempt. So far there seems to be a special divinity which shapes our ends, inasmuch as the journey is concerned. The doctor says that *nothing* will do us all as much good as going abroad. The climate here is very bad for Mamma's lungs and my throat has been troubling me now and then, so that the South of France will do us no end of good. Papa is well and cheerful, there is every chance of renting the house in town well, we have engaged the courier we wanted, who is to meet us in Liverpool—and last but oh not in the least *least,* our dear Tonni is coming—

It seems too good to last. Pray, pray that nothing shall go wrong—it seems such a good thing in every way as far as we can see now. I am very glad that I have not urged them very much to go. They took the staterooms without my knowing any thing about it, and I have been careful not to press them until they had quite decided, though of course they knew how I longed to go. As for you, of course it is going to do you good. I am very sorry that you should be obliged to go through such painful scenes, and we all appreciate that you are doing it on our account—but once you are well away from your explosive friends I hope a little peace is in store for you. It will be delightful to have you in New York so soon. I don't know whether we shall get there before you or not but I fancy so. At any rate I will send a line to your N.Y. address when I learn the day of your sailing. You will have got so many beseeching letters, that I shall only be repeating myself if I say how enchanted we are at having you come. It seems to set everything straight at once. There is so much to say that I don't know where or how to begin and I think that I shall wait now until I see you. I suppose we shall go on getting your letters now in answer to my various appeals, but when this reaches you, you will know that everything is most satisfactorily settled and that we are looking forward to your arrival.

Only one month before we sail! Think of it, dear Tonni. If I had you here I should really *explode,* I think. I go about fairly dancing at the thought that we are really going and that you are to be with us. Mamma wishes me to tell you that you lost a most beautiful and never-to-be-repeated epistle from her when the Vera Cruz went down.[2] She sends you her love and I am your devoted

Herz

For information I am going to take Kugler's Handbook of Italian Paintings & "An Introduction to Gothic Architecture." Ruskin's "Walks in Florence" we can get there.[3]

1. William Morris wrote "The Lovers of Gudrun" (1870), Matthew Arnold "Tristram and Iseult" (1852), Owen Meredith (Edward Robert Bulwer-Lytton) "Tannhäuser" (1861), and Richard Wagner "Lohengrin" (1850). This letter seems to imply that Anna has suggested Edith's working on one of the von Aue poems and Edith rejects it in favor of von Eschenbach's Parzival. Not only her reading but her confidence and ambition seem to know no bounds, as she implies that her own epic would stand among those of Morris, Arnold, and Meredith.

2. The ship *City of Vera Cruz,* traveling from New York to Havana, went down in a hurricane off the coast of Florida on 28 August 1880.

3. Franz Kugler (1800–1858) was a Prussian art historian whose handbook to European painting was an important early work of art history. The second volume of it was a handbook to the Italian School of painting, translated into English in 1851 by Lady Eastlake, an art historian and wife of Sir Charles Eastlake. It was probably this translation that Edith was taking to Europe, although, with her ability to read German, it might have been an original edition. John Henry Parker (1806–84) published his *Glossary of Architecture* in 1836, and, based on it, his *Handbook to Gothic Architecture* in 1849. John Ruskin's (1819–1900) volume was the common companion to English-speaking travelers to Europe, particularly Germany and Italy. Wharton later recalled following some of Ruskin's travels with her father.

The Jones family, along with Anna Bahlmann and Hannah Doyle, toured Europe from November 1880 until 1882. Wharton later recalled in A Backward Glance *having spent time at Cannes with the daughters of two of her mother's friends, the Countess de Sartiges and the Countess Bañuelos, and we know that Edith's then fiancé, Henry (Harry) Leyden Stevens, was a frequent guest. Perhaps consideration of these companions led the biographer R. W. B. Lewis to conclude that Edith's time in Europe was spent in the "harmless amusement" of picnics and tennis parties "in the company of agreeable people who would, she felt, no more understand her literary dreams than her friends had back in New York" (*EWAB, 43*). Edith probably did enjoy these lighthearted pleasures, but the well-annotated books in her library, purchased during the European trip, also reveal a young woman who was reading and studying, surely with Anna Bahlmann, the poetry of Matthew Arnold and François Coppée, the* Pensées *of Joseph Joubert, and*

the letters of Saint Francis de Sales, the latter three in the original French.[1]
She and Anna took long country walks, discovering natural, historical, and
village sights that Edith would recall in future letters.

Because the two were together for most of the trip, there are no letters but
this one, when Anna went off to visit relatives in Münster, Germany. Here
we see a charming example of Edith's humor and imagination in creating
scenes of Anna's travels, traits that will be manifest later in her fiction.

1. These annotated volumes, particularly Matthew Arnold's poetry, Joseph
Joubert's (1754–1824) *Pensées,* and Saint Francis de Sales (1567–1622), indicate
that Edith was thinking seriously about faith and morality at this stage of life. A
study of these copies of her books would yield great insight into the development
of her moral imagination.

Thursday August 4 [1881]

My dear Tonni,

Your post-card made a great sensation in the family coming so soon
after you left, & before we thought that a letter could reach us. Doyle
and I have imagined you in all the phases of your journey, your arrival,
the bursting of the red bonnet upon the astonished relatives, the storm-
ing of the Episcopal Palace and all the other things of which we expect
to hear full details in a letter tonight. Things have gone on quite as usual
here—I have been every morning to fetch the letters, papers &c & have
a walk with Papa. Other wise nothing has happened. Did you ever hear
a cuckoo? I never did until this moment, and there is one out in the trees
making the most musical call. I understand now "O Cuckoo shall I call
thee bird
Or but a wandering voice?"[1] I managed to order pancakes for dinner
yesterday and they were actually *buttered.* Mme Craven's book came
from Frankfurt this morning.[2] Doyle misses you very much & I will not
tell you how much *I* miss you because I don't want you to come home
before you are quite sated with the Bishop & the Anabaptists (how lucky
about those cages!) & all the other joys of Münster.

I took Mama out with the ponies the day before yesterday and they went very well.

Affly Yours, ENJ

1. William Wordsworth, "To the Cuckoo" (1804).
2. Pauline Marie Armande Aglae Craven (1808–91), daughter of a Breton nobleman and wife of a British civil servant, wrote numerous works of biography and fiction.

The Jones's European trip ended suddenly, in March 1882, with the death of Edith's father. Edith, her mother, Anna, and Doyle returned to the United States, where Anna resumed her peripatetic life. In June 1882 Anna wrote from New York to thank an acquaintance for her invitation to visit West Virginia, saying, "I fear there is no possibility of my going . . . as I am obliged to go to Newport first and to attend to various annoying matters here. . . . I have treasured up the glimpse I caught of you all and of life at Cotton Hill & it forms one of my pleasantest mental photographs. We grow old & deteriorate perhaps, but the memory of pleasant days remains — don't you find it so?" (to Myra Abbott, 26 June 1882). Bahlmann was thirty-three when she wrote those words. The letter was written from the home of her friends the Schultzes; Bahlmann herself may not have had even her own room in a boarding house at this time.

Edith became engaged to Harry Stevens in the summer of 1882, to the dismay of his mother, the formidable widow Mrs. Paran Stevens. An announcement of the postponement of their engagement was published in October 1882, and biographers have assumed that the engagement was then broken. We learn here, however, that in March 1883 Edith was still planning to be married the following summer (see EWAB, 37–46).

Cannes
March 27th 1883

Dear Tonni—

Your beautiful Easter card and your *long*-expected letter have just come. Thank you many times for both. I send you (but not as an adequate return for your enclosure!) a small photo of Cannes in the snowstorm, done by Rev'd Mr. Cirbet—I think I wrote you about him. The view is from the Provence & though not good will give you some idea of the amount of snow on the trees. All the orange trees are blighted, and will not blossom for four years, they say—Think what a loss for the people. It continues to pour in floods and torrents every second day. Last week we were packed and ready to start for Italy, but heard such terrible stories of the cold & snow that we gave up all thought of going and here we remain until about April 10 when we go straight to Paris. I am dreadfuly [*sic*] disappointed but there is no help for it.

On Easter Sunday we luckily had it fair. I went to Early Celebration at S. Paul's and then Mamma & Harry & I drove to La Verrerie Church, where a mass was sung by the Bañuelis, Mlle de Ségur, Duc de Mouchy, Duchesse de Luynes &c. All the French people & the Royalties were there. Mr. Stevens gave me such a pretty ring for Easter—a black & a white pearl.

March 31st—We all spent such a delightful evening a few nights since. We went to the Duchesse de Luynes and for two hours heard Gounod play his different compositions—Faust, Mireille, Romeo & Juliette &c, while Mlle de Ségur sang them! Think what a treat!—He was introduced to me—such a handsome old man with a white beard & excited gestures & wild eyes. He is just out of an insane asylum & looks as if he might go back any day. He said that Carvalho sang Faust better than anyone else. He did not like Nilsson's Gretchen—"Je ne dis pas qu'elle est sans talent mais c'est une femme en fer-blanc—Je n'aime pas les femmes en fer-blanc" [I don't say that she is without talent, but she is a woman made of tin: I do not like women made of tin].[1] He said some other epigrammatic things wh- I took the trouble to remember & write down.

Today I went to the Duchess of Vallombrosa's to hear Miss Somers-

Cocks, Lady Somers' niece, sing to the guitar. She is very clever at it. Did I tell you I was introduced the other day to the Ctesse de Paris & Pcesse Amélie of Orleans?[2] They are so simple & unaffected. We had to go afterwards to their villa (St. Jean) to inscribe names & it is so pretty with such a beautiful garden. But oh! The poor gardens—you can't think how miserable they look.

We leave for Paris on April 9th and go to the Westminster. I shall really be relieved to get away. It is pouring again in incessant floods today! Isn't it incredible? Lord A. Paget's yacht won the Regatta at Nice the other day—[3]

Well, I think that is all the news. Mama is remarkably well & sorry to leave her dear Cannes. I am too sorry that you have had such a hard winter. I think you do quite rightly not to come abroad next summer! And I should be so disappointed not to have you there when I'm "spliced!"—

Well, good by dear Tons. Mr. Rutherfurd is a little better but by no means well.

Affy yours,

Herz

1. Madame Miolan Carvalho (Caroline Marie Felix Carvalho-Miolan, 1827–95), wife of the stage manager who first staged *Faust,* was considered one of the greatest singers of the role of Margaret. Christina Nilsson was more famous for singing the role. Nearly forty years later Wharton would use Nilsson singing *Faust* in the opening scene of *The Age of Innocence.*

2. Princess Amélie of Orléans (1865–1951) was the daughter of Marie Isabelle d'Orléans, Countess of Paris (1848–1919), and was to become the Queen Consort of Portugal. Her husband and eldest son were assassinated in 1908, in her presence.

3. Minnie Stevens, sister of Harry Stevens, married Captain Arthur Henry Paget, eldest son of Lord Alfred Paget, in London in 1878, in one of a number of marriages between titled Europeans and wealthy American girls, the most famous being Consuelo Vanderbilt and the Duke of Marlborough. These girls and their marriages would be the subject of Edith's last, unfinished, novel, *The Buccaneers.* Had Edith married Harry Stevens, she would have been sister-in-law to the younger Paget.

My Dear Governess

The marriage between Edith and Harry Stevens did not take place during the summer of 1883, possibly blocked by Mrs. Stevens. It is likely that Mrs. Stevens would have lost control of her late husband's legacy had Harry married, reason enough to intervene, and in any case Lucretia Jones, daughter of old New York, disdained the wealthy newcomer to society. Perhaps she did not pay Mrs. Stevens the proper attention, thus causing resentment. With the engagement cancelled, Lucretia whisked her daughter away from Newport to Bar Harbor, Maine, where Fred and Minnie Jones were building a home. There Edith met two men who would be central to her life, Walter Van Rensselaer Berry (1859–1927) and Edward (Teddy) Robbins Wharton (1850–1928). With Walter she bicycled, walked, paddled a canoe, and talked, but he left without proposing marriage. Teddy continued to court her.

The next few letters suggest that Edith did not spend as much time with Anna Bahlmann in these years as she had in the past.

7 Washington Square N.
Dec 24 1883

My Dear Tonni,

Will you do me the favour of using the enclosed to get for yourself whatever books or other odds & ends you are secretly hoping to find in your stocking tomorrow? It would have been a far greater pleasure to me to do so myself, but I have been so little with you of late that I have had no means of finding out your wants, as I used to try to do at this season, & I should consider any random purchase I might make a present not worth offering. Let me have the pleasure of thinking that you will get something you really want, & which will remind you now & then of Your affectionate

E.N.J.

New York
Sunday [March 1885]

Dear Tons

For two days I have been trying to find a moment in which to tell you that I am to be married to Mr. Wharton, of whom you have very often heard me speak. I will tell you when I see you how charming he is—& meanwhile

dear Tons I am yr afft

Herz

New York
Tuesday evening
[March 1885]

Dear Tons,

I must thank you at once for your beautiful roses, & the never-failing impulse of love which prompted them. I am so anxious to have you meet Mr. Wharton, & in my hurried scrawl to you the other day, I told you so little of what he is, that I am glad of the excuse for writing again.

If my present happiness had come to me at eighteen, I should probably have taken it as a matter of course—but coming to me after Certain Experiences of which you know, it seems almost incredible that a man can be so devoted, so generous, so sweet-tempered & unselfish.[1] I shall be so glad to have you meet him, because he is one of the people whose charm makes itself felt at once, & I feel sure you will perceive quickly into what safe hands your Herz has fallen. You must before long find a moment to come & see me, & meanwhile I am

Yr affte Herz

1. She is no doubt referring to her broken engagement to Harry Stevens.

2

"Spliced"

Edith Newbold Jones and Edward Robbins Wharton were married at noon on 29 April 1885 in a modest ceremony at Trinity Chapel, New York, just across the street from the Jones home. Edith wore white satin trimmed with lace and silk mull; on her mass of hair, securing the veil, rested the diamond tiara that had been worn by Lucretia on her own wedding day, enhanced with diamonds given to Edith by Teddy. Her godfather, Frederic Rhinelander, escorted her down the aisle. Anna Bahlmann was almost certainly there; in the Bahlmann archive, now merely flakes in an envelope, we find the bouquet of lilies of the valley that Edith wore at her throat.

Henry James once said that by marrying Teddy Wharton, Edith Jones had done "an almost—or rather an utterly—inconceivable thing" (HJ to Howard Sturgis, quoted in Bell, 180). That was 1912, when Teddy was overcome by mania. The biographer Shari Benstock speculates that the first few years of their marriage must have been for Edith "a difficult period of adjustment—not only sexually, but intellectually and spiritually as well" (*NGC*, 59). Some, including Wharton's friend Ogden Codman, Jr., have surmised that it was a *marriage blanc,* never consummated. Wharton herself said that her lack of knowledge about sex, a result of her mother's refusal to enlighten her, "did more than anything else to falsify and misdirect my whole life" (*L&I,* 1088). But the marriage, at least at first, was far from a disaster. Whether or not there was a sexual union (a secret she would never have confided to Anna), these letters indicate, if not passionate attachment, at least an atmosphere of cheerful comradeship in travel, homemaking, and sport.

Within the family, once Edith Jones became Mrs. Edward Wharton, it was as if the Jones family had expanded with the addition of Teddy rather than Edith becoming a Wharton daughter-in-law. Teddy was, for Lucretia Jones, "like sunshine in the house."[1] He was handsome, blue-eyed, well bred, and kindly, physically active but intellectually undistinguished. Born in Boston, he was a distant relative to the Philadelphia Whartons. His favorite pursuits were fishing, shooting, golf, bicycling, and skating, and as a new husband he quickly learned to relish travel.

Edith had predicted that Anna would like her husband, and she was right. Anna Bahlmann and Teddy Wharton got along well from the beginning, each indulging the other with gifts and good humor. All three of them shared a love of animals, especially the Papillons, Pekinese, and other small dogs that always surrounded Edith and Teddy. Anna helped Teddy with his checkbook and his correspondence and generally fussed over him. Critically, she was able to soothe Teddy when moods of anxiety and depression beset him.

After the wedding, the newlyweds spent a few weeks alone together at Pen craig, then made their wedding trip to Paris, where they resided in an apartment just above that of Lucretia and Harry Jones. Edith spent her afternoons driving in the Bois de Boulogne with her mother, and she and Teddy wandered about Paris in the mornings, visiting galleries and museums. For the first few years of marriage they would spend most summers in Newport, where they furnished their first and second homes, Pen craig Cottage and Land's End. There Teddy visited Lucretia almost daily, surrounded by an entourage of little dogs. Winters were sometimes in New York, sometimes in Newport, and even on occasion in Europe; spring was for touring Italy and France. Edith wrote long, detailed letters about her travel, demonstrating a deep connection to history, to architectural beauty, to scenery, and to paintings and sculpture. She had internalized the advice of Joseph Joubert, whom she had read on her last tour of Europe as an unmarried woman: "He who has imagination without learning has wings but no feet." Edith's reading and study educated her perceptions; writing about her journeys exercised her precision and pleasure in language.

Perhaps not surprisingly, the letters speak frequently of the weather and of health. Weather conditions mattered in a world without air conditioning or adequate central heating, and in which women were required to wear tight corsets and layers of clothing. Extremes of heat and cold, constant dampness, flourishing pollen and mold, all could generate or exacerbate illness or simple malaise. Anna was subject to headaches and she understandably found extremes of cold and heat hard to tolerate. Edith suffered from airborne illnesses, asthma, throat infections, and "la grippe." Later on she complained of nervous dyspepsia. Lucretia often felt unwell in Paris; Teddy had frequent bouts of neuralgia that probably prefigured a ripening into severe mental illness. Medicine was an inexact science; neither aspirin nor antibiotics were available to ease the discomfort. Letters reflect the circumstances of the moment in which they are written, and weather and health were natural subjects.

This letter was written just a few months after Edith and Teddy were married.

1. Emelyn Washburn to Elisina Tyler, quoted in Lee, 74.

Paris, Hotel Westminster
July 1st [1885]

Meine beste Tons!

Harry had a letter from Fred yesterday, in which he said you were at Bar Harbour, & so I send this there on the chance of its finding you there still. And now I will begin with the history of our journey. We had a very slow trip, owing to the head-winds which barred our way from New York to Liverpool without the slightest intermission. However, we were both quite well, & our rooms very comfortable, so we hadn't much to complain of. We spent three or four days in London, where we did nothing in particular & were glad to hurry over to Paris. We have been here since June 14th, & have enjoyed every moment. The weather has been cool nearly all the time, & we have wandered about without being in too great a hurry. Mamma, who is looking wonderfully well, has the same Entresol [Mezzanine] she always has here, with Harry & her maid, & we have the corresponding apartment on *2nd,* so that we are very comfortable, & constantly together. In the afternoon Mamma & I drive in the Bois, in the mornings Mr. Wharton & I usually wander about together. The Salon is gaudy, décolletée, & uninteresting. But there is a most beautiful loan-collection of modern & old pictures at the Louvre which would go to your heart. Such specimens of Millet, Troyon, Daubigny, & Rousseau![1] How you would have enjoyed them. There were also exquisite pictures of Fragonard, Boucher, Van Loo & Greuze, & some of your favorite Italians, especially a beautiful Botticelli, the panels off a wedding-chest painted in most exquisite groups & landscapes.[2] We went today to the Hotel Cluny, which was more beautiful & absorbing than ever. The collection has been very much enlarged, & a beautiful collection of shoes added. The most interesting specimens of these were a pair of grey satin slippers trimmed with yellow, belonging to the Princesse de Lamballe.[3]

July 3rd My letter is destined not to overtake you at Bar Harbour at this rate, I am afraid. There never seems a moment to do anything in here! I am reading Zwei Gefangene by Paul Heyse, do you know it?[4] I am also embroidering a handkerchief case for Mr. Wharton & running about here, there & everywhere, so my correspondence suffers. Our plans are at last settled. Our cherished scheme of spending ten days in Holland has been given up, as Mr. Wharton is obliged to remain in Paris a week longer to be near Dr. Brown Séquard, who is treating his neuralgia.[5] I am therefore going to Hamburg early next week with the family & Mr. Wharton will join us a few days later, so that our travelling will be deferred until later. I must finish this now to get it off without further delay, but not without telling you a sad piece of news. Our dear friend Mignon, at the Duchesse de Luynes' gate, was caught & taken

My Dear Governess

to the pound, & killed before the concierge could get him out! What a wretched end to that dear little life. Write soon, dear Tons. I will write a long letter from Hamburg—

Yr own Herz

1. Jean François Millet (1814–75); Constant Troyon (1810–65); Charles François Daubigny (1817–78); almost certainly Théodore Rousseau (1812–67). All of these painters were associated with the Barbizon School.

2. All of the first group, with the exception of Greuze, eighteenth-century painters associated with the Rococo movement: Jean Honoré Fragonard (1732–1806); François Boucher (1703–70); Charles André (Carle) Van Loo (1705–65); Jean-Baptiste Greuze (1725–1805). Sandro Botticelli (1445–1510).

3. The Hôtel de Cluny is a museum specializing in medieval and Renaissance objects. The shoe collection evidently included more recent material. The Princesse de Lamballe was one of few truly virtuous women in the French court of Louis XVI and Marie Antoinette. For her kindness, Marie Antoinette made her superintendent of her household. She remained loyal to the royal family, for which she was executed during the Revolution.

4. Paul Johann Ludwig von Heyse (1830–1914), poet, novelist, and playwright, would be the first German to win the Nobel Prize for Literature, in 1910. *Zwei Gefangene* (Two prisoners) was published in 1878.

5. Dr. Charles-Édouard Brown-Séquard (1817–94) was a noted physiologist and neurologist then holding the chair of experimental medicine at the Collège de France. His work on the physiology of the spinal cord broke new ground.

The art exhibition Edith mentioned in the previous letter was an important one in Paris that summer. Put together to benefit orphans of the war between France and Austria, the exhibition contained paintings owned by dozens of wealthy patrons and included many paintings by a wide variety of European painters. They were displayed based on who owned the paintings rather than any intrinsic method of style, era, or nationality. That Edith should have made two lists of painters, grouping them by their style, indicates both her deep knowledge of art history and the orderly way her mind worked. Edith's cultivation, her appreciation for the paintings she sees, her knowledge of French history and the life of the Princesse de Lamballe are products both of Anna Bahlmann's work as finishing governess and of Edith's insatiable curiosity and study.

The Whartons returned to New York in November 1885, traveling with Lucretia and Harry Jones, beginning a pattern of spending fall and winter in New York, spring in Europe, and summer in Newport. When they were apart, Edith and Anna wrote to each other regularly. These early letters testify to Edith's powers of observation and description and manifest her love affair with Italy, its light, its history and architecture. The travelers drove along the coast of the Ligurian Sea, though it is not clear whether they managed to visit the tiny coastal towns known as the Cinque Terre. Edith reveled in the scenery and the natural wonders. She makes no mention of La Spezia as the "Gulf of the Poets," called so for the numerous poets, from Dante to the English Romantics, who visited there. Alassio and San Remo are resort towns then frequented by British and Russian travelers. The "lower church" that she wished to see in Assisi is part of the Basilica di San Francesco, built on a hill once known as Colle d'Inferno, but now called Paradise Hill.

Rome

April 14th [1886?]

My dear Tonni,

I felt quite reproached when I received this morning your charming letter of March 28th—but I feel sure you know that the only reason why I have not written to you, is that I have devoted every moment of time to sending relays of letters to Mamma. I certainly intended to send you a line from Cannes, however, for the Riviera was as lovely as it always is in Spring, "Alles grünte und blühte" [all is greening up and flourishing] (isn't my Goethe correct?) & such lovely tints in earth & sea & sky I never imagined in my life. Then we spent a week at Mte Carlo, which was even more beautiful, & certainly there is nothing on the Riviera to equal the view one gets in driving from there out to the point of Cap Martin. On the 1st of April we started in a traveling carriage with Mrs. Schuyler, Miss Langdon, & Mr. Clement March, to drive from Nice to Spezia¹—The expedition occupied about ten days, our stopping places being S. Remo, Alassio, Genoa, Sestri Levante &

Spezia. It was one long vision of beauty, from morning until night, & the mixture of tropical vegetation with the clouds of spring blossoms on the fruit-trees, & the budding green of willows, figs, & larches made the landscape really gorgeous. Mrs. Schuyler & her party left us at Sestri Levante, where we stayed over a day—Such a queer little old ~~face~~ place, with a line of frescoed & faded houses along the beach. Our Hotel, a queer old house built just over the sea, with a stone-court-yard planted with flowers, was the quaintest place imaginable, & I am quite sure my room was haunted.

We got a boat & spent the whole afternoon rowing along the exquisite shores. The sea was like glass, & so clear that we could see the anchor chains of the vessels in the port, & the little fishes darting about on the bottom. We poked into caves, where flower beds of scarlet anemones were spreading themselves open in the clear water,—we coasted around steep headlands, with ruins on their top—or we drifted along, lying in the bottom of the boat & staring at the wonderful panorama of mountains along the coast, right & left as far as the eye could reach. The finest day's drive we had was over the Velva Pass between Sestri & Spezia, & I collected a lovely lot of orchises, primroses, pink heather &c for my book.[2] At Pisa, where we went next, we found the weather so cold & dreary that we came on here for a few days. I found Rome just as I had remembered it in my infancy, but the place I had felt the greatest curiosity about, the Sistine Chapel, has been a blow to me. Imagine going in & finding a bare room, stripped of everything churchlike, & crowded with a horde of Baedeker-bearing tourists, all reading aloud little sentences to each other "sotte voce" such as—"This figure displays Michael Angelo's marvelous powers of foreshortening" or "the fresco in the lunette was freely retouched by Vasari, in the time of Pope Julius the 99th—" Another illusion gone!

The fact is, the best thing in Rome, to my mind, is the line of the ruined aqueduct on the Campagna, against the background of the Alban Mountains—& that sight, Miss Tons, is "hard to beat."

The churches in Rome are as gorgeous as gold & marbles can make them, but they are more like temples than churches, & at every step one's eye is offended by some 18th century barbarism in the shape of a statue or frescoe. From here we shall probably go in a few days to Perugia, driving over to Assisi the next day to see the "lower church" of Giotto, which has always been the desire of my heart. Then we go to Florence, Milan & the Lakes — & to Paris about May 15th. I am so sorry about the wretched brown jacket. I am sure I could wear it, for I am as thin as a rail. Too much traveling always makes me fit to exhibit at Barnum's as the Thin Lady! — I am glad, however, that you are getting fat;[3]

1. Clement March was a Boston friend. The others do not appear again in the letters or in any biography of Wharton.

2. Variously called her "book" and her "squasher," this was the herbarium that Edith, like many women of the time, kept as a record of the plants she'd seen.

3. The letter has been cut in mid-sentence.

Castellamare, Hotel
Quisisana
Sunday March 27th [1887]

Dear Tons —

Having come to one of the most beautiful places I have ever seen, it occurs to me that you will like to hear a little about it, more specially as it is very like our dear Riviera. We got tired of the snow & damp in Paris & the Riviera being out of the question we left for Turin on March 22nd, & after spending a very pleasant day there, went on the next night to Rome. There again we only halted a night, & yesterday morning took the early train to Naples. It was a beautiful day, & "alles grünte und blühte" — the hedges & the willows were covered with a light green mist, & the fruit-trees covered with white blossoms looked like puffs of smoke scattered up the hills. The journey is a very beautiful one, & the effect of the blue cloud-shadows on the hills, & the brilliant green of the corn fields in the valleys below, made the most exquisite combination of colours that you can imagine. On every hill-top an old grey village was perched, looking as sunburnt & weather beaten & mysterious as the one we explored — was it Vence or Cagnes? & in the oldest & greyest-looking, according to

My Dear Governess

Murray, St. Thomas Aquinas was born![1] We saw Monte Cassino, high up on its bare mountain, more like a fortress than a monastery, & as we got near Naples, everything assumed an Eastern look—or what one fancies to be Eastern—the houses being built very low, with flat roofs on which the people were sitting.

Naples itself is more gorgeous, more noisy, more brilliant than anything you can conceive of—& also filthier, & more detestable. Along the water is a strip of garden planted with palms, olives, & oranges—beyond this the sea & the exquisite outline of Capri. The town itself is interminably long, a Kaleidoscope of colours, a rush, a bustle, an endless shrieking & uproar. We drove the whole length of it, had luncheon at an Hotel on the sea & then came on here. Take out your map & you will see that we are on the opposite side of the bay of Naples, looking directly over the plain of Herculaneum & Pompeii at Vesuvius puffing away in the sunshine & Naples spread out along the water just facing us. This Hotel is perched on a hillside above the village of Castellamare, & we look out over a jumble of olive-orchards & tiled roofs at the beautiful bay & the still more beautiful coast. I wish you could see the Hotel. It is built very much like the funny old house at Bordighera, where we spent a night. We have to go in & out of each other's rooms in a most-sociable way, & my bedroom opens on a wide terrace, looking south towards Sorrento. From the terrace a flight of steps leads to a path bordered with roses & violets, & this in turn to the orange-garden below. The mountains seem to rise up abruptly behind us, & the steep road which passes the Hotel gate leads up under an arch of huge trees to the Royal Palace of Quisisana about half a mile higher up. We walked up there this morning. The walls on either side of the road are covered with maidenhair & beautiful mosses, which I longed to clap into my "squasher"! From the gate of Quisisana to the Palace, there is an avenue of chestnut-trees, under which is a perfect *mat* of periwinkles, violets, & maidenhair. The Palace itself is a dilapidated building, with an arched entrance which gives on a lovely neglected garden full of orange trees, violets, & broken statues covered with ivy. The Palace is built around three sides of the garden. It is painted pink & streaked with those soft brownish stains peculiar to Italian houses. How I wish you could see it all!—

On the way back, we passed a little villa, only one story high, & painted *yellow*. It was marked "to let or for sale," & just as we were looking at it an old peasant woman came along with a key & opened the door. Of course we pretended that we wanted to hire it, so she invited us in. A narrow hall gave on a double flight of steps covered with ivy & these led down to a delicious little garden full of mandarin trees. At the lower end of the garden was a long low pavilion, also painted yellow, with a dining room looking out over the sea, & another little room on each side, one marked "Solitudo," the other "Valetudo."—the study and smoking room, I suppose.[2] It was all so still, delicious, sunshiny & out-of-the world that I should have liked to take possession of it on the spot.—We thanked the old lady, & were about to leave, when she stopped us, & kicking off her wooden shoes, climbed with amazing ease to the top of a high mandarin-tree, & came down with two bunches of fruit for us!!—In what other country can one have such experiences?—Imagine Doyle "shimming" up a Pen craig pear-tree to offer fruit to our visitors!

We are going to stay here two or three days longer, in order to drive over to Sorrento & back & give Teddy a chance to see Pompeii & Vesuvius. For my part, I prefer to stay on the terrace & look at the view. The people are so filthy, noisy & brutal to animals that I hate to go among them—"Only man is vile" ought to have been written of Southern Italy instead of Ceylon's Isle.[3] We are going back to Rome for a day or two, & then we go North, to Perugia, Florence, &c. Beautiful as this is, I much prefer the North of Italy. Still, I am very glad to have seen this, & I only wish you could have seen it with me. It is so deliciously warm that we have quite forgotten the snow & ice of Paris. I am afraid in the North we shall find the weather less satisfactory, but I am curious to see Florence again after five or six years. I hope you won't think that this letter is too much of a "describe"—I know you like to see pretty places, with your mind's eye if no other way is practicable—& so I hope you may enjoy this glimpse of it with me.—We are both well, although I am sorry to say that Teddy's neuralgia is not quite got rid of, as we had hoped.—

My Dear Governess

Do write me soon, & don't let me hear of too many headaches!
Goodbye, dear Tons,

Ihr [Your] "Herz" —

1. The Catholic philosopher and theologian Saint Thomas Aquinas (c. 1225–74) was born in Roccasecca, between Rome and Naples.

2. "Solitudo" means solitude. "Valetudo," in Latin means good health, but in Italian it might also mean "anything goes."

3. From a hymn by Reginald Heber (1783–1826), "The Son of God Goes Forth to War."

Returning from Italy, Edith and Teddy spent the summer in Newport, Rhode Island. Pen craig Cottage, owned by Lucretia Jones, sat just across Harrison Street from the family home, and it was Teddy and Edith Wharton's first residence, as it had been for her brother and sister-in-law, Fred and Minnie, before them. Edith delighted in having her own home in which to try out her ideas about decoration, and subsequent letters show the Whartons collecting furniture and pieces of art and enjoying their garden. Here they installed housekeeper Catherine Gross, a native of Alsace-Lorraine, and manservant Alfred White, an Englishman born in India.[1] Both, like Anna Bahlmann, would serve the family for more than forty years, strong testimony to Edith Wharton's ability to inspire loyalty and devotion in those who served her. Here the couple began to collect their brood of dogs and kept horses and ponies, too.

The Cottage was substantial, but not as large as the Jones house after which it was named, and certainly nothing like the new, enormously elaborate "cottages" that were being built by families whose money was more ample and more recently acquired. Pen craig Cottage, with two floors of family rooms and a third floor for the servants, was uninsulated, cold and damp in the fall and winter, and hot and steamy in the summer; Edith's health suffered as she battled asthma and allergies.

1. I am indebted to Sarah Kogan for the discovery of White's place of birth.

Pen craig Cottage

Aug 4th 1887

Dear Tons—I haven't written to you these many days, because I knew
that what you wanted was perfect quiet & rest, & I was afraid that you
might feel obliged to answer my letter. Now, however, I feel that I must
know how you are getting on, & I also have a message from Mama to de-
liver to you. The message is, will you come & spend the month of Sept.
with her? Now do think favourably of this. I don't think the weather is
enervating in Sept. & I think perhaps the change might benefit you as
well & your visit would brighten up and please Mama. She has asked me
to write to you because she is so poorly herself. She has never picked up
entirely from the attack of sore-throat she had last month, & the intense,
sickening heat has used her up terribly. She has been having a masseuse
but doesn't feel much benefited by it. In fact I don't think anything will
do her much good except a radical change in the weather. I dread to
think, my poor Tons, what you must have suffered in this heat, which
I suppose has been worse with you than here. Do write me a line to say
how you are faring, & if you will agree to Mama's proposition.

I have been keeping house alone for ten days as Teddy has been at
Saratoga. His malaria is quite broken up, but his neuralgia is quite as bad
as ever. I expect him home tomorrow, & then we have a succession of
visitors for the next few weeks. I am *crazy* to have you see the Cottage,
& look forward anxiously to the prospect of yr coming to Pen craig.
Affly Yr

Herz

September 24th 1887

Dear Tons

I have had a letter from Mr. William Jay, who after prefacing his
remarks by the aphorism that "the tree is known by its fruits," goes on
to say that he would be deeply grateful if I were to enquire of you, in
his behalf, whether you have a daily hour & a half to give next winter to
his daughter Julia, aged 8 years.[1] An appeal so indirectly flattering to me

My Dear Governess

I of course transmit with all possible haste, very much hoping that you are not too entirely "bespoke" to make some arrangement with Mr. Jay. I think that he deserves encouragement for wanting his daughter to be just like me, & I hope you will do your best to produce something approaching the intellectual chef d'oeuvre now addressing you—of course, it can never be equalled! I have unluckily mislaid your last letter, & so I am not sure whether you are still at Elizabeth. However, I will put "please forward," which I hope will appeal to somebody's heart.—Mr. Jay says that the lesson may begin in the morning or afternoon, as best suits your convenience.

In haste yrs

Herz

All well here, but *very* cold.

1. Julia was the older of two daughters of Colonel William and Lucy Oelrichs Jay, the other being Eleanor, whom Anna also would teach. The Jay family, descended from John Jay, were among the many prominent Old New Yorkers who made up the social world of the Joneses and Whartons. William Jay was known for promoting coaching—driving antique and modern carriages with horses—as a sport for the wealthy, and his daughter Eleanor would grow up to be a noted horsewoman.

As the Whartons did not have a house in New York, they stayed with Lucretia Jones when they were in the city, and the following letter bears her address on West 25th Street. Bahlmann had several friends in Virginia as well as relatives of her sister-in-law, Lydia Abbot Bahlmann, and she frequently visited among them. Bahlmann's gifts to Edith on her birthday and at Christmas must have cost dearly from her small salary, and it is no wonder that she made something with her hands from time to time.

28 West 25th St.
[New York]
Thursday [December 29,
1887]

Dear Tons,

I have had to wait until now to thank you for your lovely bit of
"Hand-arbeit," as I didn't know your Norfolk address — & I write now,
to tell you how a propos a gift it was, & also to wish you on your return
the best of New Years!

As to the embroidery, it will adorn next Summer the gala room at
the Cottage, & I hope you will see it there. It is so exquisitely done, & the
colouring is so soft, that it went straight to my heart as soon as I saw it.

As to Ruskin, I forgot to say that of course I will change it for you
if you have it already, but I don't think you would have been so horribly
deceitful as to pretend that you wanted it, if this had been the case! With
another happy New Year your affte,

Herz

28 West 25th St.
Wednesday January 25
[1888]

Dearest Tons,

How sweet of you to remember that your ancient Herz was 26
yesterday. Your present was *just right* as usual — a most exquisite little bit
in itself, & doubly acceptable in that our little rooms are crying for a few
good etchings & engravings. I hope that I shall see you before Saturday,
but I know how busy you always are, & should you not find time to drop
in, I will say Aufwiedersehen in the Cottage next Summer.

We expect to get back about the 10th of June. We have taken the
Steam yacht "Vanadis," & we join her at Algiers, probably, on Feb 15th,
having decided to go to the East by way of Africa, Cyprus, Rhodes, Asia
Minor, &c, & come back by way of Greece & Sicily —
Thank you again & a hundred kisses from

Yr devoted Herz

In A Backward Glance *Wharton tells the story of how she and Teddy came to take a four-month Mediterranean cruise with a friend and cousin by marriage, James Van Alen. Although the family objected strenuously to the trip because of the cost—and we must remember that Edith's brothers controlled her inheritance—Teddy famously asked his wife, "Do you really want to go?" and, when she said that she did, replied: "All right. Come along, then." Edith kept a detailed diary of the trip, which was lost to us until 1991, when the French researcher Claudine Lesage was shown a typescript in English by a librarian at the municipal library in Hyères, France. This diary, now published as* The Cruise of the Vanadis, *is the first developed piece of travel writing Wharton attempted. Vanadis was one of the names of the Norse goddess Freyja, goddess of love, beauty, war, and death.*

Edith and Teddy clambered up and down hills, rode donkeys, climbed staircases to remote monasteries and villages, attended festivals, ate and drank strange foods and beverages, and awoke at dawn to enjoy the views from their yacht. Always on the alert for embroidery, jewelry, and pottery, they learned to negotiate crowds of villagers eager to sell anything they possessed. They had tea with local dignitaries and expatriate Europeans and watched their backs for murderers and thieves. The Whartons were young, curious, and healthy, and they were having the time of their lives.

Yacht Vanadis, Mitylene[1]
April 12th [1888]

Dear Tonni—Have you been wondering all this time why you have never had a line from me, or have you with your usual wisdom attributed it to the volumes of correspondence which I send off daily to the Frau Mama? This is, at all events, the raison d'etre of my long silence—but today, having an afternoon to spare, my first impulse is to tell you how often I have wished for you & how many times I have said to myself, "If Tons could only see this or that!" I daresay Mama or Trix or some of the family have reported our movements to you & you have heard something of all our queer & enchanting experiences. At any rate, you are to be compelled to read my journal when you visit me at Pen craig Cottage next Summer, so I will not go into an elaborate résumé of our travels. I have been very much worried about Mama all the time, & at one time was on the point of going home—but as Harry cabled me not to do so, we decided that we had no right to break our engagement with Mr. Van Alen if there was no real necessity for me at home. Of course, had we been merely travelling, I should have gone back at once. Apart from this worry, I have enjoyed the trip even more intensely than I expected. We have been particularly blessed in the matter of weather, & today we were quite taken aback by a cold rain storm, having had I think 24 days of continuous sunshine. In fact, out of the 54 days of our cruise, only five have been rainy. Since we reached the Ionian Islands the weather has been divine, & when I tell you that I have been beginning the day with a cold sea-bath & my coffee "en chemise" to keep cool, you will see that we have virtually anticipated Summer. Of all that we have seen, perhaps the Aegean has been the most interesting, because even for yachts it is still unfrequented ground, & each island has its primitive & picturesque characteristics. In one, Stampalia, all the women still wear the most gorgeous costumes—in another we found a wonderful old monastery, founded by Alexius Comnenus, & built in a cave half way up a huge perpendicular cliff overhanging the sea[2]—In another island, Tenos, we saw the great Greek festival of the Annunciation at the Church of the Miraculous Virgin "Our Lady of Good Tidings." Thousands of peasants, from Asia Minor, the Islands, Greece & Albania were there, many in beautiful dresses, & the sight was indescribably strange & picturesque. Then at Patmos, we saw the Cave of the Apocalypse, & the wonderful old fortified Monastery of St. John the Divine, built about the 10th century, & with all its defences & battlements complete.[3] Fancy smoking cigarettes & eating sweetmeats with the Head of such a venerable institution, in a room painted with Byzantine frescoes! But we are getting so used to such things that Teddy complains the edge is worn off his appreciation powers! We have just been spending two very pleasant days at Smyrna, where we had letters to several people, who took us about the bazaars &c.—It is one of the most curious places I have ever seen—a great city splendidly placed on cypress-covered hills at the head of a gulf enclosed in high mountains — & as one approaches there is nothing Eastern in the wide quays, with tramways & the huge houses with high-pitched roofs — But go ashore, & see the lemonade sellers in their yellow silk coats, the Jewesses in long silk robes & little velvet caps, the horse-cars stopped by trains of loaded camels, the donkeys with necklaces of blue beads to protect them from the evil eye, the Turkish women in bright, coloured striped garments with black veils over their faces, the "cavasses" of the different consulates in superbly-embroidered jackets & gaiters, with jeweled weapons in their belts — all these Eastern sights, contrasted with the big shops & the European civilization form the most extraordinary picture you can imagine.[4]

We spent all our time in wandering through the bazaars which, though not nearly as Oriental as the Tunisian ones, are very picturesque & amusing — Besides, it is about the only safe thing to do, as if you stir outside of the town, you are liable to be assassinated or carried off by brigands, & even, if you are known to be well-off, you are not safe in the streets. Murders are committed in broad day, & 21 people have been killed during the last month. The American Consul & his wife cannot go out without an armed cavass, & even then not far from home. I assure you that when any one walked behind us in the streets, Teddy & I kept our eyes in the backs of our heads.

All this time I have told you nothing of Malta, Sicily, or Rhodes — of the old Venetian silver I got in Zante or the wonderful bits of Greek "Handarbeit" which I was lucky enough to pick up among the peasants in the small islands. You will grow wild when you see them & some, I think, you will find easy & amusing to copy. —

We are lying now in the harbor of Mitylene where the storm obliged us to go for shelter, & from here we are going to Mount Athos, & then down between Greece & Negropont & around to the Piraeus — We shall stay four or five days in Athens, sending the yacht around to Corinth to meet us. Then to Ithaca & Corfu, & ten days in Istria & Dalmatia & then home. We hope to sail on June 2nd. Teddy & I are both very well, but I confess that this morning when we were out in the fury of the gale

& my coffee upset over me & everything stood on its head—well, even after eight weeks' apprenticeship "I weiss nicht, was sollt'es bedeuten, Dass ich so traurig war"!!!⁵

Goodbye, alte liebe Tonni—Your affte

Herz

1. Capital city of the Island of Lesbos.

2. Alexius Comnenus (1056–1118), Byzantine emperor from 1081 until his death.

3. The Cave of the Apocalypse is said to be the spot where Saint John the Divine received the visions from Christ that he recorded in the Book of Revelation. Alexius Comnenus ceded the island of Patmos to the monastery in 1088.

4. Cavasses are Turkish armed police officers.

5. "Ich weiß nicht was soll es bedeuten, / Daß ich so traurig bin," Heinrich Heine (1797–1856), lyrics to *Die Laurelei*, "I know not what is the meaning of this sorrow that fills me."

Home from their cruise, the Whartons wished to have their own place in New York rather than continue to live with Lucretia on West 25th Street. Bahlmann, who had evidently returned to New York from a recent visit to the Whartons in Newport, made herself useful by helping the couple to procure a house they had considered renting on Madison Avenue. Soon such favors would be a part of her job as Edith's secretary.

Pen craig Cottage,
Newport, R.I.
Monday Oct 8th [1888]

Dear Tons,

Thank you a thousand times for both your telegram & letter. As usual, you have proved yourself the right woman for an emergency, & have told me, in the clearest terms, just exactly what I wanted to know. The house *is* the one that Teddy saw, but he did not go over it, as we then intended to take a house for longer than May 1st, which is the term fixed in this case—Now, however, we have learned that beggars must not be

My Dear Governess

choosers, & have telegraphed an offer for it. I can't tell you how grateful I am to you for all the pains you have taken in my behalf, especially at a time when I know you had so much else to do.—You are a trump & you always were one! I am also oppressed by the guilty consciousness that I didn't give you half enough money for your telegram. Let me know if the enclosed covers it. We are going to town tomorrow night for two days— We shall be at 28 W. 25th [the home of Lucretia Jones]. If you have time to drop in, I shall be delighted, but I shall hardly expect you, knowing how busy you are just now. Teddy came back on Friday night, with only three birds! I am deep in vol. 2nd of Gibbon & much interested.[1] It is no use telling you how I enjoyed your visit—you saw it—

Love & thanks again—Herz

1. Edward Gibbon (1737–94), *The History of the Decline and Fall of the Roman Empire.*

Edith's occupation with the history of the Roman Empire while Teddy goes out hunting gives a clear picture of their different interests and pursuits.

In 1889 several wealthy summer residents of Newport filed an injunction opposing the construction of a trolley system in Newport, fearing it would spoil their pristine landscape. Year-round residents, many of whom had to travel to work in the "cottages," needed the transportation. The Rhode Island Supreme Court denied the injunction, and that year the Newport Street Railway Company opened its first line on Commercial Wharf. Teddy Wharton was deeply involved in the opposition group.

Edith, meanwhile, was writing and publishing. From the late 1880s into the early 1890s, she filled a notebook with poems, some dramatic monologues in the style of Robert Browning, and some sonnets, several of them experiments in metrics.[1] And she sent them out for publication. Scribner's Magazine *took two poems in 1889, "The Last Giustiniani" and "Happiness," and Thomas Bailey Aldrich, editor of the* Atlantic Monthly, *published "Euryalis" in December. It must have been particularly rewarding to have a man whose poetry she had admired as a child accept a poem of her own.*

1. Her notebook is in the Wharton archives at the Lilly Library, Indiana University. Most of the poems remain unpublished and unread.

Pen craig Cottage
Newport R.I.
July 10th [1889]

My dear Tonni,

I am getting on so much better that I feel I owe you something more than the scrawl I sent you a few days since — It stills rains nearly every day, but in the interval the heat has been intense, and we have all felt it very much — Mama, like the rest of us, has been hors de combat for a day or two, but not seriously so. The Dodies [dogs] have resisted better than their owners, & are all in fine condition. My rheumatism has disappeared, which is also much to be thankful for. — We are still leading the same quiet life as when you were here, & if it were not for the constant committee meetings which take so much of Teddy's time I should be inclined to forget all about the electric R.R. There is no sign of its starting yet, & rumours are afloat that it will not run this Summer. Meanwhile the Association is plodding on & I suppose by Autumn we shall know our fate, but not before. I had a charming letter from Howells the other day, telling me to send him my verses, so I suppose I shall know my fate in a few weeks! Miss Taylor is nearly finished. — The garden is looking lovely just now. The foxgloves are nearly over, but the larkspurs & hollyhocks are in bloom, and also the yellow coreopsis. The white clematis that I so ruthlessly cut in pieces has started up again, which is certainly more than I deserved. Kitten is squealing for his ball, so I must stop! Write soon again — Your account of your rooms at Brentsville sounds very cosy & shady & pleasant[1] — I am going soon to send you some Band of Mercy Pamphlets[2] —
Yr aff

Herz

1. Brentsville, Virginia, in the heart of hunting country, near Manassas, where Bahlmann visited her friends the Schultzes.

2. The Band of Mercy was a children's animal rights organization begun in Britain and, by 1889, was spreading internationally. It seems possible, based on Wharton's letter of 24 August 1889, that Anna Bahlmann was trying to start a chapter. Both Edith and Teddy Wharton were at this time involved in the Society for the Prevention of Cruelty to Animals.

Newport
Aug 24th 1889

My dear Tonni,

I am afraid you have been misbehaving, & have "kept back part of the price" as regards an accurate account of your health.[1] I hope that the little trip you propose making will be satisfactory, but I shan't be really pleased until I see you back here looking as well & jolly as you did in the early Summer. Don't feel obliged to write letters to me, just send me a postal from time to time, *truthfully* stating how you are. For my part I am a good deal better, & very little bothered about my rheumatism. Since I last wrote you there has been a fatal accident on the electric R.R. Something blew up in a car, one man was killed & another desperately wounded.[2] The Newport Association, though very sorry for the sufferers, feels that it's an ill-wind that blows nobody any good, & has promptly started a fresh suit against the R.R. —

I have had another stroke of luck—the Editor of the Century has accepted "The Sonnet on the Sonnet" & I feel much pleased at getting into the two best magazines of the country at once.[3] I shall be delighted to have you here any time in Sept. There is no need to fix the date as yet. I am reading the Inferno. It is rather hard work, as I have to use Longfellow's translation as a help, & I have never before got beyond 10 or 12 Cantos, but this time I am well on in the teens, & much absorbed of course. What images! I have ghosts who eye Dante as men "look at one another sharply at night, beneath the new moon" — the whirlwind that goes on its way "superb & *powderous*" (This word is mine, Longfellow calls it "laden with dust" or something of that sort) & that magnificent rebuke —

> "No martyrdom, save that of thine own rage
> Were for thy rage sufficient martyrdom"[4]

Longfellow's translation is perfectly unpoetic & perfectly literal, there-fore most useful & not distracting. And then the piercing sweetness of such lines as "Guardami ben, ben son, ben son, Beatrice"[5] — Well, I am almost afraid it is finer than Milton — & what would it be to any one who really knew Italian well! —

After all, I don't believe there is any greater blessing than that of being pierced through & through by the splendour or sweetness of words, & no one who is not transfixed by "Die Sonne tönt nach alter Weise," or "thick as Autumnal leaves that strew the brooks" has known half the joy of living.[6] Don't you agree with me? — I wouldn't take a king-dom for it —

Well, goodbye dear Tonni. The Newport S.P.C.A. is flourishing. — Don't have the Band of Mercy on your mind. It will probably germinate in time.

Yr loving

Herz

I will keep Trix's letters —

1. Acts 5:2. Ananias sold a piece of property but brought only a part of the proceeds to the Apostles.

2. According to the official report by the railway, on 18 August 1889, some-one on the train raised an alarm, causing the brakeman to apply the brakes. This caused noise and smoke, alarming the passengers, several of whom jumped from the car. William Anderson died of his injuries several days later. The Newport Improvement Society, of which Teddy Wharton was a member, used this event as further fuel for its opposition to the railway.

3. Richard Watson Gilder (1844–1909) was the editor of *Century*. Wharton's "Sonnet" did not appear until November 1891. Meanwhile, *Scribner's* published "The Last Giustiniani" in October, 1889; *Atlantic Monthly* published "Eurya-lis" and *Scribner's* published "Happiness," both in December 1889; and *Scrib-ner's* published "Botticelli's Madonna in the Louvre" in January, 1891. Wharton would have a longtime association with *Scribner's* editor Edward L. Burlingame (1848–1922).

4. Inferno XIV.54–55. Robert Pinsky translates these lines: "No torment but this raging of yours could goad / With agony enough to match your ire."

My Dear Governess

5. From *Purgatorio*, at the moment when Dante finally sees Beatrice. John Ciardi translates this line: "Look at me well. I am she. I am Beatrice" (XXX.73).

6. "Die Sonne," from the Prologue to Goethe's *Faust*. Barker Fairley translates it: "The sun resounds among the singing spheres with its ancient music." "Thick as Autumn leaves" is from Milton, *Paradise Lost*, I.302.

Edith and Anna continued to share their pleasure in language and poetry. We don't know what "little trip" Anna Bahlmann was contemplating, but wherever it was, her transportation was never as easy as traveling was for the Whartons. In this excerpt from an undated letter to her sister-in-law Lydia, we get a glimpse of Bahlmann's life of service to others. Even with the new Brooklyn Bridge, she might have had to take a ferry to Brooklyn and certainly to Hoboken, and to get to the ferry she would have had to take a series of horse-drawn streetcars.

> *Last week I called on Bertha Hoelscher, this afternoon I am going to see Mrs. Seitz, Schultz' sister, who lost her only son last spring. These good people live either in Hoboken or far out in Brooklyn, or up in Harlem, & the getting there takes hours. Then Mrs. Kirchner wants me to help her make her will, & I am supposed to answer letters; so that sometimes I am in a perfect whirl. This is a disgraceful piece of work to send you, but ever since I began to write you, a blatant street-organ has been under my window, & my pen would keep time, like an old circus horse that hears a band while in harness. I leave you to the pleasure of deciphering. (to Lydia Bahlmann, undated)*

Bahlmann continued to be of assistance to Edith and Teddy Wharton as well.

Pen craig Cottage
Oct 14th [1889]

Dear Tonni

A line in haste to explain my telegram. Teddy wrote to Mr. Thomson nearly a week ago to make further enquiries about the shooting, but has had no reply. He has decided, nevertheless, to leave for Brentsville on

the 17th, & as we did not know the telegraph station, we hit on the expedient of getting you to telegraph. Now will you also write a line to Reid's Hotel to ask them to look after Teddy, & if there are any other friends of yours there who could help him about his shooting, you would do him a great favour by giving him a line of introduction, which you could send him at Reid's Hotel, to meet him on his arrival there—I am afraid I am rather incoherent, but I am writing in great haste, as I want this to get off as soon as possible. Mr. Thomson's not answering has rather made a mess of things. We are all well, & everybody sends love—
Yrs affte,

Herz

"Miss Bahlmann will write" at the end of the telegram means, will you please send a line to Mr. Thomson, in case he never rec'd Teddy's letter, explaining who he is, &c—

Pen craig Cottage
Oct 16th [1889]

Dear Tonni,

Thanks a thousand times for your prompt & thoughtful letter, which will be of the greatest help to Teddy—He has not heard at all from the Thomsons, but I have no doubt that it will be all right when he gets there. He leaves tomorrow morning & will be gone about a week if the shooting is good. Did I tell you in my last hurried scrawl that we sail on Nov 13th for the Azores? We shall go to town about the 5th or 6th. Things here are going on very peacefully, as usual—We are moving trees, & when it rains I practise difficult metres!—As it rains every two days, I ought to be past master of rhythm before long—Mama had a long letter from Trix yesterday, but I have only glanced at it. I seem always destined to write to you in a hurry, & now I must trot out to attend to some work in the garden—

Ever yr aff Herz

My Dear Governess

Another of Edith Wharton's travelogues, the next letter, written from the south of France, reveals the pleasure Edith and Teddy took in traveling together, as well as Edith's increased freedom from her family's strictures as a result of her marriage. She takes in scenery and studies architecture, and she gets swept away by the history of a location, particularly one as striking as the salt flats of Aigues-Mortes. All of the reading and study she has done in advance of visiting a site combine in the crucible of her imagination with the evidence of her senses, so that when she writes she produces a rich and rounded evocation of place.

Coincidentally, around the time the Whartons visited Arles, a little-known painter, Vincent Van Gogh, had recently left the city to live voluntarily in an asylum a few miles away.

Arles

March 13th 1890

My dear Tonni

My first thought after a ramble through this queer old place is, "Now for a letter to Tonni, since I have really something to tell her about"—So no sooner said than done, & here I am at work already. We left Cannes yesterday, despite the astonishment of our family at our venturing North so early, & all sorts of prophecies of cold & bad weather— but so far we have carried Cannes weather with us, & we only pray it may continue for our little three days trip in Languedoc. So far we are much pleased. The journey from Marseilles to this place was made positively lovely by the fruit-orchards with their masses of pink & white bloom, & once in the queer streets of Arles, having crossed a moat, & entered the city walls, we felt we must be in Italy again.—The streets are very narrow, & many of the houses are charming, with sculptured niches at the corners containing statues of saints. There are even one or two Early Renaissance houses in the pretty French style, with angle turrets. Roman remains never say much to me, but under this very blue sky the amphitheater & theater are rather picturesque. Most delightful, however, is the church of St. Trophime with its exquisite doorway covered with Romanesque sculpture, & the still more beautiful cloister adjoining, a marvel of wonderfully-carved columns & niches, & such a dreamy, sunny place, with ring-doves cooing on the roof. I am very fond of cloisters, & this of St. Trophime is one [of] the quietest & most beautiful that I have ever seen. This afternoon we drove out to see more of St. Trophime, at the Abbey of Mont Majour, ~~where~~ built over the cave in which he lived—(not having Mrs. Jameson within reach I am not clear when he occupied it.)[1] Mont Majour is most picturesque, built on a knoll covered with ilex & olive trees which rises out of the level plain like an island—as it originally was—The whole place is falling to ruin, but the various churches & chapels are taken care of, & also the beautiful cloister, plainer & I should think earlier than St. Trophime, but in the same style. The great charm of it all is that nobody goes there, that it is covered with ivy & wild plants, & that from the splendid keep you look over a lonely plain, with only a rosy cloud of fruit trees hanging here & there against the horizon. I "Kodaked" away as hard as I could, & I hope successfully—but the sun rather failed me, as it was getting late. Tomorrow morning we are going to St. Gilles, to see the splendid triple door which has been tantalizing me for years in all my architecture books—Then we go to Nimes, & from there to Aigues Mortes & back, & then to Avignon. A very nice little trip, don't you think so, if only the good weather holds.

March 15th Alas, it didn't—the weather I mean. It poured yesterday morning, & as I had a little cold we didn't get to St. Gilles, to my everlasting regret, but came on here in the afternoon—"here" being Nimes. A greater contrast to the dirty but picturesque streets of Arles you can't imagine—Nimes is really a very handsome town, with wide shady avenues, handsome squares, & a most lovely public garden, which contains the Roman baths & Nymphaeum. The Maison Carrée is very beautiful, & the details of the frieze, cornice & capitals are in the most exquisite state of preservation—[2]

This morning at 11:30 we left for Aigues Mortes—It was a grey windy day, & you can imagine nothing more desolate than the flat, treeless country through which we passed. At last the train stopped, &

walking a few steps from the station we saw before us a perfect mediaeval town, with walls intact & uninterrupted, gates, towers, embrasures,
all as they were when Philippe le Hardi built them — & not a house or
outbuilding of any kind to obstruct the view, nor a roof or chimney
rising above the high walls[3] — Here are still the nine gates, the grooves
for the double portcullis in each one, the holes above through which to
send down boiling oil, the guard-rooms in the towers, reached by spiral
staircases of stone, with their hooded stone chimney-pieces, their ribbed
vaulting resting on leafy capitals, & their stone seats in the splayed embrasures of the wall. Imagine this strange town standing alone in the
midst of canals & lagoons, the water creeping to within a few feet of
its gates, & you will enter into the feelings of delight & wonder with
which we looked at it. Inside the old streets still run from gate to gate,
as Philippe le Hardi planned them, but the houses are small & insignificant — there is nothing to distract one's eye from the ramparts. Especially
beautiful is the view looking through the arch of the north gate, down
the main street of the town, & through the south gate at the grey waters
of the lagoon beyond. We had in short one of those days which Teddy &
I call "rich," & got back here tired & happy in time for dinner. Tomorrow morning we go to Avignon, spend the day there, & take the night
train for Paris. I have scarcely room left to thank you for your nice long
letter, & your news of Doylie, but I will write again from Paris — How I
wish you could have been with us to enjoy today. We really imagined we
saw the archers in the walls, & the seneschal in his balcony on the gate
tower parleying with the heralds below! —

Goodbye, dear Tons —

Affly yr

Herz

1. Anna Brownell Jameson (1794–1860) was an Irish woman who traveled
widely and wrote numerous books about her journeys. She also wrote handbooks to public and private galleries and two volumes on *Sacred and Legendary
Art* (1857), which is probably the work to which Wharton refers here.

2. The Maison Carrée, or Square House, is a Roman temple known for its pure

lines and harmonious proportions. Thomas Jefferson was inspired to re-create some of its columns for the Virginia State Capitol in Richmond.

3. In 1240 King Louis IX, known as Saint Louis, acquired Aigues-Mortes from the monks who owned the land and developed it as a Mediterranean port, from which he carried out his Crusades. His son, Philippe le Hardi, when he became king, further developed the city by building the wall and ramparts.

Pen craig Cottage

May 27 [1890]

Dear Tonni,

I have a piece of news which I think will please you—A few days ago I sent to Scribner's a little story—my first attempt at publishing prose—& to my surprise it has been accepted. Isn't this a delightful beginning? Tell Doylie when you see her—but I shall write to her myself in a day or two—How are you getting on?—Don't bother to answer this—Affly yr

Herz

"Mrs. Manstey's View," accepted by Scribner's Magazine *on 26 May, was Edith Wharton's first published story. Surprisingly, perhaps, it concerned not people of her social class but rather a poor widow: "Mrs. Manstey occupied the back room on the third floor of a New York boardinghouse, in a street where the ash barrels lingered late on the sidewalk and the gaps in the pavement would have staggered a Quintus Curtius" ("Mrs. Manstey," 117). While the narrative voice is cultured—who else would know of Roman historian Quintus Curtius?—the subject of the tale lives a narrow, pinched life, causing the biographer Shari Benstock, among other scholars, to wonder how Wharton could have "established the verisimilitude of these stories" (70). The answer to this puzzle may well be that Wharton's imagination was engaged by listening to Anna Bahlmann's tales of the people she knew and visited. That Wharton shares her news immediately with Bahlmann and her childhood nurse, Hannah Doyle, suggests her attachment to them both.*

The following letter contains the first mention of Teddy's family. Mrs. and

My Dear Governess

Miss Wharton are his mother, Nancy Spring Wharton (1820–1909), and his sister Nancy Craig Wharton (1844–1921), called Nanny. Teddy's father, William Craig Wharton (1811?–91), was by this time confined to McLean's sanatorium outside of Boston, where he committed suicide the following year. Teddy also had a brother, William Fisher Wharton (1847–1919), a lawyer serving at this time as assistant secretary of state. It is not known whether Edith ever met Teddy's father or how much she or her mother knew about his affliction. In none of the subsequent letters about Teddy's deteriorating mental condition does she mention his father.

Maggie Wingate, mentioned from time to time in these letters, was a nursery governess. Although we cannot know her difficulty at this moment, we can speculate that stories like hers sparked Edith Wharton's imagination and her fiction.

From this letter onward, Wharton signs her letters not Herz but E.W., signaling perhaps a lessening of attachment to Anna, or perhaps a shift into being more comfortable in her role as a married woman.

Pen craig Cottage
November 21st 1890

Dear Tonni,

Never apologize to me for not writing—my own sins in that respect are so flagrant as to make me very forgiving—You will be glad to hear that all your friends here are getting on well—I am *much better*, Doyle is flourishing, & Teddy & the dogs (how that combination would shock some of our friends) are as well as well can be—even dear Bijou, who got a bad biting & shaking last week from the French's St. Bernard, but stood it with his usual fortitude! Trix has probably told you what good news we have had of Mama, & how well she stood the voyage—Doyle & I have both had letters from her from London. We are having most beautiful weather, but shall soon be the sole survivors of the Summer tribe here. Mrs. & Miss Wharton are coming to us for Thanksgiving, however, so we shall be quite gay. The pansies, roses, honeysuckle & chrysanthemums are still blooming in the garden, & we had our first frost last night—

Don't worry Horatio about Dohme, there is plenty of time for him—I have just got a beautiful edition of Viollet-le-Duc from Bouton.[1] I wish you were here to see it—I am so glad that your quiet life is doing you good—Please continue to feel well—it is the greatest pleasure you can give yr affte E.W.

We go to Boston on Dec. 6th, & Doyle goes to N.Y. that night by boat. I am so much surprised at your news of Maggie Wingate. What will the finale be, I wonder?

1. Robert Dohme (1845–93) was a German art historian. He wrote several books and edited a well-illustrated series on the lives and characteristics of European artists. It is not clear which volume Wharton wanted, or whether it was in English or the original German. She refers to this book several times over the course of her travels. Eugène Viollet-le-Duc (1814–79) was a French architect whose *Dictionnaire raisoné de l'architecture française* was, according to one of his translators, "a valuable treasure of architectural art and erudition." His "restorations" of French buildings, during which he made what some considered jarring changes to ancient architectural treasures, were, and still are, controversial. J. W. Bouton was a New York bookseller, and it is likely that Horatio was as well.

When traveling, Wharton frequently dismissed guidebooks and disdained people who saw only what was recommended in them. In Italian Backgrounds *she was to write: "One of the rarest and most delicate pleasures of the continental tourist is to circumvent the compiler of his guide-book" (85). While Wharton read and appreciated history, art, and architecture, she also craved unique experiences, and in this Teddy was her willing companion. Here, as in the letter from Arles and Aigues Mortes, we witness Edith and Teddy sitting at an historic place, reading together about great events of the past. History must have come alive for them, and Edith's sweeping imagination surely enchanted her husband. Here she speaks of Florence, Siena, Torcello, and Venice and a trip "pressed down and running over with pleasures of every kind."*

My Dear Governess

Venice
Easter Sunday
March 29th [1891]

Dear Tonni,

We have spent a day into the delights of which you would have
entered so fully that the recollection of it inspires me to write to you this
evening. But I will go back a little way first in our history, for I know
you will want to hear what we have done & seen since I wrote you from
Florence. We spent a most perfect week there, & went away with that
sort of "nunc dimittis" feeling of entire satisfaction which is so rare.[1] The
weather was beautiful, the old familiar wonders were more wonderful
than ever, & one felt that every little bit of information one had managed
to acquire in the interval helped one to appreciate it more keenly than
ever. We went from there to Siena, which is one of the most interesting
towns in Italy, & in some ways even excels Perugia & Orvieto—It has
less glorious views than Perugia, but the mediaeval palaces frowning over
the narrow streets are wonderfully preserved, from their crenellated cor-
nices to the splendid wrought iron torch-holders & heavily-barred windows; & as we walked through the town it seemed to us that every other
house was a palace. Then nothing can exceed the dignity of the great
public Square, with the battlemented Palazzo Pubblicho [sic] & its tall
campanile, worthy to rival with the Palazzo Vecchio, & facing it the great
Gothic façade of the Palazzo del Governo. As to the Cathedral, Teddy
declares that he prefers it to St. Mark's—& while I of course can't give
in to such a heresy, I am bound to confess that it is one of the finest, &
the most satisfying churches I have ever seen. It is approached by a splendid flight of marble steps, leading up to a superb late Gothic doorway
of marble, which was to have been a door in the nave of the Cathedral
as originally planned (the present Duomo being only the transept!!) But
all this you can see in a guide-book—What I should have liked you to
see with your own eyes is the ivory-like sunburnt yellow of the carvings
on the façade, & inside the long vista of black & white marble columns,
leading up to Niccolò Pisano's wonderful pulpit resting on lions, & more

elaborately & intricately carved even than that at Pisa—& the afternoon light falling on the inlaid & sculptured marble of the walls, on the capitals of the piers, & on the floor of inlaid white & grey marble, with its strange pictures of prophets, Sibyls, mediaeval battles, Bible history, & heaven knows what beside.[2] How you would have enjoyed it all!

But I am forgetting to tell you that we also saw & enjoyed all the frescoes in the Palazzo Pubblicho which you & I read of in Dohme—though Lorenzetti's "Good & Bad Government" is so injured that it has to be looked at with the eye of faith[3]—We only stayed one night at Siena, for the smells in the Hotel worried me on Teddy's account, he is so dreadfully susceptible to malaria that I hate to run such risks with him—We came back to Florence for a day, & then on here. We have been here these three days, & are going off tomorrow afternoon, again driven away by the dreadful smells in the Hotel, & the impossibility of getting better quarters elsewhere. But we don't complain, for the weather has been so perfect that our time here has been just pressed down & running over with pleasures of every kind. It is wonderful to have such weather in the North of Italy in March, & we can't be thankful enough.

March 30th. But I must now come to our trip of yesterday, which I did not have time to describe last evening—We went to Torcello, leaving here at 9.30, & in the most perfect weather—an expedition I had always wanted to make, & during which, as I wrote Mama last night, I thought of you continually, knowing just how much you would have enjoyed it all.[4] It was indescribably beautiful & peaceful, & so delightful to think that while we were gliding peacefully over the Lagoon the thousands of Cook's tourists with which Venice swarms were all crowding in to St. Mark's for the Easter services, & would not be able to pursue us to Torcello! We glided under the Bridge of Sighs, & winding through numerous canals, past the Scuola di San Marco, with our old friend Colleoni sitting so proud & gallant on his big horse in the bright sunshine, we came out on the Lagoon opposite Murano—To our left was the long range of the Carnic Alps, which a recent fall of snow had covered almost to the plain, & all around us the Lagoon, calm & pearly, with here & there a bright red or yellow fishing-sail, or a little distant island stenciled

My Dear Governess

in black on the smooth water, & ahead of us the trees & campaniles of the neighbour islands Torcello & Burano. We passed Burano after an hour's row, & threaded in & out of little canals, between green banks & hedges coming into leaf, passing close to an old church with a sculptured Gothic doorway on the little island of Mazzorbo, until at length our gondola stopped at a flight of stone steps leading to the little green meadow in which the old churches of Torcello stand—I can't begin to tell you the quiet out-of-the-worldness of it all—no houses visible, no guides, no Baedekers, but only a few children who wanted to sell us violets & a fat yellow & white puppy called "Bacchus" whom they also invited us to buy; and the old basilica, & the little baptistery of St Fosca, with its encircling arcade, dozing in the peaceful sunshine, in their little meadow full of daisies & violets, & looking so old, so infirm, as if they had just strength enough left to sit & warm their old stones in the sun. I had Sismondi with me, & we sat down & read of the invasion of the Lombards, & the flight of the Bishop of Altinum to Torcello⁵—& then, how strange it was, opening the door of the nearly thousand-year-old baptistery, to see the priest in his white & gold chasuble celebrating the Easter mass at the altar, with a little acolyte holding a candle at his side, & a few fishermen & their families kneeling about him, just such as the inhabitants of Torcello might have been when the Bishop of Altinum raised it from a fishing-village into a see—All this I know you would have enjoyed just as I did—& then the little quiet canals, the old walls overhung with masses of ivy, the crumbling houses with on the other islands, with their Gothic windows choked up with bricks, the ducks floating on the water, the boats lying under their primitive thatched boat-houses—there was not a single discordant note in the whole scene! We had a delicious row home, & spent the afternoon in St. Marks, where the "Pala d'Oro" was exposed behind the high altar, & every chapel full of lights—& all the tourists away, too! This afternoon we leave for Verona—

I have capital news of Mama from Cannes, & we have decided to go to Paris by April 9th, so we shall meet in ten days. I think Teddy & I will sail for home on May 9th. Won't that be pleasant? I am pining for the Cottage already—I hope you mean to spend June with us as usual, dear Tonni—In fact, I *count on it!*—

I am late, & must close in haste to catch the mail.
With a great deal of love,

Yrs E.W.

1. Luke 2.29–32, "Lord, now lettest thy servant depart in peace, according to thy word, for mine eyes have seen thy salvation."

2. Nicola Pisano (d. c. 1284). He and his son Giovanni were the dominant sculptors of the late thirteenth century in Italy.

3. Ambrogio Lorenzetti's (active 1319–48?) fourteenth-century fresco is in the Siena Town Hall.

4. Torcello is a small island in the lagoon of Venice. Wharton describes a boat trip through the lagoon, passing several islands, in order to go to Easter service in the little community on Torcello. On the way they passed the equestrian statue of Bartolommeo Colleoni (d. 1475), general of the Republic, which was modeled by Verrocchio, the teacher of Leonardo da Vinci.

5. Simonde de Sismondi (1773–1842) was a historian who wrote about French and Italian history. His six-volume *Storia delle repubbliche italiane dei Secoli di Mezzo,* which is an Italian translation of a work written originally in French, is in Wharton's library at The Mount. One of the volumes is dated, in Wharton's hand, Florence 1891. The dedication and depth of Wharton's lifelong study of European culture cannot be exaggerated.

Teddy Wharton's father committed suicide in May 1891, a fact to which Edith Wharton never alludes, though she uses the customary black-bordered stationery. Although she doesn't share much about her relations with the Whartons, she is happy here to tell Anna news of "the gang," as Wharton referred to her household, of which she considered Anna a part. Here she describes a party in the servants' hall. The delineation of roles, though blurred for an event such as Doyle's party, was clear enough; Edith, her mother, and her husband went to watch the servants dance, but they did not join in.

My Dear Governess

Pen craig Cottage
August 18, [1891]

Dear Tonni

This is to be an English letter because I have a great deal to tell you & not much time to do it in. In the first place I know you will want to hear about Doyle's party. Imagine our feelings on Saturday morning when we found that it was pouring & meant to do so all day! We rallied our wits & turned the picnic into a dance in the servant's hall, & I would have given anything if you could have seen it. The preparations were very hurried, as you may fancy, but most successful—The supper was laid in the kitchen which was dressed out with Turkey red & flowers. They danced in the servants hall, which was hung with Chinese lanterns, & the "liquid refreshments" were served in the brushing room. There were forty-two people present, & when they were all assembled White came for Doyle, who was with me, & led her in to receive her guests! Dancing, a grab-bag, a cake with a ring, & a Virginia reel were some of the features of the evening, but it would require the editor of the Observer to do justice to the occasion! Doyle was simply radiant—

Mama & Teddy & I went in to look at the dancing, & there was Doyle polka-ing with Mamma's tall footman! Altogether it was a brilliant success—

I must tell you also that Miss Post is to recite my prologue for the tableaux, & everyone who has seen it likes it very much—A few days ago I had a long letter from the Editor of Scribner's, saying that he was much pleased with "The Fulness of Life," & thought it would be "a very exceptional success" if I would make it a little less "soulful," & in "a quieter vein"—All very well but "la plus jolie fille du monde ne peut donner que ce qu'elle a," & I'm afraid I have done the best that I can with it.[1] Certainly I don't know how to change it. We are all going on here as usual, & I am decidedly better. Mama seems very well, though of course she has felt the heat. I have amused myself learning the Greek alphabet since you left, & next month Ethel Cram & I are going to begin Spanish together without a teacher![2] After Peralta I prefer to be my own instructress. I did not learn the Greek alphabet for a freak, but with the idea of going on with the grammar when I can find a teacher—It is too difficult to do alone—

I wish you could see my little flower-garden by the greenhouse. Since the rain it has been really brilliant—I miss you very much, dear Tonni, & am looking forward greatly to all the pow-wows we can have together then—for by that time I hope to be strong as a lion—I hope that by this time you are comfortably settled at Manassas, with every-thing as you wish it to be, & *no headache* at least none when you receive this—

If you don't hear from me soon you will know it is the fault of my indomitable loathing for the pen, which gets worse every day.
Yr loving

EW

1. "The prettiest girl in the world can only give what she has," a French proverb.
2. Ethel Cram was the daughter of Mr. and Mrs. Henry A. Cram, neighbors of the Joneses and Whartons in Newport. Edith and Ethel were friends, becoming even closer after both families moved their summer residences to Lenox, Massa-chusetts.

Wharton's story "The Fulness of Life," discussed above, concerns an unhappy wife's choice, at her death, to remain in eternity with her husband rather than with someone better suited to her temperament. With its now famous allegory of a woman's nature as "a great house full of rooms" into many of which no one ever seeks entry, so that "the soul sits alone and waits for a foot-step that never comes," it has understandably been read as a description of Edith Wharton's own insufficient marriage. The above letter betrays no such self-awareness. Although Scribner's *editor Edward Burlingame was reluc-tant to take the story until it was revised, it did finally appear in* Scribner's Magazine *in December 1893. Wharton would not allow it to be collected in her first volume,* The Greater Inclination, *however, criticizing it as "writ-ten at the top of my voice," and "one long shriek" (to Edward Burlingame, 10 July 1898, LEW, 36).*

My Dear Governess

The following letter remains stubbornly undatable. We know that it pre-cedes 1893, because here Wharton is learning to skate, and by 1893 she skates easily. We know that her dog, Toots, is with them, which also places the let-ter in the early 1890s. In January 1891 the Whartons attended the Patriarch Ball in New York ("Dancing," NYT, 6 January 1891); in January 1893 the Whartons were in Newport. Because these letters are the first original docu-ments we have from this era, there is no corroborating evidence to place her whereabouts definitely in mid-January 1891 or 1892.

Whenever the trip took place, it must have been an amazing experience to climb the Swiss Alps in an open sleigh. The Whartons' young servants, Gross and White, must also have been thrilled by this kind of travel, which they would surely not have experienced had they not been employed by people as adventurous as the Whartons.

St Moritz

January 11th [1892?]

Dear Tonni,

I know that you will want to hear how we have been faring since I last wrote, & whether we have reached the top of the mountains in safety. Well, we are all here in the best of health, & even Toots, who ob-jected to the cold at first, is now merrily scampering about in the snow in her fur coat & boots!—We left Paris on the night of January 4th & reached Zürich the next morning—There we rested, & went the next day to Chur, where we slept the second night. The morning after at 8 o'c Teddy and I were packed into a tiny sleigh like a cutter, with a step be-hind for the driver to stand on, Gross & White bestowed themselves in a similar one, the luggage was piled on a third, & off we went, with bells ringing, through the frosty pine woods, up the mountainside, meet-ing only an occasional peasant driving a sled with a load of wood. The scenery was fairy-like—hills & valleys clothed with snow more blind-ingly white than you can conceive of, pine woods powdered with glit-tering crystals & feathery fringes of white, waterfalls turned into deep blue icicles, & suspended thus over the sheer edge of the rocks—while below us rushed the clear dark [river] Julia, dashing through blocks of turquoise ice & whirling around boulders of snow—& at each ascent the snow grew thicker & more dazzling, the pines rarer & more deeply buried in it—We slept that night at the village of Mühlen & the next day the ascent of the Julier began. Here the line of vegetation was left far below & we entered on a region of wild white grandeur which was absolutely awful. At each turn in the road a new & wilder vista of tossed & broken snow peaks unfolded itself, with the road winding between them only marked by an occasional tall pole in the snow—while the only sign of life was afforded now & then by the snow-laden roofs & steeple of a half-buried village which barely broke the level of the whiteness—A very short descent from the top of the Julier brought us to this place, which is at the very upper edge of the pine-belt, with bare peaks towering close around it—

But all this time, you will say, how cold they must have been! Not half so cold as I have often been in the Autumn at Newport. The air is so divinely pure & dry that one can sit out of doors for hours, with a thin jacket on, & to walk or skate one must take one's jacket off!—Many people carry sun-shades & wear straw hats. This Hotel is a huge place full of second-class English, & I am sorry to say I can get no teacher, so after 4 o'c the hours hang rather heavy, but until then life is enchanting—At 10 o'c the sun bursts above the high white peak opposite my window, & then the whole valley is lit up with warmth & radiance, the snow sparkles on the pine wood, the sky is as blue as in June, & every body dashes out to the rink or the toboggan slide, the sleigh, or some other outdoor amusement. I am devoting my whole soul to skating—I began yesterday, & today I can stand alone. Who knows what tomorrow may bring forth?—It is very funny to see the people leave off skating & watch Teddy when he begins to do some complicated figures. Luckily, there are one or two very good skaters here who can appreciate his skill, & he has great fun with them.

The air is so stupefying that when I come indoors I can hardly keep my eyes open, & am just about up to a novel or a review, so that if I had a teacher I don't believe I should do much. I don't struggle against the feeling, for I believe it is part of the cure, & I would rather be a healthy dolt than a learned miss with malaria.[1] I am sure this air must be a panacea for every ill, & I feel most hopeful about the good it is going to do me—I wish, however, you could turn up every afternoon at 4, & we could have a nice German talk over the fire! I had such a nice letter from Doyle written on Dec. 28th. Thank you again for taking her to Washington, dear Tonni.

Yr affte,

E.W.

1. This is the first, and as far as I know, the only reference we have to Edith ever having contracted malaria. Teddy is said to have had recurrences of it several times. Malarial mosquitoes were known to inhabit Teddy's home town of Brookline, Massachusetts, and also much of the southeastern United States.

The next is another winter letter, this one from Newport to Cannes, where Anna Bahlmann was attending Lucretia Jones. Ogden Codman, Jr. (1863–1951), whose Boston family knew Teddy's family quite well, was an architect, and the Whartons commissioned him to remodel and redecorate their new (to them) Newport home, Land's End, in 1893, and then their brownstone at 884 Park Avenue in New York in 1896. Codman and Edith Wharton would begin, in 1897, collaborating on a book—Edith's first since the privately printed Verses *when she was sixteen—about the relationship between architecture and interior décor, called* The Decoration of Houses *(1897). Francis Dumaresq (1854–1902) was from an old Boston family that had been in the China trade. He was at Harvard with Teddy and probably knew him even earlier than that. Dumaresq became a sugar broker and later a partner in a successful sugar refining business; he traveled frequently with the Whartons in the 1890s.*

The paintings that she mentions in this letter remained some of her favorites, particularly Jan Van Eyck's La Vierge au Donateur, *about which she had written a poem published in* Scribner's *in 1892.*

Newport

January 2nd [1893]

Dear Tonni,

We spent a very pleasant Christmas week in Boston, & while I was there I received your first letter from Cannes. I was delighted to hear that your first impressions were so favorable, the weather so beautiful, & the apartment so comfortable—We were enjoying such very wintry sports at that very moment that your description presented an almost startling contrast to our surroundings. It was intensely cold while we were in Boston, or rather when we first got there, & the river Charles froze, a most unusual event, which gave us the most exquisite skating. One day we went out with Mr. Dumaresq & Mr. Codman to a place called Waltham, & from there we skated to another place called Riverside, where we took a return train to Boston. We skated over a beautiful stretch of the river, with wooded banks on either side, & I never saw a more beautiful sight—

I had some very nice Christmas presents, & not least acceptable among them were my two dear friends, Kinder de Welt & Problematische Naturen.[1] How kind & sweet of you, dear Tonni, to remember my wish for them. My little Christmas card to you—Moore's poems (I mean C. L. Moore, not Tommy) are so late in starting that I fear you won't get them until nearly the end of the month.[2] It was Coombes' fault, he is so stupid & careless that I am really disgusted with him.[3] We got back from Boston on the 30th, & were enchanted, as usual, to find ourselves once more in the cottage. We came back to ideal weather, & you may imagine our delight when we discovered that Lily Pond was covered with the most perfect black ice. We got back by an early train, so immediately after lunch we seized our skates & flew down, to spend a most enchanting afternoon. It was very warm, & there was not a breath of wind, & what with the sunset turning the pond to mother o'pearl, & the new moon rising over the pine-grove of your pet Hazard farm, you can imagine no lovelier sight than it was. We skated again the next day, but yesterday came a storm, & a gale from the South West of the most tremendous violence, & today has been too warm for skating. We went down to our new estate, & the surf there was perfectly magnificent.

My Dear Governess

We are perfectly delighted with our experiment of spending part of the winter here. It is so restful, & the weather is so beautiful. I take two long walks & feel so perfectly well that it is a pleasure to live—& it is a long time since I have been able to say that! We don't think the dogs have ever had so pleasant a winter. They seem to be in ecstasies over our being here, & when the snow was on the ground, Jules' enjoyment knew no bounds—He raced ahead of us as far as he could go, plunging into every drift, & then tearing back with a sort of rapture on his old face. I have been coming & going so much lately that I have read nothing but trash—& stupid trash at that. In a day or two, however, I am going to settle down again to Sismondi.[4] I have had all my Brauer photographs framed most successfully, the Vierge au Donateur, the Claude Lorrain, the "Charles X & his sister," & in fact all that I brought out this year.[5] They are in plain gold frames, which I consider decidedly the most successful way of framing that I have yet attempted. We expect to be here about six weeks longer, & to sail towards the end of February. I wish I were in Cannes now, & might have some of our delightful old walks with you. Have you been to St. Cassien yet? And to Notre Dame de Vie?[6] And have you got a *native* hat trimmed with grasses? For I shouldn't know you in anything else at Cannes!—

Mary Bagley is really doing wonders.[7] Tell Mama we shall hand her back a "cordon bleu." She thinks nothing of dashing off a dinner of several courses, beginning with caviar and toast, & including *bouchés* of her own making, lobster Newburgh, croquettes, & goodness knows what besides. We had some people to dine tonight, & she really surpassed herself. I think she enjoys the excitement of it, but I am sorry to say that her nasty brute of a kitchen maid is going to leave tomorrow—"finds the place dull—too far out of town" &c—so she leaves at a day's notice.

I must stop for it is very late, & I want to catch the Wednesday mail. Goodnight, dear Tonni, with a great deal of love from

Yr affte E.W.

Teddy sends his best love & warmest thanks for his Christmas card.

1. *Kinder de Welt* by Paul Heyse, whose *Zwei Gefangene* had so moved Edith in 1885; *Problematische Naturen* by Friederich von Spielhagen (1829–1911), a German novelist.

2. Charles Leonard Moore (1854–1925), an American poet, published *Book of Daydreams* in 1883.

3. "Coombes" might be a servant, but it is more likely New York bookseller George J. Coombes.

4. She had been reading Sismondi while in Venice.

5. Claude Gelée, called Lorrain (1600–1682). The court portraitist François-Hubert Drouais (1727–75) depicted the young king-to-be Charles-Philippe and his sister Marie Adélaïde in a rustic setting, with Marie Adélaïde holding a basket of fruit and riding a perfectly groomed goat.

6. Saint Cassien is a hill about 2½ miles outside of Cannes, with a shrine on it that had earlier been a Greek Temple. Notre-Dame de Vie is a twelfth-century chapel that affords beautiful views of Cannes, about six miles distant. These are sites to which Edith and Anna must have walked frequently on their first trip to the south of France together, when Edith was eighteen and Bahlmann in her early thirties.

7. Mary Bagley was Lucretia Jones's cook. She also worked for Edith and Teddy and for Teddy's mother and sister over the years. The family was committed to retaining their servants.

Egerton Winthrop, Jr. (1839?–1916), was a dear friend of the Jones family, initially closer to Edith's parents than to her. In A Backward Glance, *Wharton credits him with being the first "cultivated intelligence" to take an interest in her reading and work and the friend who "first taught my mind to analyze and my eyes to see" (94), a judgment seemingly unfair to Anna Bahlmann. Winthrop was a widower; his sons were away at school, and his daughter, Charlotte, had recently married Ethel Cram's brother Harry, a friend of the Joneses and a Harvard classmate of Teddy's. Wharton's friendship with Winthrop continued until his death in 1916, just days before Anna's.*

The Century Club exhibition of the works of poet and painter Dante Gabriel Rossetti (1828–82) that interests Wharton here was not popular with everyone, if we are to believe the New York Times *review from the day be-*

fore: "*They come, they stare, they shrug their shoulders, they go out*" ("Pre-Raphaelite Pictures," NYT, *8 January 1893*).

The Whartons had purchased a property on the water, diagonally across the island from Pen craig, called Land's End, which would be the first home they owned together.

Pen craig Cottage
January 9th [1893]

Dear Tonni

I am so distressed to hear from Mama's last letter that your head has been troubling you so much. I had so hoped that the mild climate & the easy restful life would be a help to you this winter. I can't tell you how distressed I am. There is one consideration, however, which makes me feel that your trouble may be only temporary. Whenever I go to the Riviera my liver is utterly upset for the first fortnight, & Dr. Bright has often told me that the same thing happens to many people—so perhaps it may also account for your head being so much worse. I wrote to Mama today & gave her what news there was—namely the fact that we had been obliged to go to N.Y. for two days last week—that the weather was very cold & stormy—& that nothing else had happened—but I want to send you this line to say that, *at last,* "The Book of Day Dreams" by C. L. Moore is on its way to you. I think you will thoroughly enjoy some parts of it. Several of the sonnets are packed with imagination, & some of the single lines I find as felicitous as some of Rossetti's—& to my mind one can't say more, for you know I think Rossetti's sonnets unsurpassed in English. By the way, our tiresome visit to N.Y. was enlivened for me by going to see the exhibition of Rossetti's pictures at the Century Club. I had no idea that there were so many Rossettis in America. They interested me very much, though there is far more "plastik" in his poems than his paintings. The "Beata Beatrix" is the best known & most beautiful of the collection. I have been reading some very interesting books lately—Émile Faguet's "Etudes litteraires" of the XVII, XVIII, & XIX century. I began at the wrong end, with the XIX century, perhaps the best. Faguet, like Jules Le Maître, is too essentially a modern to be as appreciative of the XVII century as, for instance, Brunetière, who is absolutely saturated with it. Nevertheless, his study of Athalie is very interesting, though when he writes that the *style* is inadequate to the subject, I feel how utterly hopeless it is for an Anglo-Saxon to enter into the niceties of French literary criticism, until I am cheered by remembering that such men as Brunetière think very differently of Racine's style. To me it seems fit for any subject, however grand, & if it lacks the splendour & ruggedness of Corneille, it has a piercing sweetness & a sustained dignity which are all its own.[1] I am now reading another interesting book—Dowden's "Shakespere's Mind & Art." Let me know if you have read it, for I think you would like it. Like all the critics, I think he sees more in Shakespere's plays than the author ever put there—but still, it's very agreeable reading—[2]

The weather here is really awful, but we manage to keep the Cottage warm, & some merciful Providence keeps our pipes from bursting. We continue to be very much absorbed in the plans of Land's End. When I had fully matured my plans I gave them to Mr. Newton, & strange to say he found not one single difficulty, great or small, in carrying out the changes I proposed. I was ready to be told that this was too complicated, & the other too impractical—& so his unqualified approval was a pleasant surprise. Mr. Codman is coming today to pay us a little visit, & help me about my ceilings, & a few such things. How I would like to have $10,000 to spend in adorning my house! I shall not be able to furnish all the rooms at once, so I shall close the "morning room" & two of the spare-rooms next year. I shan't have much bric-à-brac, but I shall have a view, at all events. Upstairs, every single bedroom looks out to sea, & during the last southerly gale the view of the surf all along the coast was perfectly stupendous—Teddy enjoys it here very much. He hoped for some sleighing with poney, but the wind has been blowing so hard that it has swept the roads bare. We seem to have no dearth of visitors. Mr. Baldwin has been once & is coming again, & Mr. Winthrop, who is dreadfully lonely since his daughter's marriage, spends an occasional Sunday with us, & gives us no end of good advice about our house. The Dressers are still here, but the weather has been so bad that I haven't seen them for some time. Mr. & Mrs. Harry Cram sail the end of this month, & the Lewis Rutherfurds went last week in one of the southern line[s] to Genoa. —I hope soon to hear that your head has become less troublesome, dear Tonni. You can't think how it distresses me to know that you have been in such misery. With much love from Teddy and "the gang."

Yr affte

E.W.

Tell Mama that when I wrote her that the Tennant cottage had been sold for $15,000 I meant of course $1500.

1. Faguet's (1847–1916) volumes remain in Wharton's library at The Mount. The literary studies of François Élie Jules Lemaître (1853–1914), French critic and dramatist, were collected as *Les Contemporains*. Ferdinand Brunetière (1849–1906) was a literary critic and editor of *Revue des Deux Mondes*. Two of his books also remain in Wharton's library at The Mount. *Athalie* is a play by Jean Racine (1639–99). Wharton's works, particularly her novel *The Reef*, have been frequently praised as "Racinian," perhaps for their orderly construction and psychological insight. Pierre Corneille (1606–84), with Racine and Molière, one of France's great seventeenth-century dramatists.

2. Edward Dowden (1843–1913) was an Irish critic, poet, and professor of literature at the University of Dublin. His *Shakespere: A Critical Study of His Mind and Art* was published in 1875.

Wharton was maturing as a connoisseur of art. Her find in the Boston store, described here, prefigures her more famous identification, in 1894, of some della Robbia terra-cottas in an obscure monastery in Tuscany. In this case, however, it's not clear whether she ever discovered the identity of the artist "Helmsdorff."

Pen craig Cottage
Feb. 12th [1893]

Dear Tonni,

When we reached Boston three days ago I found there your delightful long letter enclosing the flowers from St. Cassien, & absolutely smelling, in all its pages, of "carnation, lily, rose," & all the flora of the Riviera.[1] I am so glad that you really think Dr. Bright is doing your head good, & I am sure that the long rest in such a climate must be a help to you in the end. I can't imagine how it happens that you never received the January Scribner, for I addressed & posted it myself. It is too bad. I am so glad you like Charles Moore's poems. I think they are very remarkable, though one could wish at times that he had a greater regard for Lindley Murray[2] —

We left New York on the 8th, & went to Boston, where we stayed until yesterday, our chief object being to see the six mantle pieces, which had been taken out of Pine Bank, cleaned, polished, & set up at a marble shop. They looked even handsomer than I had supposed possible, & everyone is envying us our good luck — I also had another interesting experience in Boston. I went to Shreve, Crump & Low (the Tiffany of Boston) to look at their furniture department, not with the idea of buying, but simply "pour passer le temps" — when what should I discover, standing in an obscure way, on a chair, but a small picture about 8 × 9 inches, the colouring of which instantly struck me. It ~~was~~ represented a little group of cupids fishing in a pool, with a lovely background of blue sky & mountains, & was so exquisitely "dix-huitième siècle" in colouring, so exactly in the style of Boucher & Fragonard, that I could hardly believe my eyes.[3] I took it to the light to look at it, & the shop-man said "that is a very old picture — it is dated 1776. We have another which goes with it." He produced the pendant, cupids romping with roses against a sunset sky, with the same delicious, indescribable but unmistakable *tone* of the 18th century picture — that faded, unreal, tapestry-like colour, which only time can give; & in the corner of each picture I found the signature, Helmsdorff, 1776. Both pictures were in very good condition, the paint a little gone here & there, but only sufficiently so to be noticed on a close examination — & the unknown-ness of the signature seemed a conclusive proof of their authenticity. If they had been modern forgeries (&, as I said, nothing but time can forge that colour) the forger would have signed them Boucher or Lancret at once; he never would have picked out a name not even to be found in Bryant's [sic] Dictionary!⁴ I was still studying them with bated breath, when the salesman added persuasively, "They are really very pretty — the price is — $35 a piece!" I wish you had seen the air of lofty indifference with which I said, "you may send them home on *approval* if you like" — but my suspense was maddening until they arrived at the house next morning, & I found they were really in my possession. Who Helmsdorff is I have not yet been able to find out. The only one in Bryant is a Helmsdorf born 1785–1850 — much too late for my man, who evidently painted under the full influence of the mid-18th century. Possibly they may be contemporary copies of some well-known painter; but I doubt it. They are such simple little compositions that they would hardly have been striking enough to copy. Their great beauty is in the backgrounds — I have investigated them carefully, & find they are painted on wood — but fancy, please, my finding them in *Boston,* of all places, & buying them for $35 a piece! No one has seen them yet, but I intend to take them to Paris & have them looked at by an expert. —

I didn't mean to devote three pages to this anecdote, but you know how anything of this sort excites & interests me, & every time I look at the pictures they seem to me more lovely. I have made a rather careful study of French pictures in the last few years, & I had the opportunity of seeing one or two unrivalled collections of them in Paris last Spring, so I feel that I know more or less what I am talking about when I say that they are really good of their kind. Well, now to go back to our history. Our visits in N.Y. and Boston were both pleasant, but it was very nice to get back to this dear little Cottage. We found all the snow melted away & the roads clear, & the weather is beautiful just at present.

Mary Bagley got back safely from her long holiday, & was here to welcome us. Mr. Dumaresq came down yesterday from Boston to pass two days with us, & we were very glad to show him Land's End this morning with a blue, Summer-like sea breaking lazily over the rocks, &

the grass really looking almost green. The work on the house has already begun. The builder is a man named Bishop, just starting here, of whom Mr. Newton thinks very highly—We are wondering very much when we shall be able to get off to Europe. The Bretagne, our favourite boat, goes on March 11th, & I doubt if we can be ready to go by that time—& after that come two horrors, the Bourgogne & Normandie, & then, I fear, the still more awful Champagne. Rather a bad outlook. Perhaps we might hustle off by the 11th, but I haven't been to the dentist yet, alas.

I am very anxious to go straight down to Italy, spend six weeks there, & then join you all in Paris. By the way, you say nothing of the apartment in your last letter. Is the lease signed yet?—Tell Mama that Bull still brings me the most delicious eggs every morning—

The creatures here are well, & I mean shortly to send you pictures of Jules & Priu [Prin?]. The latter has just been taken with his chin resting on his paws, so that his poor throat doesn't show!—I have just been reading a very interesting life of Miss Edgeworth.[5] She is always an attractive personality to me. I am glad you are able to get a few good books from the Cannes library. I shall have plenty of new ones for you to read when you come to *Land's End* next summer!—

Goodbye, dear Tonni & give my love to Mamma, & write soon again to
Yr affte

E.W.

P.S. I re-open my letter to answer Mama's question about the embroidered bed-spread. Please tell her with many thanks that I find I can make it quite large enough by bordering it with that very handsome band of open-work white embroidery which she made & gave me a year or two ago, so I would much rather keep it.

1. Wharton may here be alluding to John Singer Sargent's charming painting (1886–87) of little girls in a garden with Chinese lanterns, called "Carnation, Lily, Lily Rose," or to a line from the popular song "Ye Shepherds, Tell Me," by Joseph Mazzinghi, from which Sargent drew his title.

2. Lindley Murray (1745–1826)—whose family home in Manhattan gave rise

to the neighborhood Murray Hill—wrote eleven textbooks of grammar and usage, of which some sixteen million were in circulation in the United States in the first half of the nineteenth century.

3. François Boucher and his pupil Jean-Honoré Fragonard were known for a decorative, whimsical style called by critics Rococo.

4. Nicholas Lancret (1690–1743) also painted in the Rococo style; *Bryan's Dictionary of Painters and Engravers,* by the English art historian Michael Bryan (1757–1821).

5. Maria Edgeworth (1768–1849), an Irish writer who championed women's education. Her *Tales and Novels* was an early Christmas present to Wharton from her father.

Anna Bahlmann has been in Cannes with Lucretia Jones, but they are returning to Paris, and Wharton here anticipates their meeting, looking forward particularly to Bahlmann's companionship in visiting the Louvre. Wharton's suggestion of going to lectures by the art historian and Louvre curator Louis Courajod (1841–96) reminds us that both women continued to pursue cultivation all their lives.

Pen craig Cottage
March 1st [1893]

Dear Tonni,

By this time in all probability you are on your way to Paris—or at all events, you are likely to be there when this reaches you, so I will change my address back to Munroe & Co, which is pleasant, for it seems to bring you nearer—I fancy, too, that you will be glad to get back to Paris. Cannes is very lovely, but it certainly does get a trifle monotonous, whereas Paris is a delight everlasting to those that have eyes to see. How I shall enjoy going about with you this Spring! We shall have to begin with the Louvre & La Vierge au Donateur—that is very certain! Meanwhile, before I get there, why don't you begin with some of Courajod's delightful conférances on architecture? He gives them twice a week, I think, at 10 a.m., in a room off the Cour Lefuel in the Louvre. Walk down the quay till you come to a large door with "Cour Lefuel" above it, & you will find a notice of the days & hours hung up there. The lectures are free, & by going a little early you can get a good seat & see the magic lantern pictures better. I also wish you to do me another favour. Present yourself with two seats at the Français some evening or afternoon when they are giving a good play, & go there as my guest— & we'll "settle" when we meet! I think one of the classic matinées might please you best. And so Mama & Harry have really taken an apartment! I think they are very wise, & have chosen it in a most delightful situation; & I am very curious to see it, as you may imagine. What an opportunity it will give you for Spring walks in the Bois. You will see quite a different side of Paris life from that which we are used to. And now to tell you about ourselves. I wrote Mama ~~last w~~ two days ago of our hasty trip to New York last week to see Mr. Baldwin & Nash,—we intended to come back on Feb. 23rd, after a two days' visit, but finding that I had some wedging to be done & consequently must wait until this week before I could be "filled," we suddenly dashed off to Washington for a night to see old Doylie, who had been heavy on my mind ever since I had heard of her accident. I found her looking much better than I had expected, but as I told Mama all the particulars of my visit I will not repeat them here. You may imagine her delight at seeing us! She showed me with the greatest glee a long letter from you describing the Battle of Flowers, & her satisfaction in it made me realize how much our letters mean to her.[1] I was very glad to find her so comfortably installed in Washington, & amazed to see how she has recovered from her really dreadful fall.

We came back to Newport yesterday, having been away a week instead of two days, & were much discouraged by finding everything here buried under another deep fall of snow. Surely there never was such a dreadful winter! It is very provoking just as we are trying so hard to advance with the work on the house, for in the present state of things no outdoor work can be done. As Pat said, "It is very fine walking overhead," & nothing could be more Summerlike than the aspect of sky & sea; but the roads are really hopeless, equally bad for wheels, runners, or feet. Under these circumstances we shall be glad to get away as soon as pos-

My Dear Governess

sible, & I think we shall probably sail on the Champagne on March 25th. We used not to like her, as her machinery was always rather groggy, but she has been laid up for six weeks, completely overhauled & repainted, & has a new Capt., Laurent, one of the best on the line, a new cook, &c—so I think we shall try her. We can't get off on the 11th in the Bretagne, & the Bourgogne, on the 18th, has a brute of a Capt., who hates dogs, & made our life wretched when we last crossed on her. We had a vision of crossing on the Majestic but it is so ~~uncomfortable~~ expensive, & I so dislike the journey through England, that we soon gave it up. We have so much furniture to buy for the new house that we are in no mood for throwing money away just at present.

In a day or two I shall send you by mail a book called "Far From Today," a collection of short stories which so delighted me that I want you to share my pleasure in them.[2] I found the book by accident & know nothing of the author, but I think the style & conception equally remarkable & am anxious to hear how they impress you—especially "Sylvanus" and "Servirole," which I think I like best. I am reading a very interesting series of essays on the 14th century in Italy—but I told you about them. They are most entertaining.

The dear doggies are all as well & jolly as possible, & Jules can't get used to the rapture of having Teddy back—unluckily for poney (or for us, for I think she prefers the stable) the going at present is too bad for either village-cart or cutter, so she stands in her stall doing nothing. When I was in New York I went two or three times to a most beautiful Loan collection of pictures in the American Art Galleries in 57th St. The building is very handsome, with large galleries hung in red, more like Paris than N.Y. in their dignity & elegance of arrangement, & the collection was far finer than any I ever saw in this country—in fact compared very favourably with those I have seen in Paris. There were three really incomparable Rembrandts, a beautiful Guardi of the Grand Canal, the finest I have ever seen, a great number of beautiful landscapes by Gainsborough, Crome, Constable, &c, & some very fine Dutch pictures, by Cuyp, Terburg, de Hooghe &c—to say nothing of an authentic Bellini,

& a large room full of good modern pictures.[3] It is very encouraging to think that such a show can be got together in New York—when one is ready to "despair of the Republic" such a sight is a consolation. Most of the finest early English landscapes belong to Fuller, the wall-paper man in 42nd St!![4]

1. The *Bataille des Fleurs* was a regular part of the Carnival festivities in Nice. Parade floats were covered with flowers from the region, and many parade participants tossed flowers into the crowd.

2. *Far from Today* by Gertrude Hall (1862–1961), a prolific author of fiction and poetry who later became the second wife of William Crary Brownell, Wharton's book editor at Scribner's.

3. Dutch painters Rembrandt van Rijn (1606–69), Aelbert Cuyp (1620–91), probably Gerard Terborch (1617–81), and either Romeyn de Hooghe (1645–1708) or Pieter de Hooch (1629–84). British painters Thomas Gainsborough (1727–88), John Crome (1768–1821) or his son, John Crome (1794–1842), John Constable (1776–1837). Venetian painters Francesco Guardi (1712–93) or his brother, Giovanni Antonio Guardi (1698–1760), Giovanni Bellini (1431/2–1516).

4. The letter ends here. A full description of this loan collection can be found in *NYT,* 15 February 1893. W. H. Fuller (c. 1840–1902) was a Yale graduate and a lawyer who decided to go into the manufacture of wallpaper. He was a friend of Claude Monet's and a noted collector who specialized in the Barbizon School and in English paintings, once owning Gainsborough's *Blue Boy.* Wharton evidently found it difficult to believe that a businessman could be a connoisseur.

The Whartons are traveling in Brittany, beginning east of Rennes, where they stop to see the Chateau des Rochers-Sévigné, home of Mme de Sévigné (1626–96), the seventeenth-century aristocrat known for her vivid and witty letter-writing (Wharton's fourteen-volume edition of these letters can be seen in her library at The Mount). Dinard and Saint-Malo are resort towns along the "Emerald Coast," at the time quite popular with wealthy British and American visitors. Once again we see the sheer energy of the Whartons' travel agenda and the complicated arrangements that these trips entailed.

My Dear Governess

Grand Hôtel de Dinard,
Dinard
May 3rd [1893]

Dear Tonni,

We have been wondering ever since we said goodbye to you the day before yesterday whether you got safely to Blois & enjoyed your afternoon there, & whether your head permitted you to go on to Paris yesterday—I hope you have had as pleasant days as have fallen to our lot. We reached Vitré safely, but although the country through which we passed was very lovely, we were very much disappointed in the place itself. There were many quaint old tumble-down houses, there was even a fortified castle as well-preserved as Langrais, but the castle is used as a prison, & everything about Vitré is squalid, dusty, dirty, & forlorn. As for the inn—oh my dear! Words fail to describe its horrors! But for all these disappointments we found ample reward in our expedition to "Les Rochers" yesterday morning. The drive took us through a lovely rolling country with hedges of hawthorn & broom, & on arriving we found a most beautiful old château, placed on a high plateau overlooking a wide expanse of woods & meadows—a beautiful pastoral landscape, such as one would never tire of. As for the chateau itself, with Mme de Sévigné's room just as she left it, with its beautiful formal garden designed by Le Notre & filled with Mme de Sévigné's orange-trees—with its chapel, park, &c *all* as in her time, even the alleys that she planted, preserving the names she gave them—I shall give you the details of all these enchanting things when we meet![1] It was one of the most perfect experiences that I have ever had. We left Vitré at 2.30 p.m. yesterday & in passing Combourg saw the tops of Châteaubriand's towers through the trees, & I longed to stop & see the chateau, but it was not possible. The proper way to get to Dinard (which we decided on at the last moment, instead of Dinan, for the sake of a clean hôtel) is to go straight by train from Vitré, reaching here at 7.38 p.m.; but I perceived that by taking a different route we could reach St. Malo at 6.15, & I felt sure we could cross over to Dinard by boat in some way—so we carried out this plan, & sure enough at St. Malo we found a sail-boat, & at sunset we & our luggage were rowed across the lovely bay to this place. We are enchanted with Dinard—Our Hôtel is on the bay, looking across to St. Malo in its circle of fortified walls, to St. Servan opposite, & to the mouth of the Rance, with its charmingly wooded shores. We intend to "loaf" here today, go to Dinan & back tomorrow, & start on Friday morning for Mt St Michel. The ideal weather still continues—may it hold until Sunday is my prayer! By the way, this brings me to one of my chief objects in writing—the subject of my clothes. We have heard from both the Castiglione & Vendôme that they can promise nothing at present, so we have returned to our plan of going to Versailles & making a halt there until we can get rooms in Paris. We shall send White there to Versailles Friday with the luggage to get an apartment for us at the Hôtel des Réservoirs, & we expect to reach there on Sunday afternoon. On Saturday White will probably go in to Paris to fetch my clothes, so I will ask you to leave them in their boxes, & to give him the dress & hat—in other words, all that Gross gave you, keeping the black cape, which I shall not need until we return to Paris. We expect to spend Friday night at the Hôtel Poulard Aîné, Mt St Michel, & Saturday night at the Hôtel du Nord, Granville, taking the early express for Versailles on Sunday—this has grown to be such a long letter that I will ask you to hand it to Mama, as it contains all the news "up to date." I feel as well as possible, & as for Toots, she has been revelling in the long journey & has decided to change her name to "railway Jack." Goodbye, dear Tonni—I do hope you reached Paris without contretemps. Send me a line to Granville or Versailles.

E.W.

1. André Le Nôtre (1613–1700), perhaps the greatest French landscape architect, was gardener to King Louis XIV. His most famous work is the park of the Palace of Versailles.

My Dear Governess

3

"Un peu de faiblesse"

AUGUST 1893 TO DECEMBER 1896

The summer of 1893 brought illness to the Whartons, and the foreboding of further problems, particularly for Teddy. In late August Edith wrote of her recovery from an unnamed illness that seemed to give her "attacks," one while she had been in Tours in the spring and one more recently at their new home, Land's End, in Newport. Perhaps, as she had mentioned in her letter of 11 January 1892, she suffered from malaria, or it may have been a respiratory or heart problem. Biographers have speculated that Wharton suffered a psychosomatic response to her unsatisfactory marriage, certainly a possibility. If that were the case, it surely could have been brought on by Teddy's inexplicably erratic behavior. Edith suffered from living with Teddy's "bad nervous attacks," which we now know were symptomatic of his manic depression, but which at the time confounded both of them and made their lives miserable.

In August 1893 Teddy was in a depressive phase and the two of them did not understand what was happening. For many years when he was nervous and querulous, he continued to insist that a change in their lifestyle was all he needed. In August 1893 Teddy decided irrationally to sell their new house, which they had been furnishing and refurbishing for an entire year, but the couple did not carry out the plan. The Whartons spent summers at Land's End, out on the rocky point at the end of Ledge Road, until finally closing up the house in November 1900.

Yet all was by no means misery in Edith Wharton's life. The summer of 1893 also brought new acquaintances, the French novelist Paul Bourget (1852–1935) and his wife, Minnie (Wharton nicknamed them, for their closeness, the MinniePauls). They were introduced to the Whartons by a cousin of Teddy's, and so began a lifelong friendship, Wharton's first friendship with a working novelist. This summer encounter may have sparked Wharton's ambition and creativity so that she began writing more frequently and attempting more actively to publish.

Wharton had been publishing work in magazines, mostly poetry, steadily for about four years. "The Fulness of Life," which she had sent two years earlier to *Scribner's Magazine* editor Edward Burlingame, was her second published story. By November, Burlingame would suggest a volume of stories. Wharton liked the idea, and she continued to write stories, some acceptable to Burlingame and some not, but it was not until six years later, in 1899, that her first volume of stories, *The Greater Inclination,* appeared.

Anna Bahlmann remained in New York, teaching. In the middle 1890s, among her favorite pupils were the four children of Edith's old friend Anna Foster Robinson and Dr. Beverley Robinson. Bahlmann prepared the sons, Beverley and Herman, for school, then took charge of lessons for their younger sisters, Pauline and Anna. Young Beverley would become a lawyer. Herman also studied law, but he was never happy; in the early summer of 1903 he went out to the end of Long Island and shot himself. Bahlmann was closest with Pauline Robinson, who never married, and who visited and corresponded with Anna for the rest of her life. Pauline also followed Edith Wharton's career closely over the years, championing the author whenever New York society's opinion seemed to chastise Wharton for her books.

Land's End

Aug. 27th [1893]

Dear Tonni,

I got your letter some time ago, ~~but~~ and meant to have answered it sooner, if only to let you know, you dear, anxious soul, that I am entirely out of the woods, able to be up & about as usual, & in fact better than I have been since my last attack at Tours. *But*—there always is a *but* with us—Teddy has had one of his bad nervous attacks of last year, is in fact in the midst of it now, & I do assure you it has very nearly taken the remaining pluck out of me! We have definitely decided to sell this house, & if we can do so by Nov. or Dec. we shall pack up & go abroad at once, & take a long, long, interminable rest—but if we can't, I suppose we shall spend the winter here—However, we might do worse than that—The house is quite settled now, and really wonderfully pretty, & everyone admires it far beyond my expectations. The Bourgets have been here for about ten days, but I did not see them until two or three days ago, when they came to lunch. They are quite charming, & I shall have a great deal to tell you about them when we meet. I hope to see something more of them before they go, as they are to stay another ten days. It was enchanting to talk to them of Italy, for she is as enthusiastic & appreciative as he. They have just come from Greece, which they explored in the company of Diehl, author of our beloved "Excursions Archéologique."[1] Oh, to think of some people's opportunities!

Old Doyle is wonderfully well & seems quite contented & happy. She takes a little solitary walk along the cliffs every morning, & comes back full of enthusiasm & interest in all she has seen—Mama has been wonderfully well also, until the last few days, when I think she must have caught cold, driving around Batemann's to see the surf after that famous storm last week. At all events she is in bed today, & Dr. R. seems to regard it as a mixture of cold & liver, but not at all serious—I think, however, she will have to go back to her milk diet.

My verses on Chartres are out in this month's Scribner, & I send them to you by mail today[2]—I have at last decided to send the "Fulness of Life," which you know the editor asked for again. We hope to see you back here by Sept. 15th, & I don't suppose your work in New York will begin before the middle of Oct. At all events I am counting on a visit of several weeks, if Mrs. Schultz can spare you. I put in this proviso because I don't want you to feel that there is any obligation for you to come, I mean in the way of helping me with the house—Everything is settled & done in that respect, & if you come we shall have plenty of time for reading and enjoyment—but really all the work is over. So I leave it entirely to you to decide when you wish to come, you know no one is more welcome under our roof at all times.

Affly Yrs,

E.W.

1. *Excursions Archéologique en Grèce* (1893?), by the French historian Charles Diehl (1859–1944).

2. "Chartres" appeared in the September 1893 issue of *Scribner's Magazine*.

Bahlmann did visit in the fall, and she served as Wharton's secretary by helping to prepare a story for publication. That Bahlmann "wrote it out" indicates that Wharton did not yet have one of the gunmaker E. Remington and Sons' typewriting machines. These machines had been produced initially in 1878 and were being used widely by the 1890s. Although Bahlmann was not a paid secretary, Wharton found a way to reward her and to enhance Bahlmann's income without embarrassing her. "That Good May Come," Wharton's third story to be published, came out in Scribner's *in May 1894.*

Land's End Newport
Nov. 15th 1893

Dear Tonni,

You can do me a very great favour, & I know that you won't refuse to do so, when I tell you how much happiness it will give me—I want you to accept as a Christmas present the enclosed cheque which Scribner has just sent me for "That Good May Come." The story is so associated in my mind with the hours that we spent in writing it out together, & I

My Dear Governess

owe its opportune presentment & speedy acceptance largely to the fact that you were here to get it written out at a time when I could not have done so, that I have a peculiar feeling about your having just this special cheque & no other as a souvenir of our work together—You can send it back, of course, but I don't think you will, when I tell you that in the course of several melancholy months one of the few high spots has been the opportunity of thus sending you a Christmas present of my very own earning!—

　　We are all well & prosperous, & I am
Yr affte

　　　　　　　　　　　　　　　　　　　　　　　　　E.W.
I have just had a cable from ~~Mama~~ Harry from Queenstown, dated today: "Beastly cough. Mama well." They must have had a very long crossing.

The Whartons made an unusual winter trip to Europe, perhaps to ease Teddy's restlessness, perhaps to keep Lucretia and Harry Jones company for the holidays. They would remain on the Continent, unexpectedly, for eighteen months.

　　　　　　　　　　　　　　　　　　Paris H. de Hollande
　　　　　　　　　　　　　　　　　　Dec. 26th [1893]
Dear Tonni,

　　Just a line to tell you of our safe arrival, & to thank you for your two delightful books, which were both greatly wanted in my small library—nobody has your knack of finding out what people are in need of! You dear old soul, it was so like you to remember Toots too, with her sweet little Christmas card! As for the books, I am already deep in Symonds, which I glanced through last year at the Redwood, but never had time to read[1]—& the "Skeptics" were down on my list—so you see.

　　We had a very good voyage, as winter voyages go, but I was very tired when we went on board, & was consequently seasick for the first time in years—think what a bore! We reached Havre on Sunday at noon, but not until 9.30 p.m. did we get to Paris, worn out by the beastly delay. We found our old apartment here, which is a great comfort. We dined of course with Mama & Harry last night, & you would have rejoiced to see Mama looking so well & the apartment so charmingly arranged, so settled & luxurious-looking—I never saw the family so well installed. Miss Wallis seemed well, & she & Mama were chuckling over your Christmas cards—

Margie La Farge proved quite a good sailor & stood the voyage better than I had thought possible[2]—She is all eyes & ears here, most intelligent & appreciative, & perfectly overwhelmed by the wonder of it all—This is very short, as I want to send a line to old Doyle by this mail. Please send me an account of what you have spent for me, I think I owe you for various small sums. I hope you had a good Christmas & *no head*—We are all well, Toots included.

Yr affte E.W.

1. John Addington Symonds (1840–93) wrote widely on art, culture, and aesthetics. The Redwood Library in Newport had eight books by Symonds on its shelves in 1893; the most recently acquired was *Our Life in the Swiss Highlands* (1892), but Bahlmann's gift could have been *Essays Speculative and Suggestive* (1890), which remains in Wharton's library, or *An Introduction to the Study of Dante* (1872), certainly a subject that interested her.

2. This was probably the daughter of painter John La Farge, who was a Newport neighbor.

The Whartons traveled in Tuscany with their friend Egerton Winthrop and his niece and ward, Charlotte Hunnewell, soon to be engaged to Victor Sorchan. Harry Cram was Winthrop's son-in-law, having married Winthrop's only daughter, Charlotte, in 1892. Charlotte died in 1893, leaving an infant daughter, Charlotte Winthrop Cram. When Harry Cram died of a protracted illness less than a year later, Egerton Winthrop became baby Charlotte's legal guardian.

Once again, Wharton is concerned for her mother's health and spirits, and she changes her travel plans in order to be with Lucretia for several weeks.

This is only one of numerous hints in the letters of a closer mother-daughter relationship than biographers have portrayed.

Wharton's meeting with Vernon Lee (nom de plume of the scholar and travel writer Violet Paget, 1856–1935) was an important one for her. She credits Lee in A Backward Glance *as "the friend whose kindness made [the writing of* Italian Villas and Their Gardens*] possible," and "the first highly-cultivated and brilliant woman I had ever known." Lee arranged for Wharton to visit many private villas and gardens in researching the book, and she also critiqued most of Wharton's writing about Italy. Her talk, reported Wharton, "had the opalescent play of a northerly sky" (*BG, 132–33*).*

The trip to San Vivaldo was made so that Wharton might examine and begin to authenticate some terra cotta figures she had read about and believed to have been done by the school of della Robbia. The identification was made successfully, proving Wharton a serious scholar of Italian art. This trip would be the basis of her first travel article, "A Tuscan Shrine," published in Scribner's *in January 1895, and included later in* Italian Backgrounds.

Florence
April 8th [1894]

Dear Tonni,

I have just got your letter saying that you would like to come out & join me, & I send this line at once in reply. First I want to thank you for your ready response to my proposal. I know you would go over seas & under mountains to oblige me, & I only hope that in this case the great service you will be doing me will be compensated by some enjoyment in the trip. I send this line off in haste, as I want to tell you that Teddy has now decided to sail on May 26th, a week sooner than he had intended, (unless the Normandie sails on that date, a fact he will know in a few days.) I should therefore be glad if you could sail on May 19th, thus arriving the day after he leaves—but if it interferes with your lessons, or any of your other arrangements, to do so, it will be equally convenient to have you sail on the 26th. You must decide without reference to me, for as you know I am a very independent person & have no fear of solitude, & while I should be glad to have you arrive when Teddy leaves it will be no hardship to wait for you a week or so. We have decided to go to Paris, so you will find me there. I am sorry on your account, as I know you would have enjoyed the lakes, but we are having such a hot spring that I think we shall have had enough of Italy in another month, & besides I think I ought to be near Mama again for a few weeks before we start out on our summer trip. Well, now you know our plans; & I see no reason for cabling you, for should any changes arise, I can send a letter which will reach you by May 1st. As to your idea of coming abroad on your own haughty hook, we can discuss that when you get to Paris. I will certainly do nothing to make you feel uncomfortable, though I am not quite prepared to exonerate you from a tinge of "hastiness" in the matter. Teddy will send you in a day or two a line of introduction to the Cie Générale.[1]

And now to tell you about ourselves. Have I written to you since we left Cannes? I am not sure, but shall play that I haven't — We left on March 12th, I think, & stopped at S. Remo & Genoa, reaching here on the 15th. We have been here ever since, enjoying ourselves greatly, & revelling in the most perfect weather — but the last three days the heat has been frightful, & we are going to leave on the 15th. I have a very good English masseuse here & am making very great progress. The air here agrees with me, & I have found it a delightful change after the comparative monotony of the Riviera.

Mr. Winthrop & Miss Hunnewell have been here with us for ten days, & have now gone to Rome, but we meet again in ten days at Venice. While they were here we made charming excursions to Pistoia & Prato, & took some lovely drives into the country. Unfortunately we have had no rain & the dust has become so bad that it is no longer possible to drive with any pleasure.

I have made the acquaintance of "Vernon Lee," & shall have many interesting things to tell you about her when we meet. Mr. Harry Cram is with us now, & tomorrow we go for the night to S. Gimignano, & drive the next day to the sacred mountain of S. Vivaldo, getting back here for dinner. The day after we intend to go up to Vallombrosa, for though

My Dear Governess

it is too early for the foliage the view must be fine & it is worth seeing even at a disadvantage, especially as one can now come & go in one day. Lastly we leave here on the 15th for Rimini, thence make a driving excursion to Urbino & San Marino, then go to Ravenna & so to Venice.

I am sorry to say that Mama seems to have been poorly since her return to Paris. It is odd that she never feels well there. Teddy is the picture of health, & thank heaven has no more neuralgia. He bicycles all over the country in spite of the dust!

Toots is blooming, & sends her love—Thanks for your nice long letter. Have you read the poems of Francis Thompson?[2] They are very interesting, & I never saw a first volume so full of promise. I believe he is the coming English poet.

Yr affte

E.W.

1. Compagnie Générale Transatlantique was a shipping line that operated passenger liners between Europe and the United States. Bahlmann was to have a bad experience sailing on their ship, the *Navarre*.

2. Francis Thompson (1859–1907) was indeed a promising poet whose first volume, *Poems,* was published in 1893. He was also, however, an opium addict who suffered from tuberculosis. He published three volumes of poetry and wrote literary criticism for several publications of Alice Meynell, who helped and supported him for a number of years. His best known poem is "The Hound of Heaven."

Milan

May 2d [1894]

Dear Tonni,

I am absolutely haggard whenever I think of our carelessness in not sending you the letter to the French Steamer Co! It was simply inexcusable, & has put you to endless bother, I know. However, there is no use in crying over it now, & this letter is intended, not to only to tell you again how sorry & mortified we both feel, but also to supplement my wild scrawl from Venice by a more lucid account of our doings. We left Florence on April 12th & stopped at Bologna. We intended while there to go to Ferrara, but the day we had set aside for that purpose it poured, so we gave it up. The next day we were joined by Mr. Winthrop & Miss Hunnewell, on their way up from Rome, & we all went together to Ravenna, where we spent a most delightful day. The next day we went to Venice, where we stayed ten days. While we were there we went back to Padua, which was more interesting even than I had remembered, & also to Vicenza, a place quite apart, & full of Italian flavour. When we left Venice we stopped at Verona, & intended going from there to Mantua, but unfortunately rainy weather has set in, & so we regretfully gave up Mantua & came on here yesterday. It is still pouring today, but there are so many interesting things to be seen in Milan that one can more easily resign oneself to bad weather than in the small places. I think we shall be here for a week & make it the jumping off place for excursions to Bergamo, Pavia, &c. We have decided to get back to Paris by May 10th, as Mama is so poorly. She has sciatica in her leg & does not seem able to get over it. The cold damp weather of the last fortnight, coming after such premature heat, has probably been very bad for her, & I want to get back to her, as I know she must feel dull & depressed shut up in her room after her open air life at Cannes.

Don't you think "That Good May Come" looks well in print? At first I was disappointed, but now on the whole I'm pleased.

We are all as well as possible—Teddy looks splendidly, & as for me I have not felt so well in years. Toots is also in rude health & spirits, & quite ready to be spoiled next month by old Bahlmann. Remember my injunctions to give yourself *a good state room,* for we have been so economical all winter that I am now looking about, like the late Miss Wolfe, for investments for my superfluous income, & I know of none which would give me greater satisfaction than that.[1]

Affy Yrs,

E.W.

We shall be at the H. de Hollande in Paris. Be sure you telegraph from Havre by what train you will arrive, so that James can meet you at the station. *Don't forget—*If you are tired & land late much better stop at Frascati's for the night.

My Dear Governess

1. Catherine Lorrilard Wolfe (1828–87), who inherited a fortune, was an art collector and noted philanthropist who endowed many institutions generously, particularly the Metropolitan Museum of Art.

Bahlmann sailed to Europe and spent two months with Wharton while Teddy was in America. This letter was written shortly after her departure for home.

Lucerne
July 25th, Thursday
[1894][1]

Dear Tonni,

I send this line of farewell to Havre, although I see by the Herald that you do not have to leave Paris until Saturday morning. I hope it is true, but dare not rely on it, for it seems to me very unusual that the steamer should sail so late. Our plans are finally decided, as we have secured rooms at Andermatt & Pontresina, & we are off tomorrow morning. The servants go by rail to Andermatt, & we by boat & carriage—I shall be glad indeed to leave, for the heat seems to increase every day, & I think even *you* would find it too warm. We went up to the Gütsch yesterday afternoon late, but it was so stifling that we actually came back, finding the air closer there than on the lake. We are naturally looking forward with peculiar pleasure to our drive, under these circumstances. Gross got back last night almost dead with heat, & said she had hunted all over the station for you at Bâle, & that when her train left you had not yet registered your trunk for Paris, for she saw it standing there, so you must have reached the station after she left, & she naturally thought you must be ill.

The book-seller here got me all but one of the plays I ordered. Der Handschur, by Bjornson, is very dramatic, if one can admit the absurd premise that a man's past should be as innocent as a young girl's. Strindberg's story, "Die Leute auf Hemsö," is more than I can stand—It is the dullest thing I ever got hold of—not worth sending to you.[2]

Toots is well in spite of the scorching heat, but I know from experience that there are no extremes of temperature she cannot endure. The only difference she makes is that she does not lie in the sun these last days—judge what the heat must be! Teddy bathes in the lake, but I can't dare to, for I have never tried fresh water bathing.

Well, dear Tonni, I do hope with all my heart that all this hot breathless weather means a glassy sea for you, at least at the start. I feel that the fatigue of the two voyages were but ill-compensated by your few weeks abroad, & only wish I could have given you more enjoyment & showed you more "sights" than I did—I feel convinced that you didn't take money enough with you when you left here—be sure you let me know of all extra expenses you may have had—& you must include your *steamer tips* in the list, both coming and going, for I forgot to ask for them before you left. Don't forget. Love & bon voyage from all—E.W.

1. 25 July 1894 was a Wednesday rather than a Thursday. However, this letter and the ones that follow clearly are in sequence, and numerous internal data, such as articles in magazines and exhibitions that Wharton and Bahlmann see, all coincide with dating this series of letters in 1894. Therefore I conclude that Wharton made an error in the date or day of the week when addressing this letter.

2. The Norwegian author Bjornstjerne Bjornson (1832–1910) would win the Nobel Prize for Literature in 1903. The play that Edith read, in German translation, was "The Gauntlet." August Strindberg's (1849–1912) novel was translated variously as *The People of Hemso* and *The Natives of Hemso*.

We come now to the time in Edith Wharton's life during which R. W. B. Lewis speculated, based on the scant correspondence that he found between her and Scribner's, that Wharton had "a total nervous collapse that endured, all told, for more than two years" (74). Both Benstock and Lee have presented alternate viewpoints, based partly on Wharton's letters to Ogden Codman. Benstock and Lee argue that if Wharton was ill, she was also productive and active. The evidence in her letters to Bahlmann supports their thesis. There was illness, but far from a total collapse. As we can see from the letter of 2 August 1894, Wharton had been unwell during her time in Switzerland, but by August she was up and traveling again. Later in the month she fell ill

My Dear Governess

for a few weeks, and the doctor ordered her to take a series of "electric baths,"
which necessitated her remaining in Europe for the winter rather than re-
turning to Newport as she and Teddy had planned. Monthly letters from
1894–95 chronicle her activities and Teddy's concern, which might have been
less helpful than stifling.

Pontresina

August 2, [1894]

Dear Anna,

I found your letter from Havre when we reached here this afternoon, & was so glad to hear that the Navarre promised well & that
your room was satisfactory. I am so glad that you were not obliged to
spend the night in Havre, but could be in your comfortable quarters
until the last moment—& I do indeed hope that your good fortune
has lasted across the ocean, & kept all the winds & waves quiet. As for
you thanking me for the month you spent with me that is "un peu trop
fort." You did a very great favor & one that I shall never forget, & I fear
it was done at the cost of much fatigue & many headaches—so I think
the thanks would come more appropriately from me! I am sorry to say
that I have just heard from [Doyle's niece] Maria Buzzee that poor old
Doyle has been desperately ill again. The letter was dated July 20th, so I
fear by this time all may be over. They had taken her to the seaside, but
brought her back when she showed signs of illness, & of course the heat
in Washington was frightful. Still, I suppose they wanted to be near the
Dr. Poor old soul, I did hope to see her again. By the way, I never told
you about the destination of the three brooches—I meant the one with
the two hearts for Maria Jones, the fly for Mrs. Buzzee, & the black crystal clover-leaf for Doyle—but if anything has happened to the dear old
soul, will you send the clover-leaf to Mme Buzzee, the hearts to Maria,
& give the fly to any one to whom you want to offer a little souvenir,
now or at Christmas.

We have had a very pleasant week since I wrote you, & I am much
better than I was in Lucerne. We spent two days at Andermatt, occupying
one to drive over the St. Gotthard, then we drove over the Aberalp pass

to Thusis, sleeping at a charming little place called Disentis. This took us through most exquisite scenery. The day after we got to Thusis it poured, so we could not do anything—but the day after we drove to Splügen & back, & took our vermouth in the very room where we had that delicious coffee & roggen-brot [a sourdough bread] years ago—do you remember? The next day (yesterday) we drove over the Schym pass, lunched at an exquisite little place called Alvanen Bad, just what I had dreamed that Gérardmer would be, & drove in the afternoon through the magnificent Albula gorge to Bergün, where we slept last night. This morning we drove over the Albula, & reached here in the afternoon. We find this part of the Engadine bleak & dreary, & too cold even for me. I doubt if we stay here long. We go to Liebler's Hotel at St. Moritz Bad the day after tomorrow, but I don't believe we shall stay there more than a week—

We have almost decided to sail in Sept, on the 15th or 22nd, & I shall be very glad if we do so. Teddy is bored with this life, as I knew he would be. It is charming to drive from one place to another, but one can't do that forever, & when one settles down it seems rather purposeless.

I am sorry you had so much trouble about Déjénérescence—I never dreamed it would be out of print—There seems a fatality about that book![1] How wise you were to get that blue foulard skirt. I am so glad you did. You forgot to leave me your western address, but of course Mrs. Kirchner [in whose boarding house Bahlmann lived] will forward this.

I hope you will find your brother & his family well, & I know how glad they will be to see you. I do trust you won't have too hot a journey.

Teddy & Toots send you their love. They are *both* very well!
Affly yrs,

E.W.

Aug. 3rd p.s. I have just heard of my poor dear Doyley's death—on July 22d. I shall never forgive myself for not having been with her—if I had only been at home this Summer she would have been with me—My poor dear old soul—

Keep the little brooches till we get back, please, if you have not sent them.

1. *Entartung,* which means "Degeneration," by Max Nordau (1849–1923), a Hungarian Jew who was influenced by the Dreyfus affair to become a Zionist. His 1892 book was an influential diatribe against contemporary culture. His argument that European culture was on the decline was based on contemporary theories of mental illness. Given Edith's personal experience of living with someone who had the symptoms Nordau takes figuratively in his study of culture, it must have been a challenging book for her. Wharton reports finding her copy of the book in her 27 September letter.

Paris

Sept 7th [1894]

Dear Tonni—You must have wondered at my long silence, for I have left three of your letters unanswered. The fact is that since my return to Paris I have been very poorly—My nervous dyspepsia has returned with fresh fury, I have had to see Bouchard, & he has upset all our plans by forbidding us to sail for the present & ordering me to take a course of electric baths for six weeks—After that he says we can sail, but as soon as I had seen him we decided to give up going home until the Spring, as it would be useless to go so late in the Autumn, & besides I really don't feel strong enough—He assures me it is only a temporary relapse, merely "un peu de faiblesse," & I try to think so, but I am pretty well discouraged—However, he worked wonders before & may do so again. We shall be here two or three months, at any rate, as he wishes me to be absolutely quiet—It is a great disappointment to both of us, but there is nothing to be done about it.

I can't tell you how I felt when I heard of your horrible experience on the Navarre—Teddy took your letter to the company & made a row, but what is the use? They don't care, & their line is running down more & more every day—They said you did not see the right man, & you should have enquired the price of your room on the Navarre & made a bargain, & a lot of other reasons which were no reasons at all, & expressed a great deal of empty regret, which cost them nothing—I am more sorry than I can say about the whole business.

Your journey to Independence must have been frightful—I shall always think you might better have postponed it to next year—I only hope you will have an easier time getting back to New York—The weather here has been delightfully cool ever since our arrival & I am thankful that I can take my cure here instead of having to go to some silly watering place. I am going to take French lessons soon, & I have asked for a permit to study the engravings in the Cabinet d'Estampes, so I shall not lack occupation. As for poor Teddy, he finds it pretty dull, but is as sweet-tempered as ever, & I find it difficult to persuade him even to go & play tennis, so afraid is he of my being lonely while he is away! We go every day to the Bois for a drive, & thus Toots really gets more enjoyment out of the day than any of us—Mama is wonderfully well, & has had no cause to regret staying in Paris. As for Harry, I can't see that his cure has done him much good—He seems pretty well, but still has pain in his arm. Mr. Baldwin is staying with them now.

By the way, we have had one piece of good luck in the midst of our annoyances. We have made $5,000 "in sugar," & as we have been successful I will confide in you that in going into the speculation we risked a tiny amount for you, & your earnings are $200.[1] for which I will shortly send you a cheque—Don't rebuke me for having gambled for you, for nothing succeeds like success—I am very sorry for poor Mrs. Amory & her daughter—it seems a most cruel case & I wish I could help the latter.[2] I fear, however, from what you say, that even if they would accept help it would all go to the father, & at this distance it is so hard to devise ways & means of managing the matter satisfactorily. Could you not perhaps find out some way by which we could do something for the poor girl? Don't hesitate to tell me frankly, for we are very prosperous just at present, & it would be a pleasure if we could help anyone out of any little difficulty.

I am reading Taine's Origines de la France, & have found a nice little French library where I can get contemporary memoirs, which is a great advantage.[3]

When we were in Switzerland Gross collected a lovely bouquet of edelweiss & other alpine flowers for you, which she has asked me to send you, but I think they had better not make the long journey to Independence, so I shall send them later to N.Y.

Now, dear Tonni, don't fancy me really ill, but only temporarily *relapsed*—I hope in two or three weeks to send you a very different report, & meanwhile let me have news of yourself as often as your head will permit.

Toots sends a wag—

Affly Yrs

E.W.

1. Teddy's friend Francis Dumaresq was a sugar broker and was probably the source of this investment.

2. There is a photograph in the Bahlmann archive of a young, well-dressed woman named Mathilde Amory, so one can surmise that she was another pupil of Anna Bahlmann's. Clearly there is a story here, one which might have fed Wharton's imagination.

3. Hippolyte Taine (1828–93) was a scientific historian whose work Wharton considered "one of the formative influences of my youth" (to Sara Norton, 16 March 1908, *LEW,* 136). Here she is reading one of six volumes of *Les Origines de la France contemporaine.*

Paris
Sept 27th [1894]

Dear Tonni,

White has just forwarded me the letter you sent to welcome us on our arrival at Land's End, & we almost shed tears over your prophetic pictures of the rapture of the dogs & the other pleasant circumstances of home-coming. We are really very homesick, & would give anything in the world to be in the Land's End library at this moment with our books & dogs. I counted, too, on a long visit from you on your way back from Virginia—but es wär zu schön gewesen [it would have been so nice]! I know my last letter worried you, so I hasten to say that I am making real progress. I have no indigestion, only an occasional "migraine," but the doctor thinks that will pass off, & every one finds me looking much better. I am sure that Loulie Baylies [Bahlmann's former pupil Louise

Van Rensselaer], whom I saw for a moment last week, will tell you that I look well. She seemed the picture of health. —

We have had a week or ten days of damp warm rainy weather, which I found very trying, but today is clear & cool & I am much refreshed by the change. Teddy is having a dull life just now, for his only recreation, bicycling, has been stopped by the rain, but he is as patient as an angel, & I can hardly get him to leave me for five minutes, for fear I shall be lonely! He is looking forward very much to Cannes, & I suppose we shall go there early in Dec—I have been reading Les Origines de la France Contemporaine, which strikes me as the greatest book of the century, next to the Origin of Species. I want to read a good history of the French revolution now, but I can't stand Michelet's Jacobinism & I don't know what to get. Can you make a suggestion? After that I shall read Thiers "Consulat et Empire" & so go on down to the Franco-German war[1]—I have been trying to get French & Italian teachers, but so far without success, for every one seems to be out of town—By the way, the first volume of Entartung was found here on our return, safely packed in the book-box[2]—As to the little pin I meant for dear Doyle, give it to some one at Christmas—It is always convenient to have some little Christmas presents. In a week or so I shall send you one or two books I have been reading, which may interest you. I shall send them to New York. You will enjoy the quiet & verdure of Virginia after your Western trip, & I am glad to think of you there. Some of the sugar we bought has already been sold at a high price & I shall soon send you your winnings. Mama is perfectly well—I shall write soon again to report my progress. Affly Yrs E.W. Toots sends a wag.
[written over the first page] My article on the terra cottas of San Vivaldo is coming out in Scribner's.

1. The French historian Jules Michelet (1798–1874), whose *Histoire de France*, in nineteen volumes, is considered his masterpiece; *Histoire du consulat et de l'empire* is the fifth volume of Louis Adolphe Thiers's (1797–1877) history of the French Revolution.

2. Max Nordau's book, for which Wharton was looking in August.

Paris
Oct 23d [1894]

Dear Tonni,

You have been probably much surprised by receiving from Mrs. Jay a package of doylies, an amethyst brooch & buckle, all of which I asked her to send to you on her arrival in New York, that you might forward them to Mrs. Wharton — I meant to write you at the same time, to announce that they were coming, but I have had one of my troublesome colds which makes me so lazy about writing that I let the time pass without doing so — Well, here is the explanation of the package — The doylies are a commission, which you will please kindly send to Mrs. Wharton at once, addressed

127 Beacon St.
Boston.

As for the brooch & buckle, will you keep them till a day or two before Christmas & then send them also, putting the card for Miss W. with the buckle, & that for Mrs. W. with the brooch? —

As for yourself, let me add while I think of it that Mrs. Welman, who sails next month, will bring you my otter tippet, which I hope you will find warm & comforting for the winter, & also some warm gloves which Gross got for you the other day at the Louvre. So much for business, & now let us turn to other topics. —

As I told you I have had a cold, in fact two colds, one just after the other, so that I have been much shut up during the last ten days, & my electric baths have been most unfortunately interrupted — but otherwise I am much better. My indigestion has entirely disappeared, & when I saw Dr. Bouchard last week he was perfectly delighted with the progress I had made. I am to begin my baths next week & take them for five weeks more.

So you see we were right not to go home — By the way, I am also going to send you by Mrs. Welman a bottle of a wonderful new medicine for the suppression of uric acid, which Mr. Webster told Mama about, & which she has asked me to send you. In Mr. Webster's case it has done wonders. Mama herself is wonderfully well & does not look as if she needed that or anything else.

I have begun to read a most interesting book, the "Histoire Générale du IV Siècle à nos Jours," edited by [Ernest] Lavisse & [M. A.] Rambaud, with the different chapters written by specialists, such as [Charles] Bayet on the Byzantine Empire, [Émile] Gebhart on the Renaissance in Italy, etc.[1] It is a monumental work, there are to be 12 vols. but only 4 are out. I am in the middle of the first, which extends to the XI cent. It is intensely interesting & I wish that you were here that we might read it together—I continue my study of the history of engraving at the Cabinet d' Estampes, & have got as far as Marc Antonio in the Italian school. After that I begin with the German masters. It is most delightful as you may fancy, but I do wish I had Dohme with me. Poor little Toots has had one of her attacks of inflammation & her convalescence is very slow. She has to be fed on beef, wine, & iron, & is reduced to a little skeleton!—

I hope to soon get a line from you saying that you are safely back in N.Y.—The $200, & the cheque for Miss Amory will be sent to you shortly—Take care of yourself & have a *wood fire* in your room—do you hear?

Affly yrs.

E.W.

When I reach the French school of engraving how I shall enjoy your Goncourt! Please do not send the doylies to Mrs. Wharton before Nov. 10th, as her house in town may not be open before that.

1. Eight volumes of this twelve-volume set exist in Wharton's library at The Mount.

This letter introduces Bahlmann's friend Ella Denison, another professional woman who worked at one point as a draughtsman for Hoppin & Koen, the architectural firm that would design The Mount, the Whartons' home in Lenox, Massachusetts. Ella Denison also designed stationery for Edith Wharton and her friends. As for the "sugar gamble," while the Whartons may in-

deed have made money on such an investment, it was also a way for Wharton once again to enhance Bahlmann's income without embarrassing her.

Paris

Nov. 8th [1894]

Dear Tonni,

Teddy has just written Mr. Baldwin to send you the $200. from our sugar gamble, & $125. for Miss Denison. Mrs. Welman, who sails tomorrow, has kindly charged herself with a parcel for you, containing my otter collar, which I thought you might find useful on cold days, & also three pairs of warm gloves for the same purpose. You will also find in the same package some gloves (I think a dozen) which Mama begs you will kindly send to Mary Bagley. She (Mary B.) was to go as cook to Mrs. Victor Sorchan, whose address is 29 W. 39th St., so I suppose you will hear of her there.[1] If not you can get her address by writing to White, Land's End Lodge. Please tell Bagley that the gloves are a present from Mama—I told Mrs. Welman that you would send for the parcel.

It was very remiss of me not to notify you more promptly about the things which Mrs. Jay took out. I didn't wonder you were puzzled, but I hope you rec'd my letter soon after writing—

I have a very sad piece of news for you. Our darling Toots died last week. She was ill two weeks, a most heartbreaking time for us, but painless for her. I really can't write about it. I was up with her night after night, feeding her every hour, & hoping to the last to save her—but it was hopeless. We are perfectly heart-broken, as you may imagine.

I was getting on splendidly before this happened, but of course it has been a good deal of a set-back, & now we have decided to go away for a few days' trip to Belgium, & when we return we shall go at once either to the Riviera or Florence. I miss the little soul so horribly. I shall write a longer letter soon.

Affly E.W.

1. Mrs. Sorchan was Charlotte Hunnewell, the niece of Wharton's friend Egerton Winthrop.

Anna Bahlmann, as usual, was keeping up her cultural activities and reporting to Wharton what was going on in New York. The loan collection of women's portraits that she attended opened to great interest in New York, with many of the subjects of the portraits coming to view themselves and to be seen ("Portraits"). Bahlmann would have seen many of her employers and their friends at the exhibition.

Wharton's work was primarily writing more stories so as to have enough for a full volume. In October, Scribner's Magazine *carried her poem "An Autumn Sunset." For pleasure, she and her mother enjoyed watching a new pair of Papillon dogs.*

Paris

Nov. 20th [1894]

Dear Tonni,

I sent you such a depressed letter the other day that I know you have been fretting about me, for which there is happily no need, as I am making very satisfactory progress. Since I left off my electric baths I have had no fresh colds, & altogether I am much better. I was delighted to get your last letter, with its interesting account of the Portrait Exhibition & all your other doings, & shall read Littell with much pleasure when it arrives. I am so glad that you like the Athenaeum — I think it is a very pleasurable way of keeping up to date.[1] By the way, you must be sure to let me know about Rhys Davids' lectures. You remember the contempt with which he is treated by Sinnett, who says that he knows absolutely nothing of the true Buddhist doctrine — [2]

My reading & all my work has been terribly interrupted this last month, & now we are leaving so soon that it is not worth while to begin again with my study of engravings here, but I hope to continue it in Rome & Florence. As for Lavisse's histoire Générale it is really delightful, & I hope to introduce you to it next Summer at Newport. We have finally decided to leave here next week for Cannes, stopping at Dijon & Mâcon (the latter to see the wonderful little church at Brou, you remember, Matthew Arnold's church.)[3] From Mâcon we can go in a night to Cannes, which will be easy & comfortable. We should have started sooner, but it seemed too risky to go to the Riviera before the end of this month on account of the rain. —

Since I wrote you we have, I will not say replaced Toots, for that would be impossible, but put into her empty place two dear little dogs whose acquaintance I hope you will make next Summer. We did not mean to buy two, as you may fancy, but having seen one of them, a little brown papillon of about 6 lbs, we found that she had at home a half-sister of the same size & colour, though not so pretty, from whom she had never been separated. They were so much attached to each other that we felt it would be really cruel to buy one & leave the other, so after much hesitation we took both feeling that we were making a very rash experiment! As it happens, it is exactly like having one dog, for they are absolutely inseparable, sleeping, eating, drinking, playing, & in fact doing everything together. It is really pathetic to see them watch each other & cover each other with kisses — with it all they have taken greatly to us & are such good obedient little things that we feel quite at home with them already. Don't you think we are very fortunate to have hit upon such a funny little pair? Mama is fascinated by them, & we sit & laugh by the hour at their funny antics. —

I am very glad that Ella Denison is better, & I hope you have rec'd the cheque safely by this time — Don't bother, by the way, to send me any more cuttings from the American papers, but save your extra stamps, you spendthrift, for White deluges Gross with Heralds & N.Y. Times, so that we get all the news in that way! — I had a letter the other day from Maggie Wingate who tells me she is going to spend the Winter in New York, but does not say where.

Aff yrs E.W.

1. Littell's *Living Age* was a weekly review, published in Boston, containing articles from other magazines and journals. The *Athenaeum* was a weekly literary review, perhaps sent to Bahlmann as a gift from Wharton.

2. Professor T. W. Rhys Davids (1843–1922) gave a series of lectures, sponsored by Columbia University, on the history and literature of Buddhism. Alfred Percy

Sinnett's (1840–1921) *Esoteric Buddhism* (1883) is said to be the first modern exposition of Theosophy. He was an English journalist living in India and an early member of Mme. Blavatsky's Theosophical Society.

3. See Arnold's poem "The Church of Brou."

Paris
Dec. 1st [1894]

Dear Tonni,

Thank you so much for your kind & sympathetic letter about Toots. I really think that every one who knew her grieves for her as if she were a real little person—& indeed was she not, & of the rarest kind? We have really had "la main heureuse" [a lucky hand] in choosing her two successors. They have all her gentle, persuasive little ways & her playfulness & eager interest in us & our doings, & combined with their pathetic attachment for each other it makes them singularly good companions. The dog-doctor who has seen them says we are very lucky to have picked up two such little dogs, & I only hope we may keep them longer than we have our previous pets—

We are off for Cannes the day after tomorrow, having put off our departure several days in order to dine for Thanksgiving with Mama & Harry. We had a delicious turkey & actually some cranberry sauce on that occasion, & it seemed very homelike—The Littell arrived safely, & I read Vernon Lee's article on Ravenna with great interest, but thought it rather a pot-boiler. "The double-bedded room" was what Mr. Codman would call "curdling" wasn't it?[1]—I hope you receive the Athenaeum safely each week—I am going to send you a Christmas card in the shape of a book from the Bon Marché! Doesn't that excite your curiosity? By the way, Miss Amy Townsend, who sails in about three weeks, is to take out some gloves for Miss Wharton, & I have asked her to send them to you & shall be much obliged if you will forward them to 127 Beacon St. Please send me a "mem." of what I owe you for expressing the various parcels to Mrs. Wharton & Maria Jones—I fancy, by the way, that was a cock-&-bull story of Miss Mallen's, as I had a long letter from Maria last week, & she never said a word about the will or any money troubles.

At any rate, if there has been any difficulty it has probably been settled to their satisfaction, otherwise I am sure she would have alluded to it—

I have very little news for you this week. We went to see "Gismonda," Sarah Bernhardt's new play, which is sad trash, & last week we saw at the Odéon a revival of Dumas' intensely dramatic "Monsieur Alphonse." It was beautifuly [sic] acted & we enjoyed it very much.[2] These have been our only dissipations—The weather is so very damp & Teddy is suffering so much from neuralgia that we have decided to give up our little trip to Dijon and Mâcon & go straight to Cannes. December is a bad time for exploring French provincial towns, but we hope to make up for it by seeing more in Italy—I am very much better, so much so that I feel really most hopeful about myself—Do what you like with the $325, only don't spend it all on other people! Thank you again for your letter. I shall soon send you a picture of "Mimi" & "Miza."

Affly Yrs, E.W.

1. "Ravenna and her Ghosts," reprinted from *Macmillan's Magazine* in *Littell's Living Age,* 3 November 1894. "Double-bedded" was an anonymous ghost story reprinted from *Blackwood's Magazine* in the same issue of *Littell's.* Wharton and Bahlmann shared an interest in ghost stories.

2. The Paris reviewer for the *New York Times* disagreed with Wharton about Bernhardt's (1844–1923) performance in Victorien Sardou's (1831–1908) play *Gismonda,* saying that Sardou "had never been this triumphant," Bernhardt "never so perfect," and the staging "never more exquisitely beautiful" ("Bernhardt"). The comedy *Monsieur Alphonse* by Alexandre Dumas *fils* was not as well reviewed in the same paper.

Cannes
Dec 31 [1894]

Dear Tonni—

I need not tell you the delightful agitation of undoing your mysterious Christmas packet, nor our surprise & pleasure as one pretty thing after another emerged from the wrapping-paper. You always have the knack of "filling a long-felt want," & the delicious white shawl, the sachet, the downy rug for the "papillons," are already in constant use. As for the photographs of Land's End, we were really indescribably touched by that thought, & the results are as charming as was the intention. Teddy looks & looks at the picture of the stable & the dear doggies, with a fresh wave of homesickness at each inspection — & the sea views are very beautiful — Altogether you gave us a great deal of pleasure, & I hope your Christmas brought you as many delightful surprises as you contributed to ours —

Mama arrived the day before Christmas, as well & cheerful as possible. Mr. Van Alen, who is suffering from laryngitis, came a few days before, for a six weeks' cure — so we had a very pleasant Christmas dinner — But fancy Libler's grief at being in bed with a bad quincy sore throat, & unable to superintend the preparations for the feast! —

We are jogging on as quietly as usual here — I am much better, & Dr. Bright says I may go to Rome by the middle of February, if I am very good meanwhile — Mr. Van Alen is at this hotel, & takes his meals with us, & Teddy has a Boston friend to bicycle with, & the Bourgets are also here for six weeks, at the Californie Hotel, which is pleasant for me — & that, I think, is all the news —

I must not close without telling you how pretty we all thought Miss Denison's Christmas cards. Perhaps next winter I can arrange for some lessons for her. Meanwhile she might do some menu cards for me next summer — Just a thick gilt edged card about the size of this envelope, with "Land's End" in some decorative gold & coloured lettering on top, or in a corner — Let her try one or two & send them to me. Make the price you think right.

I hope your lessons with Miss Soley are as pleasant as they promised to be, & that everything else is going well with you.[1] Teddy sends his love, & his warmest thanks for the calendar, & I am ever
Affly yrs

E.W.

The papillons have put their rug in their basket, & they do have such cozy snoozes in its wooly depths.

Young Pussy Jones had melting brown eyes and a torrent of auburn hair.
(Smithsonian Institution National Portrait Gallery)

Mora 707 BROADWAY, N. Y.

At fifteen, Edith Jones seemed uncomfortable in her grown-up clothes.

Anna Bahlmann, with her pupil Lita leaning affectionately on her shoulder

Pen craig –
Oct 17th

My dear Tonni

Thanks many times
for your kind criticism which
has encouraged me very much.
I got your letter of Oct. 14th
yesterday & was so glad that you
were really pleased with Phantom
& June & Dec – As for the latter
it has not appeared yet – & I
don't know when it will as
I have heard nothing from
little Raymond Belmont about it –
I send you some other verses,
but I dont know whether they are
very bad or quite good – I think
they will admit of both constructions
so you may choose – You are my
Supreme Critic in these matters
& I look upon your verdict
with infinite faith & respect –
I am very glad that June &

Edith Jones to Anna Bahlmann, 17 October 1878

"an airy gallant but a Man" —
The sublime & beautiful sentiments
in that scene were quite toomuch
for my prosaic nature, & I gave
up the book as a bad job —
I never did take to Bulwer.
Well, I believe I must end now as
I want to post this note this
afternoon — & I had almost
forgotten to copy my "poesie"
for you. I was not at all
vexed at your having shewn
the "Sensuchtsromau" to Mr.
Schultz but pleased on the
contrary that you thought it
worthy to be read by a German.
Ever your —

that would have been "high
'art'" if it hadn't been for
the blot.

707 BROADWAY, N. Y.

"I hope you will think me grandement en beauté." (Mora Photography)

Top left, Henry "Harry" Stevens Jones,
"the dearest of brothers to all my youth"
Top right, Lydia Abbot Bahlmann, William Bahlmann, Alois and Anna
Bottom, Teddy Wharton in an uncharacteristically formal pose

Top, Pen craig Cottage; "I'm crazy for you to see the cottage."
Bottom, Teddy and Edith Wharton and the dogs, circa 1891

1898	Carried forward $	229	72
June 1st	9 prs. gloves for summer	8	25
" "	4½ yds mohair	3	38
" "	lawn gown	3	00
" "	1 pr. rubber sandals		40
" 6th	small wares		26
" "	making alpaca skirt	6	65
" 27th	5 prs. Oxford Ties	15	00
" "	2 " leggings	1	00
" "	4½ yds. silesia		90
" "	1 yd. linen		20
" 28th	3 prs. drawers	3	00
" "	blk. India slk. shirt	4	25
" 29th	" satin ribbon		25
" "	1 pr. gloves	1	00
July 8th	bobbin & frill		35
" "	fan		25
" 16th	4 sheets wadding		16
" 22nd	2 yds. gingham		40
Aug. 9th	velvet		62
" 15th	corset steels		15
Oct. 18th	felt hat	1	35
" "	" slippers		69
		281	23

1898	Carried forward $	281	23
Oct. 27th	2 prs. castor gloves	2	00
Nov. 4th	buckles		06
" 13th	altering dress	2	00
" 25th	flan! sacque	3	95
Dec. 17th	small wares		55
" "	rubbers		45
		290	24

This includes for		
Foot wear	$ 34	04
Underclothing	51	25
Hats	8	19
Outside wraps	13	50
Material by yd. or piece	23	80
Making	58	60
Small wares	7	88
Ribbons, lace, veils etc.		50
Gloves	14	25
Dresses & other ready-made clothing	78	23
	290	24

Anna Bahlmann kept careful records of what she spent.

Top left, Miss Eleanor Jay,
"Poor Moppy," 1899
Bottom left, Anna and Pauline
Robinson were the most faithful
of Anna Bahlmann's students.
Top right, Edith Wharton, author

In beginning a new story put in your paper, space six times and then write your title in capital letters. Space twice and make your figure for the first chapter. Space twice and begin to write.

In putting in a page when your story is started, put in your paper, space twice and write your figure to number the page, space twice and begin to write.

Begin at number five for ordinary line, fifteen for a new paragraph. One thumb space between each word or figure or dash and comma, two thumb spaces after full colon and interrogation point, three thumb spaces after period.

Black record ribbon, factory make. That one is not so heavily inked and makes the work look better.

M. S. Cook, 245 Broadway, typewriting paper. (Pro & Con

Paper, plain — 16 — 8 X 10½)

N.B. To begin a new chapter, you line-space 3 times, then write the number of chapter, then space twice.

To make carbon copy, you lay down a sheet of typing-paper; place your carbon sheet on top of that with the shiny side uppermost. Lay another sheet of typing paper on top of that. Place all three under roller of machine, taking care that as they come up under the roller, the dull side of the carbon paper is nearest you & the shiny side is farthest away.

Anna Bahlmann taught herself how to be secretary to a writer.

Offered to Miss Bahlmann
by a group of her friends and pupils,
in recognition of her many years
of faithful and successful work.

Mrs C. Alexander,	$ 2 00
Mrs Edmund Baylies	1 00
Miss Frelinghuysen	1 00
Mrs William Jay	1 00
Miss Beatrix Jones	50.
Mrs Cadwalader Jones	50.
Mrs Hamilton Kean	50
Mrs Beverley Robinson	25.
Mrs Twombly	1 00.
Mrs W. D. Sloane	2 00
Mrs Edward Wharton	1 00
Mrs Robert Winthrop	1 00.

44832

UNITED ST_____ A.

STATE OF *New York*

COUNTY OF *New York* } ss:

I, *Anna Catherine Bahlmann*, a NATIVE AND LOYAL CITIZEN OF THE
UNITED STATES, hereby apply to the Department of State, at Washington, for a passport for myself,
~~accompanied by my wife,~~

_____, and minor children, as follows:

_____ born at _____ on the _____ day

of _____ 1 _____ and _____ born at _____

I solemnly swear that I was born at *New York* _____ in the State of
New York, on ~~about~~ the *5* day of *March* 18*49* that
my { father *was* } a *naturalized* citizen of the United States; that I am domiciled in the
{ husband } *New York* residence being at *Paris—when I am* *Sept 15*
au Thomas-Edik Wharton _____ in the State
_____ where I follow the occupation of *Secretary*:
that I am about to go abroad temporarily: and I intend to return to the United States within *One*
~~months~~ { with the purpose of residing and performing the duties of citizenship therein; and that I
years }
desire a passport for use in visiting the countries hereinafter named for the following purpose:

France
(Name of country.)   *Professional duties*
                                      (Object of visit.)
_____
(Name of country.)   _____
                                      (Object of visit.)
_____
(Name of country.)   _____
                                      (Object of visit.)

OATH OF ALLEGIANCE.

Further, I do solemnly swear that I will support and defend the Constitution of the United
States against all enemies, foreign and domestic; that I will bear true faith and allegiance to the same;
and that I take this obligation freely, without any mental reservation or purpose of evasion: So help
me God.

Anna C. Bahlmann
(signature of applicant.)

Sworn to before me this *4* day

[SEAL OF COURT.]   of *Dec* 19*14*   *B*
                    Charles Wenyss
        Clerk of the *U Dist* Court at *Seine Du Froy*

*A person born in the United States in a place where births are recorded should submit a birth certificate
with his application.

[OVER.]

Facing page, A tribute to honor Anna Bahlmann, circa 1909
Above, At sixty-five, Anna Bahlmann returned to France to do war relief work.

My dear Miss Bahlmann,
I hear you are leaving
for America on the 5ᵗʰ
and I want to send you
a few words of friendship
with all my wishes
for a good voyage —
I hope we will
soon meet again, after
the victory, and
rejoice together for
the glory of the Allies

I was so pleased
to have the chance of
seeing much of you
at the Rue de Varenne
though I still preferred
la Rue de la Kasbah

Goodbye and
good luck to you!

Rodin.

CARTE POSTALE

Correspondance

Adresse

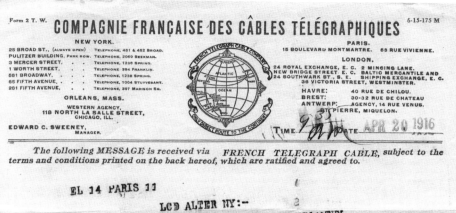

EL 14 PARIS 11

LCD ALTER NY:—

HEART BROKEN PLEASE SEND FAMILY PROFOUND SYMPATHY

WHARTON

DELIVERED FROM
65 FIFTH AVE.
BET. 13th AND 14th STS

PHONE
STUYVESANT 1004

Facing page, Georges Rodier was the administrator of
Société de Secours aux Blessés Militaires.
Above, Edith Wharton was on vacation on the French Riviera
when she heard the news of Anna Bahlmann's death.

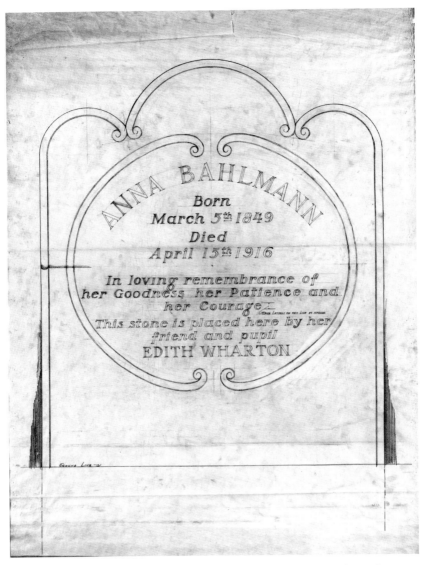

ANNA BAHLMANN

Born
March 5th 1849
Died
April 15th 1916

In loving remembrance of
her Goodness her Patience and
her Courage
This stone is placed here by her
friend and pupil
EDITH WHARTON

Wharton's niece Beatrix Jones Farrand designed Anna Bahlmann's
headstone at her aunt's request.

1. Una Soley, daughter of Mr. and Mrs. James Russell Soley, would come out in a year, so Anna must have been employed as her finishing governess.

This letter brings the first mention of Walter Berry, perhaps the most intimate and important friend in Wharton's life. They were distantly related on Wharton's mother's side, and they met in 1883, in Bar Harbor, the summer when Teddy Wharton's courtship of Edith began. A romance may have kindled that summer, but it never really took flame. Berry had another chance to woo Edith, should he have chosen it, when he played in the 1884 U.S. National Tennis tournament in Newport in August 1884—he and his cousin Alexander Van Rensselaer were the runners-up in doubles—but there is no record of Edith and Walter having met at that time.[1] Nevertheless, Wharton declared in A Backward Glance, *and in many letters, that Walter was her first friend to truly support and critique her writing (an interesting slight to Anna Bahlmann). An intense correspondence between them, mostly about literary matters, flourished from 1898 to 1904. Berry had a career in diplomacy, remained unmarried, and was a trusted friend and companion to Wharton, particularly after her divorce and her permanent residence in France. When he died in 1927, Wharton, who had been overseeing his care, wrote in her diary: "The Love of all my life died today, and I with him" (Diary, YCAL Wharton).*

1. I am indebted to Sarah Kogan for first telling me that Walter Berry was a competitive tennis player. More information can be found at the International Tennis Hall of Fame in Newport.

Cannes
Feb 22 [1895]

Dear Tonni,

Les jours suivent et se ressemblent [the days follow and are similar to one another] to such a degree here, that I have no distinct idea when I last wrote to you, though I fancy you were correct in your conjecture that there was a letter from me on that blessed Gascogne. (You may fancy, by the way, with what real agony of mind Teddy & I watched for news of her, & how elated we are by the outcome of her dreadful struggle.)[1] Well, no news has meant good news in this case, for I have gone on improving steadily ever since I last wrote, & have gained nearly 8 lbs already—Now that I know so much better how to take care of myself I hope to husband this gain instead of wasting it, as (through no fault of my own) I did last year, & in fact all our plans have been made to that end. Next week we are going to Italy, & we shall get back to Paris by the middle of April, in order that I may have six weeks more of massage there before we sail.

We are to be joined in our trip to Italy by Mr. Dumaresq, who arrives in a day or two, & by Mr. Winthrop, who is already here, & if we only have good weather our trip ought really to be a delightful one. We stop first at San Remo, then at Genoa & Pisa, making an excursion from there to Lucca & back, & so to Rome, where I suppose we shall remain four weeks—Until two days ago the weather here has been really desperate, but now it looks more promising, though the Riviera is a doleful spectacle, with all the palms frost-bitten, the heliotrope & Bougainvillea dead, & the vegetation generally in tatters. Unluckily poor Mama caught cold before the weather mended, & is not yet able to get out. I think she will go back to Paris as soon as we leave, for she has been so unlucky here in respect to weather that she is getting very tired of it.— I continue to see a great deal of the Bourgets, who are most interesting companions. The other day we lunched there to meet de Vogüe [*sic*] & it was very interesting to hear the two men talk, though Vogüe is not so good a conversationalist as Bourget, being too self-engrossed & too much inclined to "orate."[2]

I am very sorry that your Stokes project for the Summer has fallen through.[3] I think that you would have enjoyed a summer of Lenox. By the way, your mention of Lulie Baylies in your last letter reminds me to ask you to ask *her* when you have the opportunity what news she has of Mr. Walter Berry. He writes me now & then, but will not speak of his health, & as he was very ill when I saw him in Paris last Autumn I feel very anxious.—

We expect to sail in the Touraine in June, & what fun it will be to get back to our clean delicious house, & to introduce you to the pups.

By the way, poor little Miza was lost the other evening, & we never got her back till the following afternoon, when she was brought in utterly exhausted & covered with mud. The other one cried all night, & it is pathetic to see them together since the episode.[4]

1. The French steamer *La Gascogne* had been delayed by equipment failure and weather, and feared lost.

2. Eugène Marie Melchior, vicomte de Vogüé (1848–1910), was a French diplomat and literary critic with a particular interest in Russian literature.

3. Anson Phelps Stokes (1838–1913) built Shadowbrook, believed to be the largest house in America, in Lenox, Massachusetts, in 1893–96. The family had nine children, and most would have been grown by 1895. Bahlmann may have hoped to become companion to one of the daughters or perhaps governess to one of the grandchildren for the summer.

4. Unsigned, probably for lack of space.

Rome
March 10th [1895]

Dear Tonni,

I have just received your letter enclosing the dinner menus, of which more by & by—first I must thank you for writing, & assure you that I am still getting on well, & that my silence, which seems to have been longer than I intended, was not "de mauvaise augure" [a bad omen]. We left Cannes on Feb. 28, & went to S. Remo & Genoa. Mr. Dumaresq went with us & Mr. Winthrop joined us at Genoa & the Bourgets at Pisa, where we stayed three days, intending to make all manner of delightful excursions. But alas for our good intentions, or at least for mine, the weather was bitterly cold & snowy, & as I had a rheumatic throat I had to give up *everything*, even going to Lucca! The others went & came back frozen but enchanted. Still, there was much to enjoy at Pisa when the sun did finally come out, & as I had not been there for seven or eight years I found it all delightful. The Bourgets left us to go to Florence, & the following afternoon we four started for Rome—We reached here to find it bitterly cold, but the very next day the weather changed & ever since it has been spring-like & lovely. As for Rome it is one long enchantment. I know so much more now how to appreciate & enjoy it than when I was here before, that it seems like a new place to me, & every turn reveals some fresh wonder & beauty—It is delightful having Mr. Winthrop here, for he knows Rome by heart, & is the most appreciative & comprehending of companions; & Mr. Dumaresq also enjoys it very much—I take things very quietly, & have not seen much but the outside of things yet, but yesterday we made a lovely expedition out into the country to see the Villa Madama & the Villa Papa Giulio; the former pathetic in its desolation, with only one or two exquisite frescoed ceilings & a loggia adorned with jewel-like stucco ornamentation, surviving from the general destruction—while the Villa Papa Giulio is all brilliance & gayety, well-preserved & well cared for[1]—How you would have enjoyed it all!—

We have of course been several times to St. Peter's, which to my mind is the most satisfying of the churches here, but as for galleries I have only been for a few minutes in the Capitoline Museum, as I prefer to take advantage of the fine weather & reserve the museums for the inevitable change which must come in a day or two. Later we hope to get out to Frascati & Tivoli, & then I shall have much to tell you. We expect Minnie & Trix here by the end of the month, & I am sorry that we shall have to leave so soon afterwards, but I want three or four weeks between here & Paris.

Mama left Cannes a few days after we did, having been detained there by the bad weather & her obstinate cold. I have had news of her safe arrival, but nothing more—I am so surprised by what you tell me of Maggie Wingate's plans—or rather, I should say, I am surprised not to have heard from her on the subject. She has never answered my last letter, written two or three months ago, but it is quite in the cards that I should in the course of time receive a scattering epistle from her accusing me of never writing; I know her little ways!—Who are the Misses Stillman? I never heard of them.—I am so glad that you continue to be interested in Una Soley; she must be a perfect oasis to you.—

And now as to the menu-cards. I enclose the one I like best, & should be glad to have a dozen like it, on the *same* paper, but varying the colours of the letters. Only I should prefer to have the *S* of Land's End straightened into line with the other letters; it is falling down stairs for no particular reason. The others are all prettily painted, but too crooked. I think the day is past when crooked lettering was considered "quaint."— As to the dinner cards I think they show great cleverness, but I should prefer something simpler—just a smallish gilt-edged card with E.W. made into a handsome monogram with a good deal of gold—will you ask Miss Denison to try that?—The little dogs are painted with great cleverness. Of course I wish to pay her for all the specimens she has sent—Let me know how much. I think she might do such pretty menu cards by trying some delicate Renaissance arabesques, such as one can often find in details of Italian architecture or little Louis XV & Louis XVI vignettes in grisailles, copied from tail pieces of old French books— I make the suggestion as she has so much ability, & if she were a little more "up to date" in her ideas I think she might find work to do. Little medallions, surrounded by conventional designs, are more suitable to such purposes than naturalistic & humorous subjects—so it seems to me. I have only space left to give you much love & thank you again for your letter.

Yr affte E.W.

1. Villa Madama, never completed, was built in the sixteenth century by the Medicis and later belonged to Margaret of Austria, the "Madama" for whom it was named. Villa di Papa Guilio, nearby, was built a little later in the century for Pope Julius III, and even when Wharton visited it housed a museum of pre-Roman artifacts.

Hotel Bristol Rome
March 26th [1895]

Dear Tonni,

Just a line to enclose this funny photograph of Teddy & the dogs, & to say that we are all well, & have had three weeks of sufficient delight to compensate me for all the weary months of last autumn & winter. The weather has been perfect, & Rome more brilliant & picturesque &

in every way enchanting than words can express—Tomorrow we reluctantly tear ourselves away to start for Orvieto—

Since I wrote we have done & seen any number of interesting things, but they are too long to tell of until we meet—when you will have to look at a lot of Piranese prints of Rome, & hear endless descriptions.—

Minnie & Trix arrived five or six days ago, & are in a Hotel close to this one, so that we see them constantly. Trix looks thin, but seems in very good spirits, & I quite agree with you in thinking that she has improved wonderfully in cordiality of manner & in appearance. We all spent a morning in the Forum together, but as a rule we meet a[t] luncheon, dinner or tea—By the way, did I tell you that Dr. Bright makes me take tea every afternoon? I really believe it has done me as much good as any other part of his treatment.

We have bought two such funny old pictures for the hall at Land's End. How they will make you laugh! I hope you will see them in June—I think I told you that we sail on June 8 in the Gascogne—

I don't think I ever thanked you for your clear & interesting account of Buddhism, which interested me so much in your last letter. Affly yrs

E.W.

Milan

April 24 [1895]

Dear Tonni,

After the Herald's sensational accounts of the earth quake in Venice I know you will be wondering what our share in it was, & I therefore send a line to tell you that we thought so little of it that I went to sleep between the two shocks, while Teddy & Mr. Winthrop were made to feel very uncomfortable for several hours afterwards by the rocking—& that was all. Being in a distant corner of the Hôtel, à l'Entresol, we knew nothing until next morning of the ridiculous panic which prevailed—Our twelve days at Venice were one long delight—such delicious warmth & sunshine, such colour & loveliness everywhere, no words can express—We spent a delicious day at Verona, & one still more enchanting at Mantua, of which I shall have volumes to tell you & many photographs to show you—On arriving here I found your last letter, enclosing the dinner cards. They are very well done, but far too large for dinner-cards, so large that I will gladly keep them for small menu-cards—& when I get home I will give Miss Denison some models of what I want. Will you please pay her for what she has done, & tell her I shall try to get some orders for her when I get to Newport?—I will bring her some models from Paris, if possible.—

I am so glad that you liked the picture of Teddy & the sisters. It was funny, wasn't it?—I have also read much in the papers of the rapprochement between the young French and German authors.

And now to return to business. Don't get yourself a Summer "mantle," as I am bringing you one of black silk & lace which will take the place of the little one you had last summer—And, by the way, I hope you know that you have, as usual, a standing invitation to come to Land's End for as long a time as you like in June & July, with the promise of another visit in the Autumn attached as sole condition to your coming—I shall talk you to death about Italy, but when I see you failing will administer restoratives—in order to begin again as soon as you revive!—

We reach Paris on April 27, & you may not hear from me often, as the next weeks will be busy—We sail on June 8—

Yrs E.W.

The Whartons finally returned to the United States and their newly renovated home in Newport in June 1895, and then began the period of Edith Wharton's most severe illness. Bahlmann tended her during the summer but must have felt confident enough in Wharton's recovery to return to New York in the fall. By December Wharton was decidedly better, sending Edward Burlingame a little story, "The Valley of Childish Things," and enjoying bicycle trips of as much as twenty miles a day. Avoiding Boston for the holiday season seemed to be helpful for Wharton; to stay in Newport would have meant avoiding not just the weather in Boston but her in-laws as well.

Land's End
Dec. 27th [1895]

Dear Tonni,

Merry Christmas, & thank you for sending the little scarf to Ella Denison & the photograph (fancy calling it a present!) to Miss Thayer.[1] It occurred to me the other day that she had liked the dogs & might be amused by their portrait, but I am sorry I happened to send it at Christmas, as it seemed to give it an air of undue importance. As to Ella Denison (when you see her, by the way, will you please thank her from me for her pretty Xmas card) I think her suggestions to paint me two or three fans at the price you name a very good one. She may take as much time about it as she likes, & when we go to Mr. Winthrop's on Jan'y 10th I will take Minnie's book on the fan with me & lend it to E.D. during my visit, & she can take tracings of the numerous plates.[2] The best period of decoration for gauze fans is Empire & Directoire, when they were really used—& the light, attenuated & conventional style of decoration is easy to do & suitable to the flimsy material.

I am glad you liked your picture & your Welsbach, you good soul![3] Yes, the book on education came, & I am going to turn it over to you, as it turns out to be, not, as I supposed, a treatise on training the mind, but a practical methods of educating the young. However, as it's by Bain it ought to be good in its way.[4]—I am really glad that mysterious book of yours has not come. Like the children, it is better for me not to have too many presents at once—& I am now enjoying the prospect of its arrival at my leisure. Don't send it, but give it to me when I see you in town. I *know* it's going to be nice!—

Dr. Curtis wrote me that he wanted me in town for ten days in Jan'y, so we shall be with Mr. Winthrop for that length of time.

Our Christmas passed off quietly but pleasantly. We could get no one to come to us but Mr. Winthrop, but I think he really enjoyed his three days here, for the weather was perfect & we bicycled morning, noon, & night! One day I did 17 miles, & another 20½!! & all without a trace of fatigue. We had a little Xmas tree for White's children, which enlarged itself into a modest party for the servants & their friends, which

My Dear Governess

was voted a great success. Trix gave me great pleasure by sending me a photograph of that divine new Botticelli, which is a continual joy—& oddly enough I, who have never had a decent edition of Rossetti, am now the proud possessor of *two*, W. Berry having sent me the complete edition of his works edited by his brother, while Mr. Winthrop gave me the famous Kelmscott Press edition of the poems & ballads.[5] However, I didn't repine, for one can't have too much of so good a thing as that.—

We never did a better thing, as far as my health goes, than when we gave up going to Boston for Xmas. We have had two weeks of real Riviera weather—blue sea & sky, warm sun, in short just the climate that Dr. Curtis wants for me. I have been out of doors all day, & I do feel much better.—I am so sorry about your Mrs. Kirchner's daughter—I hope she goes on well.

Yrs affte E.W.

1. Frances (Fanny) Thayer was Wharton's primary typist for many years, and she and Anna Bahlmann were friends.

2. *A Book about Fans: The History of Fans and Fan Painting,* by M. A. Flory, with a chapter on fan collecting by Mary Cadwalader Jones (New York: Macmillan, 1895). Minnie was at this time employed as a reader for the Macmillan Publishing Company.

3. The Welsbach mantle was a new form of gas-powered lighting, invented by Carl Auer von Welsbach (1858–1929), whose latest model was selling in Europe and the United States. This was a thoughtful gift for a woman who both loved to read and was subject to headaches.

4. Alexander Bain (1818–1903) was a Scottish philosopher, psychologist, and educator who wrote numerous books on education, moral science, and philosophy.

5. Wharton's library at The Mount contains both of these editions of the work of Dante Gabriel Rossetti, his *Ballads and Sonnets,* which has no inscription, and the two-volume *Collected Works,* inscribed to Edith by Walter Berry.

If Wharton's present of a new reading lamp for Bahlmann was ideal, so too was Bahlmann's gift to Wharton of a book by Adolphe Berty (1818–67), who wrote numerous studies of European architecture. Wharton was in the process of launching a new project with the architect and interior designer Ogden

Codman, Jr.: a book on the relationship between architecture and interior design which would be called The Decoration of Houses *when it was published two years later.*

Land's End
Dec. 30th [1895]

Dear Tonni,

The Berty, the enchanting Berty, has just come, & if ever there was truth in the stereotyped saying, "Nothing could have given me greater pleasure," it is this particular occasion! I only wish I could coin a new phrase to express my gratitude. It is so delightful after a shower of perfunctory presents, to get one like this which shows such thought & such interest. I have been all through the delicious pages once already, & feel in consequence an irrepressible longing to pack up & be off at once to lands where such things grow. Sometimes I feel that, like Nature, I abhor a vacuum. Life is too starved here, really!—

I am glad you saw Mr. Winthrop. We really did treat him handsomely in the way of weather when he was here. The skies are clouding & a change is coming, I fear, but up to the present moment our bicycling has not failed us; & I am fresh back from doing 10 miles—
Teddy is out, & has therefore still before him the enjoyment of opening *his* little package. He will write himself & tell you his emotions—but I'm sure the contents can't come up to Berty!

Thanks again, dear Tonni, & I'll thank you more expressively when we meet.
Affly Yr

E.W.

Mr. Codman is coming on Saturday, & oh won't he be sick with envy—poor soul, *he* has no Berty!

Edith and Teddy Wharton spent spring and summer of 1896 traveling in Italy and France. Here Edith writes from Ravenna, capital of the western Byzantine Empire and of the Western Roman Empire, and also the city in which

Dante wrote much of the Divine Comedy *and where his remains rest in a* zona di silenzio, *a zone of silence. The bicycle trip to the basilica of Saint Apollinare and on to the "Pineta," the pine forest that Dante extolled as the garden of Eden, would be about a dozen miles' round trip.*

Ravenna

April 17th [1896]

Dear Tonni,

Thank you very much for your letter & for your "Littell," both of which reached me last week in Milan. I am very sorry to hear of the illness of the little Frelinghuysen boy, but I have heard nothing since your letter. I hope he may have recovered—especially as I saw Mrs. Griswold Gray in Paris, & I think she would have known if anything had gone wrong—[1]

I was much interested in the article on Mlle Dacquin—She must have been a clever woman, but perhaps, a little cold?[2]—

Since I wrote you we have had a most delightful week. Though there have been storms all over Europe we have been living in a charmed circle of fine weather, & have been able, so far, to carry out all our plans without a day's delay.—We went from Milan to Parma, which to me is less interesting than many other Italian towns of the same importance; then to Modena, far more charming & possessed of one of the most interesting picture galleries & collections of Renaissance bronzes which I know of in any provincial town—We went from there to Bologna, where we stayed a day or two, & made the excursion to Ferrara—to my mind one of the most picturesque, almost melodramatically picturesque, towns in Italy.—

Yesterday morning we came here, & tomorrow we are off for Rimini, San Marino, etc— Yesterday afternoon we bicycled out to St Apollinare, in Classe, & thence on to the "Pineta" of Dante, where we sat on the warm, dry grass under the pines & loafed away a pleasant afternoon. We have done a good deal of bicycling so far, but from here I mean to send my bicycle back to Bologna. We expect to go as far south as Loreto, & then return to Venice, where we shall arrive about the 28th.

We shall probably be there a week or ten days, & I have hopes that the Bourgets may join us there.—

We are all well, especially the kittens [dogs], who take all the chances & changes of travel with an extraordinary equanimity—They are delighted with Ravenna, as our hotel has a charming old garden, with a high ivy-covered wall fringed with wall-flowers, & full of winding walks for good kittens—

Teddy sends his love and I am ever

Yr aff.

E.W.

1. The Frelinghuysens were a large, well-connected New Jersey family, many of whose members served, and to this day serve, in public office. The boy in question may have been Peter Hood Ballantine Frelinghuysen (b. 1882), son of George Griswold and Sara Ballantine Frelinghuysen. Mrs. Griswold Gray would be a cousin by marriage. The Frelinghuysen family also had a presence in New York and Lenox.

2. Littell's *Living Age* for 13 April 1896 contained an article about Mlle. Jenny Dacquin, friend and muse of Prosper Mérimée (1803–70), whose *Lettres à une inconnue* were written to her.

The Whartons progressed by horse-drawn carriage down the coast of the Adriatic as far south as Ancona, in an area known as Le Marche, then back inland to Bologna.

Venice

May 1st [1896]

Dear Tonni,

I have just received your letter of April 21st enclosing Ella Denison's note, for which please thank her when you see her. I am very sorry that she has been ill & has had to interrupt her work—I only wish I knew what to do next to help her. You will let me know, won't you, if she needs help this Summer? Give her whatever is necessary, & let me know afterwards.—

I am glad that it is all right about your little Frelinghuysen. I know how you must have ached over him during his ordeal—I am glad, also, that your plans for the Summer are definitely settled, & that you have some new pupils down on your list for next Winter.—

As to ourselves, we have had a very interesting fortnight or so since I wrote. I think my last report was from Ravenna, was it not? From there we went to Rimini, & spent two days in enjoying the marvelous church of Isotta & Sigismondo, which by the aid of the little summary of Guaste's book I had made before leaving America, we were able to study very carefully[1]—From there we drove to San Marino & back; then we went to Ancona, itself one of the most extraordinarily picturesque places in Italy—From there we made the excursion to Loreto & back, unluckily on a rainy day, which deprived us of what must be a glorious view; then to Pesaro, the most out-of-the-world place I have ever been to, I think, where the inn is in the old palace of Cardinal Zongo, an immense old, echoing, vaulted, Castle-of-Otranto kind of place, with perspectives of architecture painted on the walls, & bolts & bars on the doors that re-called the days when bravos [hired assassins] & stilettos were every day possibilities.[2] From Pesaro we went to see the enchanting Villa Monte Imperiale, the "maison de plaisance" of the dukes of Urbino; & the next day we went to Urbino itself. We had to start at 8 o'c in the morning, & so inaccessible is the place that for the last six miles or more of the drive our horses had to be reinforced by oxen—We got there at last, however, & spent a delightful afternoon in the wonderful palace, which [John Addington] Symonds pictures so delightfully, as you will remember— Urbino, itself, though gloriously situated, is a dull & uninteresting town, but the palace is incomparable. We got back to Pesaro by moonlight, & the next day returned to Bologna & civilization. In spite of a fortnight or more of hard travelling, dirt, discomfort, & awful food, I ended my trip feeling better & stronger than when I started. Indeed, I can hardly realize how much I have gained since I sailed—

I can keep going for twelve hours & feel as fresh as ever the next morning, & you don't know what a different aspect it gives to life!— We have been in Venice for three or four days, & expect to "move on" next week towards the Lakes, in order to have some time bicycling. — Personally, Teddy & I would prefer to remain here a month longer, but Mr. Winthrop, who is still with us, is always rather restless, & so we have decided to begin our rambling again, & perhaps come back here in June for a few weeks.

I think we shall undoubtedly return to America a year from now. I see more & more clearly that nothing else is possible for Teddy, & if I remain strong I shall find the life there much less wearisome. It is pathetic to see Teddy's interest in picking up bits of furniture for Land's End, & all his affections are centred there.

This more than usually illegible scrawl is due to the fact that I am sitting on a low sofa, before a very high table, & writing *upward,* instead of on a level, but I am none the less, as always,

Yr affte E.W.

The "girls" do well & send their love—We are very glad to hear that Meyse is with Mr. Clark—

1. Cesare Guaste (1822–89) wrote about Italian history, art, and literature. The church to which Edith refers is the Tempio Malatestiano, which houses the tomb of the tyrannical sixteenth-century ruler Sigismondo Malatesta and his beloved mistress Isotta degli Atti.

2. *The Castle of Otranto* (1764), by Horace Walpole (1717–97), is widely considered the first Gothic novel.

Baveno

May 21st [1896]

Dear Tonni,

We have just heard from Mrs. & Miss Wharton that they are about moving to Lenox, & while the subject is fresh in my mind I want to ask you to go & see them when you get there.[1] Their house is nearly opposite the church, in a very central position, so that you will have no difficulty in finding them, & I know they will be very much gratified by your looking them up. I need not tell you how cordial & friendly they both are & how much they enjoy being dropped in on & showing their

My Dear Governess

pretty house & garden to any of our friends, & I am sure their being at Lenox will make a very great difference in your summers there. — I have written to them that you were to be there, but as I could not give them your address I said that I would tell you to look them up. —

Since I last wrote you we have spent a very pleasant fortnight at Verona, Villa d'Este & this place. Here we have met some Boston friends, Mr. & Mrs. Peabody. Mr. Peabody has joined us in our bicycle excursions, so that we have had a very pleasant little partie carrée. The bicycling about here is delightful, & we have made some charming excursions. To give you an idea of what I am up to, listen to this picture of what I did one day last week. We started off at 8:15 a.m. & drove 12 kilometers to a little place called Gravellona. There we took the train for Orta, where we arrived at 10 o'c. We spent the morning in sight-seeing, & in the afternoon we bicycled back to Baveno, a *20 mile* ride, not reaching home until 6 o'c, & after all this I simply felt a little tired & stiff the next day. Now isn't that a real triumph? —

Tomorrow the Peabodys & Mr. Winthrop leave us, & we shall stay here for a few days longer. We expect to return to Venice about June 1st, to meet Mr. Dumaresq, & also Minnie & Trix. After that I don't know what we shall do, except that we shall go off somewhere in pursuit of bicycling.

I have got for you a black lace scarf, such as these lakes produce, which I shall send "at the earliest opportunity."

Let me [hear] from you soon & take care of yourself & keep well. The dogs send their love.
Affly Yrs.

E.W.

1. The Whartons already owned their house, called Pine Acre, in the center of Lenox. They were probably moving there for the summer.

Edith Wharton's brother Frederic had long been known as an adulterer. Minnie Jones ignored her husband's infidelities, and they lived apart for sev-

eral years, but at last the situation became untenable, and Fred's behavior impelled Minnie to divorce him. He quickly married his longtime paramour, Elsie West. The divorce caused a deep rift in the Jones family, with Wharton and her brother Harry siding with Minnie and Trix; Harry even adopted Trix legally so as to ensure her fair share of the Jones inheritance. Wharton's mother sided with her eldest child, causing a breach between mother and daughter that was never healed. Over the years the family ties would shred further over money, inheritance, and later Harry's marriage to an equally unsavory woman who did all she could to separate Harry from Edith. We may think of New York society as being straitlaced and conventional, but it is worth noting that all the Jones children would have passionate love affairs, two would have divorces, and what was once a relatively close, traditional family would end up with only the two sisters-in-law, Edith Wharton and Minnie Jones, and Minnie's daughter Beatrix, remaining together. Wharton was a good daughter to her mother, and it must have hurt her terribly to be thus rejected after her years of care. Although she lived until 1901, Lucretia is mentioned only once more in Wharton's letters to Bahlmann. It is possible to understand Edith Wharton's harsh words about her mother in A Backward Glance *as having arisen less from childhood experiences than from this painful break.*

Milan

June 3d [1896]

Dear Tonni,

I have two letters to thank you for, the last of which I received on arriving here the day before yesterday—And, by the way, in the other you asked me if you should send me Das Glück im Winkel but you need not take the trouble, as I can easily get it here, or (which will probably be the case) wait until I get home to read it.[1] Thanks all the same; while we are on the subject, have you seen Sudermann's play "Fritzchen," in the last number of Cosmopolis? There is no study of character in it, but simply the presentment of a "situation" & that so impossible in our social conditions that, as the French say, it left me cold—

I think I wrote you last from Baveno, did I not? We stayed there until two days ago, & then came here, intending to return to Venice. But the weather is very warm, & now that we have heard that Minnie & Trix are not coming abroad (we had intended meeting them in Venice) it seems scarcely worth while to go back there; so we have decided instead to go to Aix-les-Bains for two or three weeks—I promised my two medicos at home to take some douching, & this seems a good chance of doing it.

Turin, June 4th

I was interrupted by Teddy who dragged me out to buy some Louis XVI arm chairs at *15 fcs* a piece, which you will see next year in the morning-room! & here we are at Turin, where we stay until tomorrow afternoon.——

Well, where was I?? Oh, on the brink of making an important announcement. Do you know that we think a little of going home this Autumn? Your eyes will probably start out of your head, for you know how discontented and bored I was last winter, & how I hailed the opportunity of sailing. But the fact is that we find, just as we did before, that the prospect of spending a whole year in Hotels is really too appalling! Besides, now that I have grown strong again, I miss the little occupations & activities of home, which for the last two or three years have been such a burden to me, & the utter désoeuvrement [idleness] of Hôtel life weighs upon me more than I can say. Time was, as you know, when I should have been glad to make my home in Europe, but it was made in America, & I have fitted myself into it tant bien que mal [for better or worse], & taken its creases more than I realized until I left it again—At all events, when we do get back to it, I mean to try to overcome the restlessness which has grown on me ever since I have been ill, & make the best of my life in the place where I have finally decided to spend it—Oh my, what big words! But I am reading myself a lecture while I write, & I wish you would keep this letter & show it to me when I get one of my nomadic fits!—Well, we shall decide definitely on our plans in a week or so, & when we do "you shall be the first to hear of it," as young ladies say when they are engaged—

You have of course heard by this time of the wretched business of

Minnie's having been obliged to divorce my brother, & of the deluded & perverted view of the situation which he has influenced my mother to take. For months past I have been doing my best to keep off this catastrophe, & to try to make my mother see what an unjust & mistaken attitude she was being led to take; but you know how completely she is controlled by the emotion of the moment, & how little capable she is, owing to her long seclusion from the world, of forming an independent judgment—well, all that Harry and I have done has been useless. My brother has married the woman with whom he has been living, & all the circumstances of the last few months have been so inexpressibly painful & distressing to me that it increases my wish to be at home & away from it all—

If we go back we shall not spend the winter at Newport, which would never do for Teddy, but take a house somewhere—N.Y. or Boston—for two or three months—

Dear Tonni, it is just about a year since you joined us at Land's End, & I tried to crawl down to the shore with you one day & had to go back to bed in consequence; do you remember?—I wish you could see me now! Bath at a quarter to 8—then breakfast (not in bed any longer, thank you!) writing letters, etc; out by 10 or 10:30, trotting about until luncheon—out again until tea time, then a rest, & down to dinner as fresh as paint, if you please! Isn't that something to be proud of? And I mean to stay so, too, for now I really know how to take care of myself.

I am sorry your prospects for next winter (I mean as regards rooms) are so cloudy still, for in spite of your philosophic view it must bother you, I know. But I hope that something will present itself before long. What became of the flat house where "Viola Roseboro" lives?[2]

When you receive this you will be among the delicious green trees & meadows of that lovely Lenox, & I know how much you will enjoy it.

Give my love to the Whartons when you see them—Teddy sends you many messages.
Affly

E.W.

My Dear Governess

1. "Happiness in a Quiet Corner," a play by the German author Hermann Sudermann (1857–1928), which opened to dismal reviews in New York in February 1896. Edith Wharton would translate Sudermann's play *Es Lebe das Leben* (The joy of living) in 1902. *Fritzchen,* a one-act play, portrayed a man going off to a duel that he was certain to lose.

2. Viola Roseboro' (1857?–1945) was a colorful figure, an actress, a writer, and a well-known habituée of theatrical and artistic circles in New York City. One of her most important friendships was with the artist John La Farge. It has been suggested (Skaggs) that she was the model for Myra Henshawe, the mysterious character in Willa Cather's *My Mortal Enemy.* By the 1890s Roseboro' was working at *McClure's* as a reader, much beloved by aspiring writers.

Versailles
Aug. 8th [1896]

Dear Tonni,

I hasten to answer your letter of July 27, which I have just received, in order to explain to you why we have singled out Park Avenue as our domicile. I must have been in great haste when I last wrote you, or I should have told you that we have not "taken" the house at all. It belongs to me, I have been its proud possessor for several years, & as we hear that Park Avenue, in spite of the disadvantages you mention, is not absolutely uninhabitable, especially in winter, we have determined to try living there for two or three months. Certainly the situation is not "ideal"; but then, we have the advantage of not paying any rent, or at least only forfeiting the small rent which the house brings me in. This is our reason for trying it, & as we shall only be there in mid winter, when the windows are generally shut, I hope we may not find the trains unbearable. But if we do, & if we like living in New York, we shall look about later for another house. We want to have our own furniture about us, & to hire an unfurnished house uptown is an expensive amusement — too much so for us! Hence our experiment. — Thank you none the less for warning me about Park Avenue. You must certainly not choose *your* flat there, for the noise would drive you mad; but I do hope you will come up in our quartier, it will be so very pleasant for us, & we can have such nice long book-chats. — By the way, I never told you, I think, how much I liked the fragment of a poem by Coventry Patmore, which you sent me. I have never read his "pomes," repelled, I believe, by the title of the principal one, "The Angel in the House" — but this bit is fine.[1] Yes, the little Joachim du Bellay song is charming, but I like even better that sad, exquisite "Vaunneur de blés aux vents."[2] You know it, don't you? — I am having ample leisure at present for Shakespere & the musical glasses, for what do you think I've done?[3] Fallen off my bicycle while going at express speed, & sprained my ankle so badly that as the Dr. cheerfully remarked, "Vous auriez bien mieux fait de vous casser la cheville"! [You would have done better to have broken the ankle!] This exploit I performed five days ago, & "the limb" has still to be kept horizontal, but it is getting better, & I am to hop about with a stick in a few days. The worst of it is, it was all my own fault. I was thinking of something else, & rode down onto the side of the road (to avoid a cart) without moderating my pace. The consequence was, my wheel slipped in the deep dust, & down I came. It is maddening for several reasons, first because regular exercise is so important to me, & secondly because Mr. Codman is here with us, & we were so much enjoying our trips into Paris & our explorations of the palace with him. — The weather is delightfully cool, so that one feels active & enthusiastic, & it's a bore to be tied to a stake. However, I'm well, & my massage did wonders for me.

I am glad to hear of Trix's success. She has another big place now, a Mr. Scott's.[4] It is capital to have her start off so well, & she is the more likely to keep it up.

I am glad you have seen so much of Mrs. Wharton — She is a most soothing person, & always restores one's failing faith in the happy side of life. — Thanks for your offer, but I don't think there is anything you can do for me in town — I do hope you will find something habitable near us —
Affly Yrs,

E.W.

1. Coventry Patmore (1823–96) is best known for his sentimental sequence of poems in praise of married life and traditional womanhood, *The Angel in the House*, first published in 1854 and expanded several times.

2. Joachim du Bellay (c. 1522–60), French poet, one of the first to write sonnets in French. Many of his poems have been set to music.

3. "Shakespeare and the musical glasses" alludes to the line in Oliver Goldsmith's (1730?–74) *The Vicar of Wakefield* (1764), suggesting that she has time to think about all sorts of disparate subjects.

4. Edward T. Scott's home in Bar Harbor, Maine, was one of Beatrix Jones's first commissions as a landscape architect.

Versailles

Sept. 1st [1896]

Dear Tonni,

It is so long since I have heard from you that I am feeling a little bit worried about your precious health, so send me a line of reassurance as soon as you conveniently can—I fear the great heat last month was too much even for your tropical nature, & that your head has been more troublesome in consequence.

I suppose that about this time you will be going to town to look for a "tenement"—hardly had I written the above, when Gross handed me your long letter of Aug. 20th, in which you tell me that you are leaving the next day for New York on that happy errand! Talk of telepathy—!

I am so glad to hear from you, & to know that you are getting along as well as thunderstorms & extremes of heat & cold will permit—& I do hope you have been successful in your search of a flat near us, for it sounds so nice to have you live "private," with a nice German to house-keep for you, & all your own possessions around you. I find that I must abbreviate this letter to catch the mail, so I will skip at once to the subject of my ankle. It has been pretty troublesome, as inflammatory rheumatism settled there just as it was getting better; but now it is on the mend, & I am able to bicycle a little—

But to come to my purpose in writing—It is, to ask you not to get yourself a "costume d'hiver" until I get home. My heavy blue cloth dress of last winter, which I wore very little, is rather tight for me, & I am going to ask you to accept it, as it is such good material that I do not think I could do better for you. It has a skirt, jacket & satin body, & I think can easily be arranged. I write this, lest you should be starting your Winter dress-making.

We are going to Lenox as soon as we arrive, so we shall see you there, which will be delightful—Let me know if there is anything I can bring you out. We shall be here till we sail, & Gross is always running in to Paris, so it will be no trouble to any one. I rejoice with you that Trix has found her work in life so young. We most of us spend the best of our days hunting for it.—

We have had such sad news of White's wife. She has a hemorrhage, & is threatened with consumption. He is to take her to the mountains & later she must go away for the Winter—but just at present she is better. With much love,

In haste yrs,

E.W.

We are all very well.

P.S. Mrs. Jay's sister Mrs. Henderson lived for 3 years on Park Avenue near 70th St. & the Jays speak well of the situation. They have been here.[1]

1. Mrs. Jay, a former employer, was a good choice of authority to convince the worried Bahlmann that all would be well in the Wharton's new home at 884 Park Avenue, near the noisy trains.

The Whartons lived at 884 Park Avenue from 1897 to 1910. After a few years in her own apartment, and when the Whartons had acquired the adjoining house [882] for their servants, Anna Bahlmann moved in with them. Wharton's discreet thoughtfulness in providing for Bahlmann without embarrassing her is evidenced once again by her gift of a winter garment, which would have made a substantial difference in Bahlmann's budget.

Versailles
Sept. 19th [1896]

Dear Tonni,

I am so glad to hear about the eyry in 95th Street! I wish it had been a little closer to our perch, but I suppose it isn't easy in that impossible city to find just such a little chez toi [your own home] as you want. You have the sun & cleanliness & a civil landlord, which really seem the three essential points, & perhaps the drawbacks will be relatively few — I am sure of one thing, & that is that you will enjoy intensely having your home, after all these years of boarding & staying with people — I do hope it will be the greatest possible success, & it will make a great difference in our New York experiment to have you (relatively!) near us. —

This is only a line, to congratulate you on having settled your plans for the Winter, & to say that we are all well, & making progress in our preparations for going home —

We have only two weeks now, & I shall be very glad when they are over, or rather when *we* are over — the Atlantic! It will be pleasant to go home for the first time in so many years feeling really well & able to cope with life (Unberufen![1] Say it quick!!) & I am looking forward in many ways to being in New York for a short time.

The Dodies send you their love & count on seeing you in Lenox — How pleasant it will be to meet there, you dear soul.
Affly Yrs

E.W.

1. A German expression for warding off evil: "May no evil befall us" or "Heaven shield us from harm."

The Whartons returned to America in October, unable to go to Newport because their house was rented, or to Lenox because Nannie Wharton was ill.

New York
Tuesday [October 1896]

Dear Tonni,

It was so sweet of you, & so *like* you, to think at once that I might need you & to be ready to cast your engagements to the winds & fly at once to the rescue of your elderly infant. Teddy & I were both greatly touched by it—but I don't think I can trump up a decent excuse for taking you away from Lenox.—After some deliberation we have decided to go straight to the Muenchinger Cottage Newport & shall leave by boat today if it is not too stormy.[1] Miss Kneeland was kind enough to ask us to Lenox, but alas, she did not want us until the 16th, & we could not very well languish at the Cambridge for a whole week.[2] Besides, there are rumours that our tenant may leave from the 15th to the 20th, & we wish to be on the spot to take over the house, get together servants, horses, & so on—It looks, therefore, as if there was no chance of our meeting just at present. I am so sorry that the Lenox visit has fallen through, & so distressed about the cause. I think Teddy feels more worried about his mother than his sister, & he is so thankful to be here. You will see him at Lenox in a few days.

Now to yourself?—When you leave Lenox, could you come to us for a few days, supposing we are by that time at Land's End, which may almost be counted on?—If so, it would be very delightful.—

We spent an hour or more at 884 Park Ave yesterday, & I know you will be glad to hear that seven or eight trains passed without affecting our nervous system. What happens is a short roar & rumble, & a puff of white smoke. Some people might mind it very much—to me it would not be in the least disturbing, much less so than the jingle of a cable car, for instance. And where else in New York could we get a very solidly & expensively built little house, with all "modern improvements," floods of light & sunshine, & close proximity to the Park, for a rent of $1,200, which (in strict confidence) is what the house costs us?—On the whole, we are very hopeful about our venture. We had a beautiful voyage like a yachting trip & are all as well as possible. Send me a line to New York & thanks for your letter & telegram. Affly Yrs E.W.
address simply Newport R.I.

My Dear Governess

1. The Muenchinger was, according to Mrs. Harry Lehr, one of only two acceptable hotels in Newport and the only place that society members would occupy, the other being reserved for members of the trade who came to sell them wine, jewels, and the like: "Amanda Muenchinger was as exclusive as Newport itself; she would never dream of harbouring anyone not already admitted to the sacred inner circle" (114–15).

2. Miss Adele Kneeland (1856–1937) was a friend of Wharton's, and also, later, a competitor in Lenox's annual Horticultural Show, where she inevitably won for her phlox. I am indebted to Cornelia Brooke Gilder for this and several other identifications of Lenox residents.

While the Whartons were thrilled to be back at Land's End, they also encountered illness. We do not know with what "dread disease" Teddy's sister Nannie suffered, but she did recover. The Jay family, both of whose daughters were pupils of Bahlmann's, were nursing their older daughter, Julia, who was stricken with typhoid fever. She, not so lucky, died just days after this letter was written, leaving her sister Eleanor (Moppy) an only child.

Land's End Newport, R.I.
Nov. 8th [1896]

Dear Tonni,

Have you ever read a narrow-minded, priggish book called "Hours with the Mysteries," [*sic*] & if so, do you remember a delightful hymn, translated from Tauler or Eckart, the chorus of which is "Ju—ju—ju—Ju—bilation!"?[1] because that is the way we felt yesterday when at length we moved in to Land's End.

We had expected to get possession last Monday, but the old man stayed on, & not till yesterday did we come into our own. It was a heavenly day, like June at its best, & I can't tell you how lovely the house & place looked after our long absence, & how good my bed felt after Hotel mattresses for over eight months! We found the house in perfect order, & it is so nice getting shaken down & hugging the books & getting a nod & smile from the pictures every time one passes them—

Teddy came home last Wednesday, leaving his sister, as we hope, well started on the road to complete recovery—though with that dread disease there is no real security—However, this attack seems quite over, & the news since Teddy left continues very favorable.

Meanwhile our hearts are aching for the poor Jays. Moppy is at the Brooks', as of course you knew, & Mr. Brooks told me yesterday that Mrs. Jay had written very sadly—I can't think how she will stand it, poor soul!—if anything goes wrong.—

I am very sorry we are not to have a glimpse of you here this month. The weather is so mild that you would have enjoyed it, I know. We shall not go to town until December, when we are going to stay with Mr. Winthrop for a few days—& we expect (or I should say "hope") to move into our shanty about Jan'y 15th.—

Let me know from time to time how you are getting along in *your* shanty—

Affly Yrs

E.W.
The "gang" is so glad to be at Land's End!

1. Robert Alfred Vaughan (1823–57), *Hours with the Mystics: A Contribution to the History of Religious Opinion* (1856).

Land's End
Nov. 24th [1896]

You dear soul, I had my misgivings about your health, & of course I can't help feeling worried about what you tell me of it.—I hope you are truthful in saying that you are really better, but I must read you a little lecture on overdoing things. Don't let yourself get so dreadfully overtired early in the Winter. You will always be the victim of people who use & abuse you when they might as well be using someone less valuable than you are to all your friends. Now do ménager yourself a little, & above all don't go & imagine gratuitous things like that idea that the Jays have engaged you for Moppy because they felt obliged to. If you could have heard what both Mr. & Mrs. Jay said of you last Summer at Versailles you would have no such scruples. Dear little Moppy! When we get to

My Dear Governess

town, you must bring her to lunch with us every now & then. I have written her that she & I are to be great friends this Winter.—Before I go any further, by the way, I must tell you that I am in no way responsible for the gloves which I sent you. I supposed Miss Wingate had written you that they are from her.—And, while we are on the subject of the things I sent you, please, when you use the headache remedy, be *very* careful to follow the directions, & especially to not to open it anywhere near a light or fire, as it goes off pop if you do.

And now, one more business item; how about your fire-wood? I have a superstition about keeping you supplied with it, & if you should thwart me (as you are quite capable of doing, you old Jesuit) I know it would bring me bad luck. I used to be able to find out from Mrs. Kirchner, but now I must apply to you direct, & ask you to provide yourself with the wood, & send me the bill—a very crude way of doing, but I see no other. And moreover, you are not to get wood that has been "marked down" because it won't burn, or any other cheapness, but the kind that I always send you, & the proper quantity—what is it? A cord or two, I think.—

Teddy got back from Lenox last Friday, & Nannie was then doing much better. I do not think the tone of the telegrams so satisfactory these last two days, but trust it may be only a passing cloud. Teddy goes back on Saturday.

Now, is there any chance of your being able to spend the holidays with us this year? You need not give your answer in a hurry, for we shall certainly be in town for a few days next month, & we can talk it over then. It would be so pleasant to have you here, that I hope you can manage it, if you think it would be really a rest for you, & not an extra fatigue.—I am glad you think the Park Ave tenement looks so well. If you have leisure some day & would like to take a look inside, the worthy Mrs. Brown, who mounts guard over it, will be charmed to admit you. I think we shall move in soon after January 1st. Our alterations promise to be very successful.

Don't bother to answer, & do take care of yourself.
Affly Yrs,

E. W.

Land's End
Dec. 24th [1896]

Dear Tonni,

I read yesterday such a harrowing account of the overworked post office employees that I hardly dare add this straw to their burden; but you *must* have our Christmas wishes on the day itself, so here goes! I was sorry about that hateful headache that interfered with our final meeting—I know how you must have worried, & I didn't go to see you because I thought I should only be an additional bother.

Gross was so charmed by your little "installation" that I fully expected her to abandon me & set up one like it; & when I told Mr. Codman of her description he announced his intention of taking a flat next year in the same house!

We are probably going to be alone this year for Christmas, I am sorry to say. Mr. Winthrop can't come, & unless Mr. Codman turns up we shall have no guests.

It is bitterly cold & there are mountains of snow, but the sunshine is glorious and we are all as well as possible—

The dogs all send you their respectful greeting (*I* put in the adjective) & hope you will have lots of bones tomorrow & a nice warm fire to snooze by, & Teddy & I join in wishing you all sorts of good things, & in telling you again what a dear soul you are & how very much we love you.

Your affectionate

E.W.

My Dear Governess

4

"Harvesting laurels"

APRIL 1898 TO APRIL 1907

During her thirteen years of married life, Edith Wharton had published more than a dozen poems, three stories, and one travel article, most of them in *Scribner's Magazine*. In 1897 her avocation in letters ripened to a career as an author as she undertook her first sustained effort of researching, writing, and managing a relationship with a publisher in order to produce, to her satisfaction, a book. In collaboration with the architect Ogden Codman, and with coaching from Walter Berry, Wharton devoted most of the summer and fall of 1897 to working on what would finally, after a half-dozen different names, be called *The Decoration of Houses*. In it the two collaborators—whose friendship was sorely tried by the joint effort—set forth their ideas on proportion, harmony, and design, hoping to wrest interior decoration from the hands of dressmakers and allow "the vulgarity of current decoration" to give way to "architectural fitness" (*DH,* 3). By the fall Wharton was writing almost daily to Scribner's editor William Crary Brownell (1851–1928) specifying title, design, binding, proofs, galleys, and the like.

The Bahlmann family endured a trauma in September 1897: Anna's nephew Louis, William and Lydia's son, committed suicide. Like Teddy Wharton, Louis suffered from manic depression, and there must have been some talk of institutionalizing him. Anna's sympathetic letter of condolence to her brother and sister-in-law mentions also that Anna herself has had some trouble with a knee, which was at the time "done up in elastic bandages." She was on her way to recuperate for a month or so at "Pussie's house," and: "I can't imagine a better way or place, now that her fashionable guests are gone and the 'season' is over" (to William Bahlmann, 18 September 1897). So for at least a month, Anna Bahlmann was at Land's End, and it seems likely that she typed the manuscript of *The Decoration of Houses*.

The production of the book at a time when Bahlmann's mobility was challenged probably marked the beginning of her employment as Wharton's secretary. Bahlmann took on the work part-time while she continued teaching. She educated herself in the use of a typewriting machine and carbon paper and the preparation of a manuscript for publication. Gradually she also acquired the task of responding to Wharton's business mail on her behalf, and eventually, in the late 1890s, she moved into the servants' quarters of 882–884 Park Avenue. There she served as secretary and, when the Whartons traveled, as household manager. She never gave up her teaching or her other charitable and friendly work caring for the sick, performing errands and secretarial services for friends, and serving on the relief committee of the Women's Association of German Teachers.

As Wharton's secretary Bahlmann opened and sorted the writer's professional mail — ten or more letters a day — deciding which letters she could answer and which required her employer's attention. She typed manuscripts, although this was not her task alone; eventually Wharton's writing was so prolific that it took several typists to prepare it for publication. Bahlmann only rarely proofread manuscripts; this work was done by Wharton herself or, in her absence, by her sister-in-law Minnie Jones.

Along with *The Decoration of Houses*, there were other literary endeavors. In the early part of the winter Wharton had translated three stories from the Italian for a Scribner's volume, *Stories by Foreign Authors: Italian*. Two poems and two stories also appeared in *Scribner's Magazine* in 1898.

There are no letters from Wharton to Bahlmann during the period when Wharton was working on *The Decoration of Houses*, probably because they were so much together. By the time the letters between them resumed in April 1898, *Decoration* had been published and Wharton was taking pride in its favorable notices. One of those notices was written by her friend Walter Berry, who had helped in organizing and writing the book. Another was written by the Boston artist Edwin H. Blashfield (1848–1936), who said: "The book is a thoroughly welcome one and should be a very present help to the many who realize that the material environment of home life has a real influence" (quoted in Tuttleton, Lauer, and Murray, 7).

The Whartons went to Washington, D.C., touring and spending time with Berry. Although they were in the capital and the United States had declared war on Spain just three days earlier than the next letter, Wharton typically mentions nothing about politics or world affairs.

> [Gordon Hotel,
> Washington, D.C.]
> April 24th [1898]

Dear Tonni,

Teddy tells me he has been worrying you by telling you I have not been so well, so I send a line at once to say that I am better again; & besides I am so busy harvesting laurels that I haven't time to think of my vile body. I think I wrote you that Lippincott's Magazine had written for a short story or a novel of 50,000 words; I have had a splendid notice in "Literature," the best of all in the Brooklyn "Life," a column in the N.Y. Times, & endless other favourable notices; not to speak of an application for my photo from the Bookman, who is publishing a review of the book this month! All this will amuse you, I know.

Teddy is going to N.Y. tonight to meet Minnie, but in case he doesn't see you, I write to say that we shall probably be very glad to have Buchtenkirch in 884 this Summer, as we have almost decided not to make any alterations for another year. You may consider it *positive*, I think, unless you hear to contrary in a day or two.

I am really better & biking again daily.

> Yrs. E.W.

Wharton was indeed feeling well by July, despite a recurring illness that would soon be diagnosed as heart trouble. This same month she wrote to Edward Burlingame at Scribner's that she had enough stories ready for a volume, asking how many he would need.

Land's End Newport R.I.

Sunday [July 1898]

You anxious soul, I know you are impatient to hear how I am getting on, so I send this line post haste to tell you that we have been ungrateful enough to flourish like green bay-trees since your departure. "Coddy" arrived in the afternoon, funnier than ever, in blue spectacles, with a huge palm leaf fan in his hand, & Mr. Updike turned up for dinner in very good form, with lots of new stories.[1]

In addition to these diversions, the post brought me so much good news that I had to keep exclaiming "unberufen"! after each letter. —

1st. The announcement that my business complications are successfully concluded, just as I wished them to be.

2d. Letter from Scribner accepting the Muse's Tragedy.

3d. Announcement that the Pelican appears next month.

4th. Another unexpectedly satisfactory letter.

To celebrate all of which I jubilantly finished "Souls Belated" upon libations of warm milk! Needless to say that the dogs showed their usual unselfish participation in these incidents — in fact, Rickly celebrated the occasion by going off on a midnight "bum."

I only hope you have fared nearly as well since you left here, but I'm afraid you sizzled in the train, didn't you? Do take things coolly & quietly while you are in town & go to the Alexanders' as soon as you can.[2]

I expect Mr. Jay tomorrow, so you see the supply of protectors is practically inexhaustible.

Take care of yourself & keep those fat infantine cheeks.

Affly Yrs

E.W.

1. Daniel Berkeley Updike (1860–1941), founder of the Merrymount Press in Boston, became a close friend of the Whartons. His press would print several of Edith's books, beginning with *The Greater Inclination* in 1899.

2. Probably the family of Charles B. Alexander. Anna taught one or more of their three daughters, and Mrs. Alexander was one of the donors to Anna's gift (see introduction, p. 18).

Land's End

Sept. 20th [1898]

Dear Tonni,

I hope you are behaving in sympathy with me & having no more headaches in order to celebrate my glorious improvement. In spite of two days of dripping stifling fog, more oppressive I think than any we had this summer, my run of luck has not yet broken (unberufen!) & Mr. Sturgis, who came in the day before yesterday after a fortnight's absence could not believe that I was I.— Dr. McC came yesterday, & was quite as much astonished, although he cleverly pretended that of course he couldn't give any opinion yet etc, etc—[1]

Still the upshot of it was that if ~~we~~ I go on improving at this rate for the next fortnight there is to be no rest-cure, & we are instead to take White's cottage at Saranac for November & part of Dec. Isn't this a good idea?

I think it came to me after you left, & the Dr. was much pleased with it. Europe he absolutely forbids, on account of the effect of the sea voyage on my heart; he won't even promise that I may go in April!— I am sorry to say that New York is also ruled out, as the rest-cure can be given up only on condition that all the other terms are fulfilled, & he is inexorable about Washington. Still, we shall be in New York for a visit, & you are not to forget that your Xmas week is to be spent with us.—

I do hope you are enjoying Manassas & feeling better. You must have found me a very uncompanionable person when you were here, but to tell you the truth I was à bout de forces [exhausted] that first week after we came home, & have only just recovered my nerve possession, so to speak.

Thank you again for the trouble you took for me about Ella Denison.

Mr. Berry leaves tonight & we shall be quite alone for the first time since May, I believe!

Affly Yrs

E.W.

Running over Rickly has made his stomach stick out so that he has no "style" [?] at all!

1. Dr. George McClellan was the grandson of the founder of Jefferson Medical Center in Philadelphia (*EWAZ*, 159).

Despite her hopeful prognostication in the previous letter, the Whartons did travel to Philadelphia for Edith to take a rest cure. Famously, this time in her life has been characterized as a neurasthenic incident, but it is clear from the letters that Wharton was being treated not by Weir Mitchell, who was not even in Philadelphia at the time, but by Dr. George McClellan, who believed her heart to be the cause of her health problems. She was markedly still in control of her work and her surroundings, and she even brought her dogs. Bahlmann, in New York, was assisting with the preparation of The Greater Inclination, *Wharton's first collection of short stories.*

Philadelphia
Nov 1st [1898]

Dear Tonni,

I know you will be impatient to hear all about my installation here, so I send this line off to tell you that we had a very comfortable night journey from Newport, that I have *no* headache, & that my little apartment here is charming: a sunny cheerful corner, with a sitting room looking down Broad Street, & a nice bedroom & bathroom adjoining.—Mrs. Robert Gammell had ordered my sitting room filled with roses, so that the first impression was charming; & then I found your books & letter, & another nice letter, & altogether everybody had done everything to mitigate my exile.[1]—Dr. McClellan came in soon after we got here, & found that my heart had improved slightly in the three weeks since the consultation, & this is of course very encouraging. — Teddy is going back to Land's End in a day or two, & shortly after that you will see 884 Park Ave open its palatial doors, & *Moke* & his suite move in. The little dogs of course are here. —

I am more than obliged to you for all the trouble you have taken in divers ways about my books, & *so* glad to get the Meredith. Thank you many times, & please send the account to Teddy when you get it. — Of course I want Diana & Richard, whenever they can be got; & I may as well add Evan Harrington & The Shaving of Shagpat, which I had forgotten, because they make the set complete; but I don't care to pay more than $1.50 a piece for the two latter, as I have no particular desire to have them. — [2]

Thanks also for the the Psyche type-writing—Keep the ms, please, & destroy it as soon as I let you know that I have rec'd the proofs.[3] By the way, Mr. Updike is to print the book, & just after writing to Ella D. I heard that Scribner has also given him the designing of the book-cover, a thing they seldom do. I am not sorry, as I thought Ella could hardly in so short a time hope to turn out anything satisfactory; but I have written her to go ahead & make some designs, & if she shows taste I can doubtless get her some orders later. My régime is not decided yet, so I can't tell you what it will be.

Affly Yrs. E.W.

Your bonnet will be sent to you as soon as Gross goes to N.Y. to unpack the trunks.

1. Mrs. Robert Gammell was a Newport neighbor.

2. George Meredith (1828–1909), British poet and novelist most famous today for his cycle of sixteen-line poems *Modern Love* (1862) and his novel *The Egoist* (1879). All the novels mentioned here are his.

3. An interesting piece of information. Wharton's story "The Lamp of Psyche" had been published in *Scribner's* in 1895, and it is said that Burlingame wanted it

for her collection, *The Greater Inclination,* but Wharton refused (*EWAB,* 37 n. 5). Here it seems as though Wharton might have been preparing it to go into the volume.

1329 K Street
[Washington, D.C.]
Jan. 24th [1899]

Return that Müntz, Dear Tonni? Thank you, no. I have been pining for it ever since it came out, & it exceeds my expectations.[1] You have "la main heureuse" in the way of presents, & as if to make this one doubly welcome the heavens have been pouring down sheets of rain all the morning, so that I have had full opportunity to test the delights of my precious book. It is better than fine weather.

I had a good journey here, & felt very well on Sunday. Yesterday the "getting settled," trying a new masseuse &c, tired me a little, & today I am housed by the bad weather; but as soon as I begin to go out regularly I think I shall make good progress. This house is charming, & Teddy had done wonders in arranging it. Washington is certainly a better "winter resort" for an invalid than N.Y.

On Sunday & yesterday we had real Riviera weather, & the driving through the wide avenues & out to the Soldiers House was delightful. There is new green grass coming up in the Square under my windows, & the pansy plants are perfectly green. Isn't it wonderful?

Thanks again & much love.

Yr Affte,

E.W.

1. Possibly *Histoire de L'Art Pendant la Renaissance* (1895) by Eugène Müntz (1845–1902).

Washington
Sunday morning
[January? 1899]

Dear Tonni,

You will be startled at your gifts in the telepathic line, when I tell you that one of the first poetic excursions that Mr. Berry & I made after I got here was into Lefroy-land![1] He has only the volume of '85, without the thirty later sonnets, & he did not know of the "complete poems" until I told him about them—so that, to a person not accustomed to your tricks of divination, there is something almost uncanny in the arrival of the said volume this morning!—Thanks are needless, dear Tonni, for you know the added pleasure of getting a thing one wants just when one most wants it!—

Judging from the flattering remarks of my friends & family, Washington must be making me into a thing of beauty; or, to look at it in another light, I must have been a pretty haggard object when I left New York.—I feel a great deal better, & long to stay another month; but the dentist waits like a malignant spider at the other end of the line, so I suppose we shall have to go back by the end of this week.

Teddy has been away for three or four days, attending to things in New York & Newport, & yesterday I was cheered by a telegram announcing that Fred had bought Pen craig at the auction for a sum which is satisfactory to us; so that we are relieved of that burden at one stroke.—I will not write you of politics, for the subject is too depressing; but I wish I could put you pillion-wise on my bike & carry you off this minute to a grey-brown oak-wood all carpeted with windflowers & violets.—[2]

Later: Well, the wood was lovely; such a cool brown stream rushing over big stones & fallen tree-trunks, & such warm stillness, with little buds bursting almost audibly all around one. Here I am back, full of sylvan air & saps & juices, not to speak of a glass of crab-apple cider that we stopped to drink half-way up a long hot hill on the road home. It is all delightful, & the world isn't a bad place—now & then.—

And hereupon I am going to sit down & read Lefroy,[1] while I wait for Teddy, who arrives in about an hour. Thank you again, you dear soul.

Take care of yourself & write soon. We shall probably go home on Friday.

Affly Yr

E.W.

1. Edward Cracroft Lefroy (1855–91), a poet whose *Echoes from Theocratus and Other Poets* was published in 1885. After his death, the poet's friend Wilfred Austin Gill, along with John Addington Symonds, published in 1897 a volume including a biography of Lefroy, the text of *Echoes,* and other poems.

2. Wharton rarely discussed politics in her letters to anyone until the First World War. Here she may be referring to the aftermath of the Spanish-American War and the inevitable run-up to the war in the Philippines.

The Whartons were still on K Street in Washington in April when Wharton wrote to William Crary Brownell complaining about inadequate advertisement of The Greater Inclination, *which had been published six weeks earlier. Nevertheless, the book was approved by critics. John D. Barry, who wrote the "New York Letter" column in* Literary World, *in his second mention of the book praised Wharton's talents and suggested with prescience that her subject matter might be appropriate to a novel: "Now that Mrs. Wharton has tried her wings so successfully, there is no knowing how far they may carry her in the future" (quoted in Tuttleton, Lauer, and Murray, 14). F. J. G. of* Book Buyer *wrote, "There are many flashes in the tales . . . which make one pause in sheer joy at the felicity of the touch. . . . In every instance you feel that the successful phrase, the happy aphorism, gives a clew to character, an aid to your knowledge of the temperament of the individual" (quoted in Tuttleton, Lauer, and Murray, 15). As in the previous year, Wharton was indeed harvesting laurels.*

After a brief stop in New York in May, she and Teddy sailed for London.

Dear Tonni,

I know you will want to hear the Dr.'s verdict, & so send you a line by this steamer — but not a real letter, as I am miserable with a slight touch of influenza. — Well, I saw Dr. Brunten yesterday & he confirmed the usual diagnosis: no organic trouble anywhere, but a state of extreme "depression" caused by anaemia & goutiness (is that a word?) He thinks my condition is the result of influenza, as he has had many similar cases. He has ordered me to Ragatz for three or four weeks, with an after-cure in Switzerland, I don't yet know where; & we have decided to leave England in about a week, in order to get off to Ragatz about June 20th, as the Bourgets are going & will arrange to be there at the same time.[2] The most amusing part of the interview was that, when I showed him a table of the diet I have been following, he folded it up, & put it in an envelope which he sealed & handed to me, saying: "Don't look at that again & eat *everything*" — and when I gasped, "What, sweets, sauces, salads, everything I want?" he laughed & said again, "Everything." — Be sure you tell Bagley this, for I know she will be delighted to do some *real* cooking with seasoning in it, & tell her she must have a lot of splendid new dishes ready for us when we get home! — My influenza does not keep me indoors, as the weather is lovely, but makes me languid & headachy, so I won't tell you much today, except that I feel encouraged by Dr. Brunten's opinion. —

We have been enjoying wonderful pictures & other delights, & I hate to give up part of our time in England, but really I am not strong enough to do much sight-seeing. We are going to see Grosvenor House & Holland House, & take tea with the Alma Tademas, & lunch with the Duchess of Sutherland.[3] We will hope to sail on Sept. 9th. Best love to kittens & yourself. E.W.

1. The London home of the American Mary Ethel Burns, Viscountess Harcourt (Towheed, 61 n. 3).

2. Ragatz, Switzerland, was a resort on the Rhine that featured beautiful scenery and hot mineral waters in which people bathed for their health.

3. Grosvenor House and Holland House were two of the largest and stateliest of the stately homes near London, and Grosvenor, home of the Duke of Westminster, was said to have a large collection of art. Probably these visits were not to the people who lived there, but to the homes themselves. Lawrence Alma-Tadema (1836–1912) was a highly successful painter born in the Netherlands, trained in Belgium, and resident in England since the late 1860s. The Duchess of Sutherland (1867–1955) was a novelist who published under the name Lady Millicent St. Clair-Erskine, the first of her three married names.

Despite Edith's lingering flu, she and Teddy kept an active schedule. Their escort for the queen's birthday parade was Henry White (1850–1927), the husband of Edith's childhood Newport neighbor (and Anna Bahlmann's former pupil), Margaret Rutherfurd. At this time he was in the middle years of a distinguished career in diplomacy, serving as chargé d'affaires for the United States Legation in London.

34 Brook St

June 5 [1899]

Dear Tonni,

How we both wish we were basking on the Land's End verandah with you & kittens all, this red-hot evening! Think of the heat in London being greater than it has been in fifty years at this season: 86° on Saturday & 83° today. Luckily there is a breeze, & out of doors it seems fresh when one is driving, but it is very stuffy in this little hotel.

We have done many interesting things since I wrote, but I think my chief pleasure has been derived from the National Gallery, which puts all other collections to shame. We go there again & again. —

On Saturday Harry White took us to the Foreign Office to see the trooping of the Colours in honour of the Queen's Birthday. It takes place on the Parade behind the Horse Guards, against the leafy background of St. James's Park, & I suppose there is no prettier military pageant to be seen in Europe. First the state carriages with scarlet liveries drive up to the Horse Guards with the Princesses & royal children, who appear on the balcony in the centre; then the Guards form a hollow square (they march up headed by their Drum-majors in state uniform entirely of cloth of gold;) & lastly the royal procession comes flashing through the trees of St. James's Park; the staff in a blaze of gold & scarlet, Lord Wolseley riding alone, with the blue ribbon of the Garter & the commander-in chief's gold baton in his hand; the Prince of Wales, Duke of Cambridge & Dukes of Connaught & York, the military attachés of the embassies in gala dress, & a throng of royal grooms in scarlet.[1] This splendid procession marches slowly around the Parade, saluting the Colours, while the bands play God Save the Queen & every head in the crowd is uncovered; then the staff & the royalties draw up in line, & the guards salute the Colours, a most elaborate ceremony involving marching & counter-marching, band-playing, & such flashing of swords, helmets, & gold lace, such caracoling of chargers & general glitter as one seldom sees outside of old ceremonial pictures.

But if I go on at this rate there will be no time to tell you of our other experiences. Today we took tea at the Alma Tademas, who live in the dreary suburb of St. John's Wood. They have a sweet little garden full of flowers & fountains, but the pergolas are of *cast-iron* painted black, & the house, which is supposed to be very "artistic," would give you the shivers. The studio has a domed ceiling of aluminium & Mexican onyx windows!!

We have decided to leave here on the 7th, as Dr. Brunten is anxious that I should get away from London, which seems to disagree with my throat & nose. We are going to spend a day at Salisbury, to see Wilton, the Pembroke place, which they have given us leave to visit, & then we shall go to Paris, reaching there on the 9th. I saw another specialist today, Sir John Williams, who examined my insides & pronounced me perfectly sound — it seems merely a case of general debility, & Dr. Brunten told Teddy I had been "starved" — so I am now eating wildly right

& left. I shall be glad to get to Paris where I can cycle. We hope to leave for Ragatz June 20th & sail Sept. 9th.

With love from Teddy

Yr Affte

E.W.

1. Garnet Wolseley, First Viscount Wolseley (1833–1913), was commander in chief of the forces. He was noted for his service in the colonial wars.

Edith and Teddy Wharton went to Ragatz, Switzerland, as ordered by her doctor, and continued traveling in Switzerland and Italy with the Bourgets. Wharton enjoyed the leisurely opportunity to talk shop with novelist Paul Bourget, and his conversation inspired her to write. Their trip gave rise to some of her best descriptions of Italy, which she no longer sent to Bahlmann in her letters, but rather saved for publication. "An Alpine Posting-Inn" appeared in the Atlantic Monthly *for June 1900, and "A Midsummer Week's Dream" in* Scribner's *in August 1902. And in an early demonstration of Wharton's talent at getting paid more than once for each piece of writing, both would be collected in* Italian Backgrounds *in 1905. In the following letter the Whartons have just come south from Switzerland through the lake district.*

Anna Bahlmann, meanwhile, was housesitting for the Whartons in Newport, happily pasting laudatory reviews of The Greater Inclination *into a scrapbook. She had a near-accident in Wharton's trap, a light, two-wheeled vehicle pulled by a pony or horse. Wharton suggests here that she take the larger vis-à-vis, which would have four wheels and seats facing each other. There is no word of the Dreyfus court-martial case that was being tried in France, though we know that Wharton believed the Jewish army captain to be innocent.*

Madonna di Tirano,
Valtellina
Aug. 4th [1899]

Dear Tonni,

I fear I must have let a fortnight elapse without writing you, an omission which was unintentional & which I much regret. My excuse is that after we left Ragatz for Splügen I took advantage of the quiet of the latter place to do some "littery work," which rather interfered with letters. We spent ten days of delightful rest at Splügen in splendid air & utter solitude. It was there, by the way, that I got your letter giving us the account of your carriage accident. What a narrow escape, & how cool & plucky you were! I was dreadfully distressed about it. I hope you will do just as you like about having the vis à vis as often as you please. Don't think of going out in the light trap if the other is more comfortable. How good you were to take such care of the Miteys. Mr. Mitou offered up devout thanksgivings when he heard what an escape his little wives had had, thanks to their good Bahlmann.

To take up the broken thread of our travels, we left Splügen two days ago & drove down to Chiavenna. Yesterday we met the Bourgets at Colico & took [the] train to Sondrio in the Valtellina. There we rested for a few hours & late in the afternoon drove up to the enchanting place from which I write. It is simply a cluster of houses around the wonderful marble pilgrimage church of the Madonna di Tirano. We are lodged in the old monastery of the church (now an inn) & my cell looks across the Val Tellina at the snow peaks of the Bergamesque Alps. The wealth of beauty of Italy at this season is indescribable. The flowers, the vines, maize & melons, are a tangle of almost theatrical luxuriance. This place is especially lovely as it is so remote & primitive. The heat is great in the middle of the day, but the mornings and afternoons are pleasant.

Tomorrow we drive across the Aprica pass to the village of Edolo, in the Bergamasco, from there another day through Val Camonica to Lovero on Lake Iseo, & then to Bergamo & probably back to the lakes. The Bourgets knew nothing of this part of Italy, so we are really all on an exploring trip.

We are trying hard for rooms on an earlier steamer, but so far without success. I am very homesick for my own house, & should like to get straight on board the steamer on leaving Italy.

I am *very* well, & don't mind the heat so far.
With love from Teddy.

Yr affte, E.W.

P.S. We sail Aug. 26th. Just heard we can have rooms.

An interesting piece of information comes to light in this letter, which is that Wharton's play, The Tightrope, *evidently had been completed and was being passed around theater circles—or at least to the actor-producer Sir George Alexander—in London. At this point Wharton was trying to write and publish plays, working with the theatrical agent Elisabeth Marbury, who much later would attempt unsuccessfully to produce a play of* The Age of Innocence. *While several of her shorter plays were produced locally, she did not have success with either* The Tightrope *or her version of* Manon.[1]

Lunch at Lady Jeune's was an important occasion. Susan Mary Elizabeth Mackenzie Stanley, Lady Jeune (1849–1931), became Lady Saint-Helier when her husband was made the first Baron Saint–Helier. She was one of London's leading literary hostesses of the time. It has been reported that Henry James introduced the Whartons to her, but this letter indicates that Edith Wharton came into Lady Jeune's circle some years before her better-known 1908 entrée into a London season.

Not much correspondence between Wharton and Bahlmann from the first few years of the new millennium has survived. The two women were increasingly together as Wharton wrote ever more prolifically: short stories, a novella, plays, travel essays, and an ambitious novel set in Italy.

1. Sir George Alexander (1858–1918), actor, theater manager, and producer, was at the height of his career in 1900, having produced several plays by Oscar Wilde but also the famously failed *Guy Domville* by Henry James. The literary agent Elisabeth Marbury (1856–1933), longtime companion of the designer Elsie de Wolfe, represented such diverse clients as Frances Hodgson Burnett, Oscar

Wilde, George Bernard Shaw, and Edmond Rostand. Both she and fellow American Charles Frohman (1856–1915) promoted the work of J. M. Barrie.

34 Brook St.
May 15th [1900]

Dear Tonni,

I am sure that you are prepared to hear that we have had a chequered existence since our arrival, & you will therefore not be surprised to hear that William [a servant, possibly a footman] was seized with the measles the day we landed & that I have been through a bad cold. We had a tremendous piece of work getting William to the hospital & so on, owing to the slowness with which the English official mind moves; but he is there now, & doing well, my cold is over & the present is comparatively serene. —

The weather here is bitterly cold, so cold that we hug the fire & wish for our furs; but luckily it is clear & London looks beautifully. We have, of course, given most of our time to pictures, but we went to see Mr. Alexander's play the other night, & found him very friendly & pleasant. I am to see him on Friday & I suppose talk of a play. He told Miss Marbury (not knowing she knew me) that he thought "The Tightrope" the best play (written by an American) that he had ever read. Then it seems there is a chance that Frohman's version of "Manon" may have fallen through, so Miss Marbury is going to see what she can do about mine. Last Sunday we lunched with Lady Jeune, where we met Thomas Hardy & Stephen Phillips. The former is a charming dapper little gentleman, with a very sweet voice; Stephen Phillips looks like a dark handsome heavy boy of eighteen.[1] We also met there a delightful Miss Stanley of Alderley, a brisk old lady who has asked us to lunch with her today, & who lives in a seventeenth century house down near the Thames. —

The exhibitions of pictures this year are not as interesting as usual. There is a large show of Romneys at the Grafton Galleries, the best of which is owned by Pierpont Morgan; & the Ruskin Collection of Turner watercolours are being shown; but beyond that not much.[2]

I wanted to send you this report by tomorrow's steamer, but I haven't time to add more. We don't know yet when we shall go to Paris. Mama is doing very well.

With hugs & kisses to those angels Pluffs & much love from both of us to yourself, dear Tonni,
Affly Yrs

E.W.

1. The English novelist and poet Thomas Hardy (1840–1928) was reputed to be shy in company. Stephen Phillips (1864–1915) was enjoying fame, having recently published his poetic drama *Paolo and Francesca* to enthusiastic reviews. Wharton would critique the work and his later verse drama *Ulysses* in 1902, finding the latter wanting in dramatic value (Wegener, 66–70).
2. The British painter George Romney (1704–1832). The art critic John Ruskin (1819–1900) championed, and collected, the unconventional work of J. M. W. Turner (1775–1851).

Edith Wharton's mother, Lucretia Jones, died in Paris on 1 June 1901. Although Wharton had continued to visit her mother, the two had split bitterly over the divorce and remarriage of Wharton's brother Fred. Teddy, who was in England looking after his own mother, was able to cross to France and attend the funeral. Lucretia Jones's death reopened the family quarrels, and Wharton had to fight to get a fair inheritance for herself and for her niece Beatrix Jones. Meanwhile, in Lenox, Massachusetts, where Teddy's mother and sister had a home, the Whartons found and purchased Laurel Lake Farm, on which they would build The Mount. They chose the architect Francis L. V. Hoppin to design the house and Beatrix Jones to design the gardens. Bahlmann was going overseas.

Lenox, Mass.
Friday [June 1901]

Dear Tonni,

This is just a farewell hug from your affectionate family, who wish you all manner of good luck on your travels & who are convinced that the only reason for your not having it is that you so richly deserve it.

Still, if you will try to live down your better self for once & be as extravagant and immoral as you know how (or rather *don't* know) you may yet manage to cheat Providence & have a good time; so my parting advice is, whenever you feel a bad head coming on, *go out & spend some money!*

And now there is one thing I must ask you to promise. If anything goes seriously wrong, in health or any other way, *promise* to cable us at once. I promise I won't rush out to you, or do anything to inconvenience my precious self, but I will send or arrange or in some way contrive to look after you — & if I found you had kept back anything from me I should be so distressed afterward! — But I will *not* close with such gloomy hypotheses. There is one thing certain — & that is that you will be glad to be breathing in a good sea breeze tomorrow, after the fiery ordeal of these last days.

It has been bad here, but I simply thrive on it. Unberufen — but the hotter it grows the hungrier grow I. — I get a ride every evening & work all the morning, & haven't felt as well & fat in years. The house is settled & Mr. Hoppin & Trix come on Monday to start things up — so you may think of things here as going very placidly just now.

May they be the same with you, dear Tonni, & do be prudent in everything except enjoying yourself!
Yrs affly

E.W.

Gross covered the kittens' baskets with Holland "against the heat," & they won't get into them!!

During the two years between letters, Wharton wrote furiously and happily. Her second collection of stories, Crucial Instances, *was published in 1901, but her biggest effort came with* The Valley of Decision, *which she finished triumphantly in 1902 just weeks before her fortieth birthday. To it she brought her immense erudition and knowledge of Italy and Italian history. Complex, historically rich, with a theme she would tackle later on in other ways — how do societies change? — it is Wharton's most difficult, least-read novel today. She was particularly pleased with a review that said, in Wharton's words, "that the book should be regarded as the picture of a period, not of one or two persons, & that Italy is my hero—or heroine, if you prefer"* (to Sara Norton, 24 February 1902, LEW, 59).

In September of either 1902 or 1903, while the Whartons were at The Mount, Wharton's friend Daisy Chanler was seeking a finishing governess for her daughter Laura (an artist who would later marry the son of Stanford White). Wharton's reply is worth recording, for it demonstrates her confidence in Bahlmann—by now in her early fifties—and also the fact that Bahlmann, even while working as Wharton's secretary, nevertheless continued with her other employment. Edith Wharton was as firm a businesswoman on Anna Bahlmann's behalf as she was on her own.

> My old governess, Miss Anna Bahlmann, is an admirable finishing governess, & thoroughly fitted to interest a girl of Laura's age in literature, German or English. She even inspired me with a passion for Novalis, not to speak of the Nibelungenlied in the original O.H.G. [Old High German].[1]
>
> She is here now, & I asked her about hours. She says she will be very glad to take Laura if an afternoon hour suits. She has no morning hours left. Of course, if she got an offer for the hour beginning Nov. 15 (the usual date of the winter term), she might not be willing to wait till Jan 1st, unless you cared to pay something in advance. She has not said anything about this to me, but I know she is in great demand, & it is usual to pay from Nov. 15th or Dec. 1st when making arrangements for the winter. But of course this you could learn by correspondence with her.—She is here giving lessons, & her address is Spencer Cottage, Lenox.
>
> (to MTC 25 Sept. [1902?])

In the following letter the Whartons have been traveling in northern Italy while Edith worked on a series of articles on Italian villas and gardens, commissioned by Richard Watson Gilder of Century Magazine, later published as a book. Bahlmann was living at 882 Park Avenue, working as Wharton's literary secretary and representative and also as general house manager. "Middy" was probably the housekeeper.

My Dear Governess

1. Novalis was the nom de plume of Georg Philipp Friedrich Freiherr von Hardenberg (1772–1801), a philosopher of German romanticism.

Venice
April 4 [1903]

Dear Middy & Bahlmann

We were very glad to get your pleasant letter the other day, & to hear that the weather was warm & that you had both been enjoying yourselves in the Park. Your presentiment that we should not sail on April 25 has come true, but our going is only deferred for a week, we start on May 2d on the Zeeland from Antwerp—The reason is Smith's delay, as I wrote you—we send White on a fast steamer on the 22d April, with two footmen, & he will arrive on the 28 or 29, & expects to have Lenox ready for us by the time we land, as our boat is very slow—

We have had some charming days since I wrote you—On leaving Florence we met the Bourgets at Bologna. We left them again to go to Padua & do the Brenta & they rejoined us here[1]—On the way down the Brenta our horses saw the steam train & jumped into the river, but luckily we skipped out in good time, & my camera full of precious photos fell on the bank, while the lunch box went into the water! So you see we don't always have bad luck. Mitou, who was on the trip, took it all philosophically, but regretted leaving the carriage—

Another day we went to Battaglia, & drove to a charming villa in the Euganean Alps, which I also photo'd. I shall have quite a nice collection.

We are going to Milan today & expect to be there or in the neighbourhood for about two weeks & then to Paris—

I think I wrote you how ill poor M. Wingate has been. She is better, & has been out driving, but she is still very shaky, & I tremble to think what her illness must have cost her—

The servants are to be ready to go to the Mount when White arrives, please.

Affly Yrs

E.W.

I had sent you today 4 vols (Ariosto) wh. I bought here, & wh. were too big for my trunk. It is an 18th century ed., in a paper binding, & I don't suppose there is any duty, but please pay whatever is required.

1. By "doing the Brenta" she probably meant traveling alongside the river Brenta from Padua to Venice, where she would have passed—and probably visited—many famous villas along the way.

Teddy Wharton had a return of his nervous condition in 1903, causing Edith to write sympathetically to William Crary Brownell, on 16 August, "I was very sorry to learn that things are going badly with you—I understand what it means, for my husband is very poorly & I have had an anxious summer— I can't do consecutive work" (LEW, 86).

In 1904 the Whartons bought their first motorcar, a Panhard-Levassor, and with it their lives changed. No longer subject to train schedules or horses whose well-being needed to be considered, they could travel much more quickly and directly to their destination. With Edith having recovered from another illness and what she called "the dreariest winter I ever spent" (to Sally Norton, 5 May 1904, LEW, 89), and with Teddy feeling better, they embarked on a motor tour of southwestern France, with a dip into northernmost Spain, then back north and east up to Bourges, about 120 miles south of Paris. There they picked up Edith's brother Harry and took him on a tour of the Loire Valley to see the famed chateaux. No longer does Wharton linger for Bahlmann's enjoyment over description of the places she sees, sufficing instead with lists of the towns they visit, perhaps hoarding her impressions for a more lucrative medium. As she mentions here, she is between literary projects, having recently finished the essays for Italian Villas and Their Gardens *and also a volume of short stories,* The Descent of Man. *And yet she is already talking to Mr. Brownell about other stories, and by summer she will be writing* The House of Mirth.

Grand Hôtel et Grand
Hôtel de Blois
April 12 [1904]

Dear Tonni,

Many thanks for your letter of April 1st, which I found on reaching here last night—also for two others which I have not yet answered, though you will have seen from an occasional post-card that we were alive & had not forgotten you. The fact is we have been travelling pretty continuously ever since we left Hyères, for though we made Pau our headquarters for ten days we went off on long excursions & on a three days' tour through the Basque country & down to Fontarabia; & after our return we started almost at once for Paris. We left Pau five days ago, coming up through central France at a leisurely pace, to avoid over-tire & do some sight-seeing by the way. We spent the first night at Agen, the second at Périgueux, the third at Limoges—Between Périgueux & Limoges we made a charming détour to the valley of the Drônne, to see the extraordinary old château of Bourdeilles, belonging to the family of Brantôme, & thence to the little town & abbey of Brantôme, from which we sent you some post cards. Then we went to Bourges, where we had asked Harry [Jones, Edith's brother] to join us. To our surprise he accepted, & it was so funny, when we puffed up to the humble & dirty dirty inn, to see him sitting on a bench at the door, more monumental & splendid than ever! Then we found he had actually *never been* to Touraine—at least not since he was a boy. So we decided to give him a coup d'oeil [a glimpse], & yesterday morning we left Bourges for this place, seeing Cheverny & Chambord by the way. He was perfectly delighted with everything—the motor, the dirty inns, the bad food, the châteaux, the whole adventure! This afternoon we shall take him to Amboise & Chaumont, & tomorrow we all return to Paris, via Chartres, Rambouillet & Versailles, lunching at Chartres. I think the trip will do him a lot of good!—

To return to Bourges—some day you must see the Cathedral there. You know I am "rebelle au Gothique"—but it completely conquered me. In no great Gothic church have I seen such complete expression of the spirit in which the huge mediaeval church was built—such soaring majesty, such depths of awe & solemnity, & so few ugly excrescences & restorations. When we went into it, just at twilight, it seemed to stretch away into infinity.

The trip has done Teddy & me a lot of good. I eat anything (& *such* things!) & sleep as if I were drugged—but mental effort is impossible, & so I as I have no "littery" work on hand now I am taking a complete rest, even from letters. I never did anything I enjoyed more than this motor travelling & I am really glad now we had to give up Italy, for it forced us to come to France & see things we should otherwise have missed. The scenery through central France is exquisite, till about half way between Limoges & Bourges, & we saw such an out of the way region, where the peasants still wear their smocks & the women their pretty caps or winged head-dresses.—

To leave the subject for a moment—Thanks for looking up the elusive Ellen. I should not bother about her any further, as she will probably turn up by May 1st, when I told her I would begin paying her wages. I assume that Louisa intends to come back, as you have said nothing to the contrary. If Mr. Blight leaves 884 before June, as he may very likely do, since I hear Miss Blight is coming abroad, you can put the two women in there & they can do what is necessary about the house—though of course, if Louisa can keep her place till June 1st it will suit me better. And this reminds me—if please let everything in 884 be left as it was when we prepared it for the Blights—don't take out anything that was put away, or make any changes, as that can be attended to before we move in next autumn. In any case, the house will have to be repainted.

If the Blights do *not* move out, & Ellen & Louisa are out of place by May 1st, pay them their wages & let them look out for themselves till they go to Lenox—I will let you know early in May when I want the house opened.

Another thing—do get Miss Thayer to take another $50 on account. I shall be giving her lots of work when I get back, & she might as well draw on me now.

[letter is cut here and a line or two omitted]

My Dear Governess

Mr. Canfield's funeral![1] I have a horror of flowers at funerals, & had I wished to send any, should of course have cabled you to that effect. But it was done in all kindness, like all she does.

It is so nice to think of the splendid care those dear kitties have had all winter—I hope they are properly grateful—
Teddy sends love—

Yr affte E.W.

Tell me about the German play—I hadn't heard of it—

That Boston broker's letter isn't anything but a bid for a job. Throw away all such stuff unanswered—[this is the other side of the paper that was cut off]

1. Augustus Cass Canfield, a member of New York society, had died at age fifty while golfing in South Carolina.

On 13 July 1905, Edith Wharton's good friend Miss Ethel Cram was fatally injured when she dropped the reins of the pony cart she was driving and was kicked in the head by the pony. She never regained consciousness, but lingered for many weeks, much to the distress of her family and friends. This was surely one of the inspirations for the major moral dilemma in Wharton's third novel, The Fruit of the Tree *(1907), which she would begin writing in a few months, and in which she treats the question of whether a mercy killing is ever right. Her second novel,* The House of Mirth, *was coming out serially that summer to great critical acclaim and financial success. She was writing every morning before getting out of bed, leaving the pages for her maid to bring to Bahlmann, who organized and typed them. Wharton joined Teddy in enjoying the summer pleasures of The Mount and entertaining, among others, the expatriate Henry James (1843–1916), who was finishing a tour of his native country.*

The distinguished novelist was a relatively recent friend of Wharton's, although she had been introduced to him several times, and her sister-in-law, Minnie Jones, had counted him among her circle of literary friends for years. The two authors had exchanged letters and books somewhat tentatively, but in 1903, when they lunched together in London, each affirmed an eagerness to know the other better. By 1905 they were close enough that Anna Bahlmann could apply to James for advice and assistance in planning her visit to his adoptive England, where she hoped—in vain—to see Osterley House, a stately home designed by Robert Adam in the eighteenth century. Bahlmann received a charming letter in reply. When James came to the United States to make his tour to gather material for The American Scene *(1906), he stayed with the Whartons at The Mount and the friendship was sealed.[1] James brought with him his friend Howard Sturgis (1855–1920), about whom we will read more later.*

Bahlmann was traveling in Europe with her younger friend Ella Denison. Given what we know of Bahlmann's finances, and her pride, it is not surprising that she would find a hotel that the Whartons recommend to be well beyond her sense of what she could afford or what she would feel comfortable asking them to pay for on her behalf.

1. Millicent Bell's *Edith Wharton and Henry James* provides the richest account of their friendship.

> The Mount
> Lenox, Mass.
> Aug 4th [1905]

Dear Tonni—It was a great pleasure to get your long & satisfactory letter of July 23d, & the cheerful little p.s. about Vaux-le-Vicomte the next day. I am so glad you have seen that, & seen it thoroughly & successfully, & I shall write and tell Mrs. Gay how much I appreciate her sending you the permission.[1] Thank you for the pretty post cards—

Everything in your letter gives us both pleasure, except the fact that you are suffering with your foot (for which I wish you wd see Dr. Austin, & mention my name & Mrs. Wharton's), & the other fact that you are worrying over your little economies, after all we have said & done to make you feel that *we* shall not be comfortable while you are away unless we feel that you are. The prices at the H. Balzac seem to me very reasonable, & I can't imagine when you know how much I wanted you to go there, why you should now feel any compunctions for doing so. I only

My Dear Governess

beg you not to spoil any comfort you may get out of it by what you call "economies in other directions." Take cabs instead of omnibuses, don't walk off your legs & Ella's, & remember that you are "doing" Paris in hot weather, that you are neither of you robust, & that the constant excitement & interest of your life is in itself a source of fatigue.—

Since you appear to regard us on the brink of ruin I will casually mention that my "rents" are to be higher this winter than ever before, & that I am making money indecently with my pen! So spend all you know how & don't worry—& don't drink water in Paris, by the way. Get *Eau d'Evian*—it is much better than St Galuier—no matter if it costs more—It is folly to drink Paris water— And don't be in the best place in the world for coffee, & deny yourself that!—

We have just come back from a delightful nine days' trip in the motor, during which we had good weather, & the car ran perfectly. We went to Groton, Manchester, Danvers & Beverly, staying with friends at each place—& made, besides, a long day's excursion into Maine, & to Portsmouth. Mr. Lodge went with us, & Mr. Morton made the run back with us yesterday.[2]

The drought has been broken by a few showers, & the place looks better, & the garden is quite lovely—really full of bloom. We returned to sad news of Ethel Cram—one side is paralyzed, & she is dying, though, alas, *so* slowly! If only she could be released—but she is unconscious, & apparently suffers no pain. The strain on the others is the worst part of it.

Mrs. Winthrop came home just before we left, looking fagged out after her long journey & her prolonged anxiety about Tina.[3]—I suppose you saw the poor Dixeys had lost their only boy, who had gone out as a secretary of legation to Corea[4]—It is really a sad year for Lenox.—

Thank you for attending to all my errands. I enclose another for you on another slip. No matter about the [comb?]—just throw it away. Mme Lebrevier has had my letter, & all is well about the dresses.

We are delighted to hear that Ella is enjoying everything so much— but if you feel done up & want a rest, go to Cook's, or the Ladies Guide Ass[oc.], (Mr. Waddy cd tell you where to go) & engage a companion to go about with her—Don't spoil your holiday by trying to do too much.

You must not be worried if I don't write long letters hereafter, for I am rather overwhelmed by my letters — I have had *30* to write since returning yesterday, besides proofs to correct! I miss your faithful hand. —

Teddy sends his love & says: "tell her to take cabs *all the time*." Affly Yrs.

E.W.

Dogs all well — By the way, I should like you here about Sept 27 for a week if you can manage it, as we are going away —

1. Matilda Travers Gay, wife of painter Walter Gay (1856–1937). The couple were friends of the Whartons living in Paris. Vaux-le-Vicomte, a seventeenth-century castle outside of Paris, was magnificent and had a fascinating history sure to intrigue Bahlmann and Denison.

2. Friends George Cabot (Bay) Lodge (1873–1909) and Johnson Morton (1862?–1922). Morton would later travel with Teddy in his futile pursuit of peace of mind and good health. They probably visited Teddy's brother William and his family while in Groton.

3. Albertina Winthrop, daughter of Robert and Katherine Taylor Winthrop, would survive whatever problem she was having and marry a Dutch diplomat.

4. Mr. & Mrs. Richard Dixey, whose son Arthur Sturgis Dixey was only twenty-five when he died of dysentery.

The Mount
Lenox, Mass.
Aug. 19 [1905]

Dear Tonni — And so you are already in London! Your letter has just come, saying that you were going there on the 18th; but, as your lodgings may not prove satisfactory, I think it safer to send this care of Munroe. I am glad you are able to give a little longer time to England, for I know it will be a treat to you personally, & it will be good for Ella too. Now perhaps you can permit yourself one or two more excursions, & please don't be stingy about your expenses, for ~~I hav~~ we have never been as rich as we are this year, & last week we had $900 drop in unexpectedly from some rise in rent that we had forgotten! So you see I am not dealing in generalities, but in solid facts. —

My Dear Governess

Tell Ella to put £6 for herself in a coat or cloak, or anything of the kind she wants. One can get that sort of thing only in London, as you know. I shd advise Marshall's or Peter Robinson's. I hope you are going to get my Xmas to you in the shape of a good winter coat or dress for £8 or so—won't you?—We are all well & the weather is heavenly. I took 7 first prizes at the [Lenox] Garden Flower Show last week.—

Poor Ethel Cram lies in the same state—over five weeks after the accident—still unconscious, & doomed to die, but, alas, not for weeks, I fear. To me she has long been dead already.

Mrs. Robert Winthrop, Miss Bigelow, & little Kitty all ask after you affectionately, as do Mrs. Wharton & Nannie.[1]
Ever Yr

E.W.

1. Kitty was Katherine Lanier Lawrence (1893–1936), granddaughter of Charles Lanier (1837–1926). Her mother being dead, Kitty lived with her grandfather and was cared for by Miss Bigelow. It is possible that Bahlmann provided Kitty with some lessons. I am indebted to the historian Cornelia Brooke Gilder for identifying these Lenox friends.

> The Mount
> Lenox Massachusetts
> Friday [Sept. 1905]

Dear Tonni—I waited till yesterday to write, in order to give you the latest news, & yesterday was one of those Niagara days when things come with a rush from breakfast till bedtime. I am sorry, because I wanted to have a letter for you at Quarantine, but I don't dare send this, as the time is so short.—To begin with practical matters if you would like to come to Lenox next week, we shall be delighted to have you on Tuesday, & you can stop here till Friday, & I will do whatever you wish about getting you a room, if you will telegraph me what to do. It will be no trouble, so let me know in good time—I understand from Mr. G. Winthrop that you propose spending the Autumn here, & I am delighted at the prospect.[1] Of course in Oct. we can have you here for a good part of the time.

Mr. Hoppin was here last week, & asked me to tell Ella that she need not come to the office till Wednesday next, as she will want a day or two to rest after the voyage.—I enclose a note for her, as I am not sure if she kept her rooms.—He brought me her letters, with which he is quite delighted, & so was I.—You have certainly given her a wonderful opportunity, & I only hope you have not tired yourself too much in the effort.—I rec'd your Hampton Court postal, & also yr letter describing yr perfect day there. I stupidly dreamed at one time that you were sailing on the 8th instead of the 2nd, & I fear I sent my last letter too late for it to reach you—I mean the one in which I suggested you & Ella to get yourself Christmas presents in London. I don't see how I made such a mistake.—

Yes, please bring my box from the bank when you come.—the dogs are all well & send much love, & it will be a great pleasure to us all to see you here.

Affly Yrs, E.W.

I have nearly had writer's cramp owing to the lack of yr helpful hand. Ethel's condition is still the same.

1. Grenville Winthrop (1864–1943), Mrs. Robert Winthrop's son, was a noted art collector and at this time a widower with two young daughters who would have been of the right age for Bahlmann to teach.

With more than 100,000 copies of The House of Mirth *sold, Edith and Teddy Wharton returned to Europe in March of 1906, spending time in both England and France. In Paris they stayed with Edith's brother Harry, and Wharton made the acquaintance of two women who would become friends, the famous hostess Rosa de Fitz-James and the countess and poet Anna de Noailles. Rosalie von Guttman, Mme de Fitz-James (1862–1923) was the daughter of a successful Jewish banker. Nearly thirty years younger than her husband, she was known for hosting one of the most interesting and successful*

salons in Paris. Anna de Noailles (1876–1933) was the daughter of a Ruma-
nian prince and famous as much for her conversation as for her poetry. These
introductions marked an important entry for Wharton into Faubourg liter-
ary and aristocratic society, and also a diversion from the travel and sporting
pleasures enjoyed by Teddy.

Teddy having acquired a new motorcar, they returned to England for a
tour with Henry James into Devonshire and Somersetshire. It may have been
delightful for the Whartons, but James left them earlier than planned, writ-
ing to his brother that he had "impatiently and prematurely and gleefully re-
turned today" (NGC, 153). Sometimes Wharton's energy was more agitating
to James than it was pleasing.

34 Brook St. London

May 9th [1906]

Dear Tonni—We are back from our ten days' motor-trip, which was
quite delightful except for the unseasonable cold, & by a sudden impulse
we have decided to go back to the continent & motor there until we sail.
Teddy had the great good luck to pick up a second-hand Panhard which
is really a wonderful car, & we have enjoyed it so much that we thought
we should get more fun out of two ~~days~~ weeks more motoring than out
of the same brief time given to the London season. Our tour was really
wonderful, considering how short a time we were gone. We saw, comfortably & without hurry, Chichester, Benchurch (I. of Wight), Win-
chester, the New Forest, a passing glimpse of Salisbury (which we already
knew & therefore did not linger over), Bath, Wells, Gloucester, Chelten-
ham, part of the Valley of the Wye, Malvern, Worcester, Broadway &
Stratford-on-A., ending up at Cambridge where we spent two delightful
days & saw Ely!—Tomorrow we go down to Windsor to spend a night
with Mr. Sturgis, & the next day to the Alfred Austins in Kent, & from
there we go to Folkestone, & join the motor at Boulogne.[1]

I shall have a great deal to say to you about English cathedrals, of
which I knew nothing before.

We are pining for little Nicette, & shall be so glad when we get
back to France & she can join us.—I hope dear Mitou is as well as when

you last wrote. — White had a letter from Alfred, in which he said he had seen Bagley, & that she still looked very poorly. I hope the work will not be too much for her this summer. White has found two good footmen, & sails on May 19th, taking one with him. We bring the other.

Affly Yrs E.W.

1. Alfred Austin (1835–1913) was then poet laureate, though most, including Wharton, agreed that his poetry was undistinguished. He had written to Wharton in praise of *The Valley of Decision* and they had met before in Fiesole.

One of Edith Wharton's closest women friends was Sally (Sara) Norton, daughter of the noted art historian and public intellectual Charles Eliot Norton (1827–1908). The Nortons had a summer home in Ashfield, Massachusetts, a long day's drive from The Mount. Edith and Sally visited each other and maintained a friendship and correspondence for many years. In fall of 1906 Anna Bahlmann wrote a little note to Norton at Wharton's behest, and added a line that gives a hint of Wharton's continuing energy and perhaps what it was like to work for her as well: "In an aside I may add that she seems very well, having taken these two rainy days to rest. Of course her kindness & her powers of organization are directed in twenty directions, so that while her body rests, her mind does the work of ten people" (ACB to Norton, 30 November 1906). Although Wharton frequently had Bahlmann write short notes for her, she wasn't always satisfied with the results. In 1903 she had felt the need to apologize to Sally for something Bahlmann wrote: "It is just like Anna to write that kind of note! Unless I dictate every word, she never gives the impression I want her to" (9 August 1903). Occasionally Bahlmann was too deferential or too scrupulous to adopt the same tone in her letters that Wharton could in her own.

In 1908 the Whartons were installed in George Vanderbilt's Paris apartment with six servants, two dogs, and their chauffeur. All the servants were taking French lessons, and Charles Cook, the chauffeur, from Lee, Massachusetts, "found his way around Paris as if he had lived here for years" (Teddy Wharton to Sally Norton, 26 February 1907). We get only a brief glance in this next letter of the three-week automobile trip through France that the Whartons made with Henry James, to be memorialized in Edith Wharton's A Motor Flight through France *(1908). It was on this trip that Wharton and James went together to the home of Georges Sand, Nohant, surprised and mystified to discover a house much more "dignified and decent" than Sand's autobiography would suggest (MF, 41–45). Sumptuous meals in old-fashioned courtyards, explorations of churches and cathedrals inspiring reverence, distant views of Lyons at night, "outspread below in a wide network of lights against its holy hill of Fourvière (MF, 147)—all this they enjoyed in the doing, and Wharton again in the telling.* A Motor Flight through France *would be her fifteenth book in eleven years.*

58 Rue de Varenne Paris
April 13, [1907]

Dear Tonni,

Your last letter overtook me at Dijon two or three days ago, & I was very glad to hear such good accounts of Bagley, & to be able to look forward to her good repasts again at the Mount. Please tell her so with my regards.

We got back yesterday from the most successful motor trip we have ever made. Twenty two days on the road, & only ~~one~~ two days of rain, & one the last, so we were approaching Paris, & not missing anything new or wonderful. The motor ran like a bird from start to finish, & we saw more beautiful places than I can begin to tell you about. The trip has cured me completely, as motoring always does, & I now feel perfectly well, & weigh—what do you think? 138!! This is higher than I have climbed in 15 years!

We get good accounts of Gross, & expect her back in about eight days.

This is a half sheet, the other half clearly having been ripped off. No closing greeting.

5

"Turning-points"

JUNE 1907 TO JULY 1914

There come turning-points where one has to go sharply round the corner without looking behind." So wrote Edith Wharton to Anna Bahlmann in 1908, justifying Wharton's unplanned flight from Lenox to London and Paris in early fall. Indeed, the years from 1907 to 1914 brought many turning points for Wharton, and she took the turns with determination and grace.

The summer of 1907 was spent at The Mount, hosting numerous friends and finishing the design of Wharton's latest novel, *The Fruit of the Tree*. Among their many guests that summer and fall, the Whartons entertained a friend of Henry James and Sally Norton, the journalist (William) Morton Fullerton (1865–1952). Fullerton and Wharton had met earlier in the year in the salon of the Countess Rosa de Fitz-James, and Wharton found him "slightly mysterious" (*NGC*, 170). Soon she would be enchanted by the man who had already enchanted many women—and a few men, including Henry James—before her. Fullerton was born in Connecticut, raised in a Boston suburb, and educated at Harvard, where he studied with Charles Eliot Norton. By 1907 he was the Paris correspondent for the London *Times*, he had been secretly married and divorced, he had enjoyed numerous lovers, and, the week before visiting the Whartons, he had contracted a secret engagement with his cousin Katharine Fullerton. Leon Edel, James's biographer, said of

Fullerton: "He was in every way an *homme de coeur*, a discriminatingly promiscuous Victorian-American, who dressed with dignity and lived the life of an egotist as if he were a mixture of a Restoration rake and (in his verbal solemnities) Dr. Johnson himself" (Edel, 411). He shined his seductive light on Wharton, and so began the four years of turmoil, of happiness and sexual initiation, of betrayal and devastation, that was Edith Wharton's first—and only—full-blown love affair.

In conjunction with the desire for Fullerton that pulled her away from her marriage and American home, there was also Teddy Wharton's escalating mental illness to propel her. It wasn't simply their intellectual incompatibility that tore them apart. Teddy was genuinely proud of his wife's accomplishments and indulgent enough to allow her the freedom to pursue her work. Edith, in turn, would have continued to find occupations that would keep Teddy's interest while she involved herself with the intellectual pursuits that he found dull. But by 1907 intense emotional moods, sometimes highly energetic and sometimes nervous, anxious, and depressed, increasingly ruled Teddy's life and made him difficult and embarrassing to be around. When in the throes of megalomania, he chased women blatantly, gambled, and mishandled his wife's finances; eventually, by 1911, he threatened her physical safety. Anna Bahlmann, who had a way with Teddy, was frequently called in to stay with him and keep him calm, but her presence was not always sufficient. Eventually, Edith Wharton felt compelled to divorce.

The third major change that occurred during these years, when Edith was seeking a path that would make both herself and Teddy happy, was the decision to move to Paris full time. There and in London she had a circle of friends who shared her humor, supported her writing, and indulged her love of travel and conversation. The couple retained their home in Massachusetts, a place they both loved, and the hope was that management of The Mount would provide Teddy with enough to occupy his interest. Meanwhile, Edith could participate in the Faubourg salon life and travel as she pleased.

And so these seven years, beginning when Edith Wharton was forty-five, brought major changes. Reading the letters, however, one learns little of her inner life. She could not confess her tumultuous love affair with Fullerton, and she did not need to tell Bahlmann about Teddy. One must read carefully to understand her state of mind; Wharton had grown into the woman of her long-ago poetry, a woman who kept her passions to herself and showed a cool face to the world.

The Mount
Lenox, Mass.
June 19th [1907]

Dear Tonni,

Many thanks for looking up terrace furniture for me. I don't think ours looks as badly as White represented, & I fancy I can fill up the gaps well enough at Pittsfield, as they had last year better models than Flint's Catalogue shows.

I fancy you are having rather more hot weather than you want in Virginia, for it was 84 here yesterday—unheard of for June. Today, however, is much cooler.—

Teddy & I have gone into the boarding house question thoroughly for you, & I have decided on your fate, which is a very nice room on the top floor at Curtis's.[1]—Lee is out of the question, on the very selfish ground of my own convenience. I need your help so often in summer that it would really be a trial to me to have you so uncomfortably out of reach.—The boarding-houses are no better than last year—probably worse—& we have made an arrangement at Curtis's, whereby you will pay $10 a week, & I will make up the difference. Please don't protest at this, for I should not be comfortable knowing that you were not—it troubled me all last summer, & now I shall know you are well fed & decently "roomed." I visited the room yesterday p.m., temperature 84, & found it cool, & just opposite there is a little passage with [a] window at [the] end at right angles with the main hall, so by leaving yr door open you can always get a draught. There is a sort of built-out hanging-closet & a shelf with a few hooks & a chest of drawers—not much space to put things away, but a lovely view over the trees down toward the southwest. We looked at the Aspinwall also, thinking you might use the "bus," but there the price was higher for a horrid little gable room that wd not have been possible.

Come here for a few days first, & you can arrange details comfortably at Curtis's.

Remember me to Mrs. Schultz. I hope she is better.

Affly Yr E.W.

1. The Curtis Hotel stands in the center of Lenox, near Teddy Wharton's mother's house. A hostelry has stood on the spot since the 1770s and has welcomed many famous guests, including Catharine Maria Sedgwick and Fanny Kemble. The Aspinwall, mentioned later, was a more luxurious hotel, recently built about three-quarters of a mile up a hill from town center. It burned down in 1931.

3 Pl. des E. Unis
Dec. 13th [1907]

Dear Tonni,

It is so long since we have crossed on a fast boat that I feel as if I had made one step from Mr. Winthrop's motor, on the dock in New York, to Harry's yesterday, at the Gare St. Lazare! We had terribly rough weather all the way, but it did not lower our speed, though the Adriatic, which left the day before us, & which we overtook the second or third day, had a terrible time, & was reduced to 7 knots an hour. So that there are advantages in a fast boat, especially in winter.—We were very comfortable, & the kittens approved of everything, as they were allowed the range of the passenger deck, instead of being relegated among the emigrants—so all went well. The weather was so mild & beautiful when we landed at Havre early yesterday that we sighed for our motor, which is here having its winter body put on. Chrysanthemums & *tea-roses* were in bloom in the little gardens, & Normandy looked as green as in April!—What an adorable country it is.

I find Harry looking thin & pulled down, but luckily he has developed a passion for motoring, which keeps him out in the air; & he & Teddy have already gone off to the country this morning.

I hope poor Miss Thayer has got over her attack of bronchitis, & that things generally are going well. You will certainly have plenty to do till after Xmas—I saw to that, didn't I?

We shall probably go to the country next week for a day or two, to the Walter Gays', & move into the R. de Varenne on our return, just before Xmas. I am glad to be here, & especially so on account of Harry, who seems to me less strong than he ought to be.—This is just a scrawl to tell you of our arrival, & carry you best Xmas wishes from the whole party, biped & quadruped (the latter of whom are lying on my bed as I write, with a spoonful of Castor-oil in each round little tum!)

Affly Yrs. E.W.

Please send Aimée Bodignel $5 from me for Christmas. The new kitten shawls are too lovely—they are lying on them now. Did you make them? They are the prettiest I have ever seen.

Paris
Dec. 18th [1907]

Dear Tonni—

Your note came yesterday enclosing the documents from home, & I was glad to hear that everything was going on well, & especially glad for your sake that you were having balmy weather while we were at sea.

It has been quite beautiful since we got here—bright sunshine nearly every day, & such exquisite evening lights on the Seine. On Sunday Harry took us out in his new motor for the day. We went 80 kil. down into Normandy, to see a really lovely Louis XIII chateau with a moat around it, called Brécourt. It is for sale, & Harry, who thinks a little of buying a place in the country, wanted to see it with that in view—but charming as it was, there were objections. On the way we followed the Seine for some distance, & it was all lovely, the fields still green, cattle grazing out in the pastures, & chrysanthemums & roses still in bloom in the road-side gardens!

Harry seems well, I think, though on arriving we thought he looked rather poorly. He enjoys motoring intensely, & I think it will do him a lot of good.

Tomorrow we are going to the academy to see Maurice Donnay received by Bourget, & in the evening to a dinner which the Bourgets are giving to Donnay & some other gens de letters.[1] — The H. of Mirth is having, I am told, a really unprecedented success in the Revue de Paris, & I shall perhaps be able to get my little Noailles article published on the strength of it![2]

This is just a word to carry you, rather tardily, our best love for Christmas & all our loving wishes for 1908. The doggies join in these messages, & wish you to be specially told that their "mats" are kept on the library sofa, being thought too handsome for bedroom use!

Please give my love to Miss Thayer. I do hope she is better. — We move to the Rue de Varenne on the 23d to celebrate Xmas there.

Affly Yrs

E.W.

Will you call up Dr. Cutler (8 E. 54th) & tell him that after repeated trials I find my new reading glasses rather a strain to my eyes, though I see so well with them, & I should like him to send me a copy of the *old prescription,* that I may have some glasses made here at Meyrowitz's. He will remember that when he gave me my ~~last year's~~ former glasses (the ones I now want to go back to — I think they are really *two* years old) Meyrowitz in N.Y. lost the prescription, & I have never had it. He will understand.

1. The playwright Maurice Donnay (1859–1945) was to be elected to the French Academy that day.

2. *The House of Mirth,* translated by Charles Du Bos (1882–1939), was published first in the *Revue de Paris* as *La Demeure de liesse,* then later in book form as *Chez les heureux du monde.* Wharton's essay about the poetry of the intense and gifted Comtesse de Noailles (1876–1933) never came to fruition.

There is no word in these letters from December 1907 either of Teddy Wharton's relapse into nervous depression or of Edith Wharton's intensifying intimacy with Morton Fullerton. In April 1908 Teddy sailed to the United States with Alfred White for more treatments. While he was away, Edith kept up a very busy social schedule, and she saw a great deal of Morton Fullerton as he became her guest at teas and dinners, her escort to lectures and theater, and her companion on day trips to the country. None of this did she mention to Bahlmann in these letters. We do not know whether there were other letters, letters sufficiently compromising that Anna Bahlmann chose to destroy them.[1]

1. The most evocative description of Wharton's affair with Fullerton can be found in Lee's chapter 11, *L'Âme Close* (308–48).

3 P. des E. Unis
April 26th [1908]

Dear Tonni,

I did not answer yr cable at once, because a letter from me was on its way, going into the house-maid situation; & I wanted to wait & see if Emily cd at the last moment perhaps pick up a friend in England.

Since I last wrote the weather has been incredibly bad, cold, rainy, & snowy; and I am so glad Teddy has escaped this unnatural spring, which is far more wintry than anything the winter brought. It is too bad to have such weather come during the Easter holidays, when work-people & tourists need the sunshine so much.

I continue to be very happy & comfortable here, & now that Mr. James has come life is very animated, as every one wants to see him. He arrived three days ago, coming straight to Paris on account of the bad weather, instead of my meeting him at Amiens in the motor, as we had planned.[1] We are very thankful that we gave up the little trip, for there wd have been no pleasure in it. —I am happy to say that I have persuaded Mr. James to sit for his portrait to Mr. Jacques Blanche, who has made a very fine picture of Thos. Hardy.[2] It appears that there is *no* portrait of him, & as Mr. Blanche is most anxious to do him, I have a feeling the picture may be a success. Don't you think people ought to be grateful to me for managing this?

Teddy writes me cheerfully from the Hot Springs, & the baths seem to be doing him a great deal of good.—He thinks he will go straight to Boston after they are over.

Will you please subscribe at Brentano's, for *six months,* beginning June 1st, to the following:—Graphic, Illustration, Spectator, Revue de Paris, Mercure de France?—I think I won't renew the Country Life, as it is really not much use in our climate, & rather discourages[3]

1. This corrects Leon Edel's account of 1908, wherein he indicates that James and Wharton met at Amiens (351).

2. The society painter Jacques Émile Blanche (1861–1942). While Wharton liked the portrait, James's initial reaction was that it made him look "very big, and fat and uncanny and 'brainy' and awful" (quoted in Edel, 351).

3. The page ends here and there is no next page.

During the summer of 1908 the Whartons returned to The Mount, where Edith was increasingly unhappy at not hearing from Fullerton, who continued to advance and retreat in his lovemaking to her. In Paris, Fullerton was equally dishonest with his cousin Katharine, who had come to see him and was anxious to know the status of their engagement. He was also entangled with a former lover who was blackmailing him. Between Morton Fullerton's inconstancy and Teddy's instability, Wharton was deeply distraught.

Suffering from insomnia and headaches, she wrote numerous pleading letters to Fullerton, to which he failed to reply. On 26 August, the day after this bland, chatty letter to Bahlmann, she wrote to Fullerton: "Dear, won't you tell me soon the meaning of this silence," and went on painfully to speculate on what she might mean to him that he should treat her this way. "I could take my life up again courageously if I only understood; for whatever those months were to you, to me they were a great gift, a wonderful enrichment; & still I rejoice & give thanks for them! . . . Yes, dear, I loved you then, & I love you now, as you then wished me to; only I have learned that one must put all the happiness one can into each moment, & I will never again love you 'sadly,' since that displeases you."[1]

Wharton was suffering deeply. But ever a working artist, she was also reading, writing, and editing stories for The Hermit and the Wild Woman *and* A Motor Flight through France. *By late July she had sent six chapters of* The Custom of the Country *to Scribner's. And as was frequently the case for her in times of emotional turmoil, she began to "warble" again—that is, to write poetry. This eventually led to her second volume of poems,* Artemis to Actaeon, *which Scribner's published in 1909.*

Bahlmann left Lenox in July to vacation in Europe, and so began a period of a year in which the two women were apart. In Weimar and Frankfurt she traced Goethe's life.

1. EW to WMF 26 August 1908, *LEW* 160. Several poignant letters from this summer can be found in *LEW.*

The Mount

Aug. 25 [1908]

Dear Tonni,

In a fit of indolence I missed the Tuesday steamer yesterday—but as your letters now go through Munroe it doesn't much matter.

The Weimar epistle was a great joy to me. I feel almost as if I had been there now! And I am so happy to think that it gave you what you had dreamed it would. The post-cards certainly convey a great deal of the charm and the unchanged-ness.

I am glad on the whole that I didn't get my letters off yesterday, for today comes a note from S. Norton, to whom I had sent your Weimar letter & the card, knowing she wd appreciate them. Mr. Norton is seriously ill—not likely to recover, I fear—& she asks me to tell you that she read him your letter in a moment when he was free from pain, & that he was so interested, & enjoyed your description so much, & your "touches of humour," that she wishes you to know of it. So there's her message!

Mrs. Wharton has been in her room for ten days with one of her vague digestive collapses, after being so wonderfully well. No doubt she'll pull up again soon.—Poor Mrs. Winthrop is suffering very much

from neuritis, & seems to take it as inevitable & not be helped by anything she might do. The fatalism of the helpless rich!—

We are all well here, & the chicken palace is nearly finished. The
place looks extremely well, & the garden is at its fullest.[1]

Mrs. Joe Burden thinks of taking 884 on a three years' lease.[2] It is
to be settled in about a fortnight.

The little doggies send you their love. They are very well, & have
had some good motor trips since the car came home.—I wonder where
you are now? Perhaps following Frau Buchholz across the Alps![3] I wish
I could think you had yr friend with you. I don't like your being alone
in Italy.
Affly Yr

E.W.
I wonder how Frankfurt seemed!

1. This letter and the next confirm for the first time that the Whartons—under
Teddy's direction—built both a henhouse and a piggery on their Lenox property.
Scott Marshall's comprehensive study of The Mount indicates scant documentation for the farm buildings, requiring him to speculate about their construction
(151).

2. Lenox neighbor Harriette Griswold Burden. I am indebted for this and
other identifications of Lenox residents to the historian Cornelia Brooke Gilder.

3. Julius Stinde (1841–1905) wrote a series of popular novels in the 1880s about
the typically middle-class Buchholz family and their travels.

*A rare letter from Teddy Wharton, who was feeling better, to "Miss Anna"
reveals his humor and his genuine affection for her—and perhaps also some
of his weaknesses, including spelling and punctuation.*

The Mount
Aug 27th 08

Dear Miss Anna,
We send you the enclosed clipping. It's evidently you, how could you
have done it! Mrs. Burden may take 884 for three years, so you will

My Dear Governess

have a nice neighbor. I think she hopes also that you might be induced to teach her little girl. I miss greatly your valuable assistance with my cheque book, but nevertheless I go on somehow. Later. I fear Mrs. Burden thinks the house is too small, so that wont work. We have the motor & its going well. Puss is hard at work. She looks well & seems pretty well but she don't sleep well but no one can stop her working. Gross is wonderfully well & also Bagley—You seem fr yr letters to Puss to be having a really perfect time. Little Miss Denison's trip was a great success. You will rejoice to know Mitou & Nicette are both finely. They went on a picnic yesterday & had a glorious time. The place looks lovely. I wish you could see it. The pig-house is finished & about a week more will finish the Henery, the roads & pathes there are coming into shape, & the big field by the lake is being put into perfect condition, & you wont know it, when you come here on yr. return. Dont hurry back but go on enjoying yrself & if you want money cable me. Things have gone well with us, thanks to Herman & we are all right.[1] I suppose we shall go back to 58 Rue de Varenne.

Always yrs faithfully,

Edward. R. Wharton
The Gang send their love. Bono is finely.

The following is a transcription of the newspaper clipping pinned to the page by Teddy:

The report that the record of Goethe's birth had been cut from the municipal record at Frankfort-on-the-Main by a vandal recalls a similar theft in the same city a few years ago. A party of young women were being escorted through the old Goethe house by the official guide. On the top floor of the quaint house the chief object of interest is the miniature stage which Goethe had painted and erected when a boy. The guide droned off the story, the girls "ah'd!" and the return trip was begun, when the guide, looking about, saw a fragment of the sacred scenery on the floor, where it had undoubtedly fallen from the nervous hand of the vandal. The whole party was detained for examination, but the souvenir fiend was not discovered.

1. Edith's cousin and financial manager, Herman Edgar.

The Mount

Aug. 31st [1908]

Dear Tonni,

Your post-cards from Göttingen, Frankfurt, & Baden made me feel that I am still in your tracks. How I wish I could see Baden again! I recall it as one of the most exquisite morsels of earth that I know. I am so glad you went there. And your postcard of the Schloss recalled to me such a nice hot climb up that very wooded steep in the picture.

I suppose since then you have been "wallowing" in Stuttgard & Munich — now, no doubt, you are dangling your feet over Italy. What a descent you'll have on it in the September weather — if only the rain has held up!

We have had deliciously cool autumnal weather here these last days — fires every evening, & a sparkle in the air. Everybody is well, & life jogging along as usual. The garden prizes have been awarded, & there were 29 this year, so I think we ought to feel encouraged.

Clyde Fitch has been here for a few days, with the John Corbins (— he is one of the directors of the "New Theater"), & we have had some pleasant motor trips & some good talk.[1]
[Here a large section of the letter has been cut]
visitors in the motor.

Affly Yrs, E.W.

Love from the happy & healthy little dogs.

1. The American dramatist Clyde Fitch (1865–1909) adapted, unsuccessfully, *The House of Mirth* for the stage. John Corbin (1870–1959) was a drama critic and, at the time this letter was written, the "literary manager" of the New Theater in New York City.

The Whartons had known Eunice Ives in Lenox, where she spent summers with her parents. In 1903 Eunice married the publisher Walter Maynard (1871–1925), and the families remained friends. Robert Grant (1852–1940) was an old Boston friend of the Whartons', a novelist and judge with whom Edith corresponded from time to time, and Mr. Richardson was probably the Boston lawyer William King Richardson. All during this summer and fall Wharton was suffering from Morton Fullerton's failure to write to her, though she could not let on to anyone. To Bahlmann she says nothing of this heartache, nor is she able to write her usual chatty letters.

The Mount
Sept 6th [1908]

Dear Tonni,

The Rothenberg post-cards were quite charming, & made me pine again! I *must* see Germany soon.—

Nothing new since last week, but good health & good weather continue. This week we have the Walter Maynards & Mr. Richardson of Boston, & next week the Robert Grants.—Yesterday we had a pleasant picnic at Twin Lakes, which I think the dogs enjoyed as much as any one, if not more!

I hear Hoppin is to build a large house for the Tytuses at Tyringham, so I suppose Ella will have some work here next year, perhaps.[1]—

You must excuse my writing very short letters, as I am pretty hard at work still. I try to write regularly to let you know how we are getting on, but I can't always send a long letter.—I hear from Paris that "Les Heureux" are selling splendidly, & I have a lot of short stories coming out in various reviews & papers.—Enjoy yourself, & spend all the money you can.

Affly Yrs

E.W.

1. Mr. and Mrs. Robb de Peyster Tytus. He was in the Massachusetts State legislature.

The Mount
Sept 9th 1908

Dear Tonni,

The Munich, Verona & Venice post-cards came today, to tell me that the great flight has really been made, & that you are face to face with all the glories of the world.

I am distressed at the very serious crease in the rose-leaf caused by your loss of your trunk; & I shan't be at peace till I hear that you have found it. But if it has *not* been found, don't let that *or anything else,* mar your Italian days; but get everything you need; and don't worry about the expense, or anything material & transitory. We are horribly prosperous, & you can draw on your letter of credit et au delà without a thought.

Above all, as Alexander VI said of Italy, or rather of the Papacy, "Let us enjoy it."[1] My experience is that to have the thing one wants, ever in life, comes to about one mortal in a million—so take Italy with both hands, & eat it leaf by leaf.

All well, no news—I wrote only a day or two ago. Glorious weather here still.

Affly Yr

E.W.

1. "Since God has given us the Papacy, let us enjoy it." The quotation is properly attributed to Pope Leo X (1475–1521) rather than Alexander VI, a Medici pope rather than a Borgia.

The Mount
Sept. 19th [1908]

Dear Tonni,

Your announcement of your departure for Greece left me so breathless that I believe I missed sending you my weekly bulletin last Tuesday! At any rate, the wonder was all of approval & admiration. I applaud every snatch at *more life,* & I am so glad you caught this big opportunity by the forelock & made him carry you down the Aegean on his broad back, between his glorious wings![1] What joys, what sensations, will be yours! Some day when you've calmed down I hope to hear how it all came about. Not that it matters much, in comparison with the bright fact that it *did* come about; but I want to hear the details nevertheless.

We are going through a strange phase of heavy hazy weather, laden with smoke wh is said to come all the way from forest fires in *Michigan,* & wh extends out to sea, & delays incoming ships like fog. The drought is terrible—over a month since we had our last brief shower. And really there has been only one rainy week since I came home in May.

We are all well, but there is no news, ~~expect~~ except that we have the V. apartment again for the winter. No applications yet for 884.—Tina van Riyan's husband has been sent to Japan, & they come to America next month, so Mrs. Winthrop will see her for a short time. But I believe ~~she~~ Mrs. W. feels very badly over their going so far away. She seems very poorly, & looks 100 years old. —

I have been reading Tyndall's Essays, with delight. Somehow I had never come across him before, & I had no idea what a far-ranging suggestive mind he had.—What a good name Schnitzler's novel has![2] It must be worthwhile.

We all send love & good luck to the intrepid pilgrim.

Yrs Ever,

E.W.

1. More life: Wharton may be making an allusion to Goethe's last words, "More light!" Forelock: Kairos, Greek spirit of opportunity, was said to have wings to fly swiftly and a long forelock so that men could seize it and be carried away. Bahlmann had a friend named Albertina Hase who was living in Greece in 1902 and 1903; it could be that she went to see her.

2. The English scientist and natural historian John Tyndall (1820–93). Wharton will recommend him as salutary reading for Morton Fullerton when, in 1912, he is stuck on a writing project, and she will quote him in *The Writing of Fiction* (1925). She is probably speaking of Austrian novelist and dramatist Arthur Schnitzler (1862–1931), *Der Weg ins Freie* (The road into the open).

On 13 October, Henry James responded to what must have been two truly desperate letters from Wharton in which she described her situation with both her husband and with Morton Fullerton, who was a good friend of James's.

"My dear friend! I cabled you an hour ago my earnest hope that you may see your way to sailing with Walter B[erry] on the 20th. . . . I am deeply distressed at the situation you describe & as to which my power to suggest or enlighten now quite miserably fails me. I move in darkness; I rack my brain; I gnash my teeth; I don't pretend to understand or imagine. And yet incredibly to you doubtless—I am still moved to say "Don't conclude!" Some light will still absolutely come to you—I believe—though I can't pretend to say what it will be. . . . Only sit tight yourself & go through the movements of life" (Powers, 101).

Wharton took her friend's advice to sail to England as soon as possible, and this decision caused her to miss seeing Bahlmann, who was just returning from her own European tour. Wharton's guilt is palpable, but the opportunity to sail with Walter Berry, to escape her difficult husband, and most especially to reunite with Morton Fullerton while her husband was thousands of miles away, was too tempting for her to resist.

23 East 33rd Street
Wednesday night
[28 October 1908]

Dearest Tonni,

The disappointment of not seeing you before I sail! If I *could* do it now, I'd change my passage—but I made sure I should have at least a few hours with you. And first of all I want to explain why I am rushing off like this, just as you come back. It seems heartless, unsympathetic, & unnatural—all of which, I *know*, Miss Thayer thinks it is!

Well, I've had insomnia badly for two months, & Dr. Kinnicutt, who came to Lenox early in Sept. tried different things, of a mild kind, but said "If it goes on, you must have a change." It did go on, & get worse, & I came to town to see him about three weeks ago, & he said more emphatically: "Do go away at once." The trouble is that the least

My Dear Governess

little sleep drug stupefies me the next day, & unfits me for any writing, which is such a joy & interest to me—& that makes me restless & bored. So I felt he was right.

At the same time he urged Teddy *very* strongly to go back to the Hot Springs for another cure, before going to his shooting in Dec. Teddy has had the best summer he has had in years, as the result of his Hot Springs visit, so it seemed as if he ought to do this. Therefore I shd have had to stay alone in Lenox all Nov., or go with him, & I disliked the idea of that, as the hotel is very much over-heated, food very indigest-ible, &c. So I decided I wd go out to Europe six weeks ahead of him; but I should have waited over another week in N.Y. expressly to see you, if it had not been that Mr. Berry (who has been appointed a Judge of the International Tribunal at Cairo) suddenly decided to sail on the Pro-vence—that is, as soon as he was appointed, he settled on that date as the *latest*. It gave me the opportunity of having a companion instead of crossing utterly alone, & as I knew no one going out in Nov. I was very strongly tempted, & decided I had better go with him.

If I had felt well I shd not have minded being alone, but the insom-nia has pulled me down, naturally, & it made *all* the difference having him with me. Dr. K. thinks my bad hay-fever was one of the causes, & he assures me it will all be over in a short time with complete change, as my general physical condition is so good.—But I want to break it up before it becomes anything like a habit, because it unsettles my whole mental life, & leaves me so good for nothing.

Miss Thayer will tell you that it hasn't yet affected my spirits, or prevented my writing what *she* considers a very funny story!!

I write this in great haste, as I was so sure of seeing you today that I didn't allow myself time. But you shall get a real letter from the steamer.

Dear Tonni, I do hope you understand that it is *not* heartless or inconsiderate of me to go off like this, & that it wrings my heart not to see you, & hear from your own lips the story of your summer.

Teddy will tell you all the details; I only want to assure you that I wouldn't have gone without seeing you for a few days first if I hadn't dreaded the long solitary days at sea & the sleepless nights. I have a feeling that you'll understand, & not be hurt, & above all *not worry.* That's the thing I want most. I am *well,* essentially, only this special thing has to be cured.

Your devoted

E.W.

I enclose a few business works on another page.

Despite being unwell for much of the summer and fall, when she arrived in Europe, Wharton jumped in to her usual fast-paced, almost frantic schedule of visits and travel. First, in her continuing investigation of the sites of other people's writing, she and Walter Berry went to Croisset, home for more than forty years to novelist Gustave Flaubert. There she would have seen the garden, in which Flaubert was known to pace up and down his allée *of lime trees, bellowing lines from* Madame Bovary *in order to hear and feel the rhythm and sound of his own prose.*

Grand Hôtel du Rhin

Amiens

Sunday Nov. 8 [1908]

Dear Tonni,

Here I am at Amiens en route for London! We had a beautiful warm calm voyage, & I slept a lot better at sea—Cook [her chauffeur] met us at the dock, & Mr. Berry & I motored up to Paris (of course with the angel dogs), & stopped on the way to see Croisset (where Flaubert lived), & Rouen & les Andelys.[1] I had two hurried days in Paris for Mr. Berry said he wd go over to England with me if I wd go today (as he had to be in Cairo so soon, at his post.) So we have just motored down to Amiens, & are taking the train here, as the run to Boulogne is rather too long. Cook has gone on with the car & will come to London tomorrow.—In London I shall find Mr. James, & he and Mr. Berry & I will have three good days there. Then Mr. Berry leaves for Egypt, & I go to Rye to stay with Mr. James, & then—

Monday Nov. 9th
London.

We arrived last night, & I found a charming apartment awaiting me at the Berkeley. The weather is still glorious, & my rooms are flooded with sunshine, & last night I slept *like a top*. Hurrah! — Today I have my hands full of friends, if the expression is permissible, for Mr. Lapsley is coming up from Cambridge to see me and Mr. Howard Sturgis from Windsor, & they & I, & Mr. Berry & Mr. James, are all lunching and dining together. — London is really very cheerful at this season, for so many people are in town.

I shall spend a few days at Rye with Mr. James, & then go to Mr. Sturgis's for a week, & then come back to London to stop with Lady St. Helier, who has asked me for as long as I will stay, & who always has pleasant people at her house — so it will be very cheerful for me. — [2]

When I got to Paris I found that Harry was off motoring; but I left Mitou and Nicette with his concierge, who is perfectly devoted to them, & where they will be quite happy.

I am glad now that I decided to sail when I did. I am decidedly better already, & sleep is coming back to me without the assistance of "dope," which I can't take because it interferes with my work.

Give my love to Miss Thayer, & tell her I enjoyed my talks with her — I hope you are settling down comfortably, & I am sure Teddy has given you plenty of work to do.

Affly Yrs

E.W.

Address Munroe

1. Les Andelys was the stronghold of Richard the Lionheart at Chateau Gaillard.

2. Lady Saint-Helier, whom Wharton had first met in 1900, entertained many literary and artistic friends, and it was at her home in Portland Place that Wharton was introduced to the historian Sir George Trevelyan and held conversation with such literary lights as Thomas Hardy and John Galsworthy.

The friends who met Wharton and Berry in London were some of her dearest and the closest of her "inner circle." Howard Sturgis, whom Wharton had met in Newport shortly after her marriage, had become a close friend when Henry James brought him to The Mount in 1904. Born in London of Bostonian parents, Sturgis lived all of his life in England at his family estate, Queen's Acre (Qu'acre), where he knitted, crocheted, and wrote novels. Wharton referred to him as "the kindest and strangest of men" (EWAB, 140–41). Gaillard Lapsley (1871–1949), introduced to the Whartons by Walter Berry, was also an expatriate American. Educated at Harvard, Lapsley was a don in medieval English history at Trinity College, Cambridge. Henry James, of course, was by now a dear and trusted friend. These were the men who encouraged Edith Wharton with her writing, consoled with her over Teddy's increasing psychopathy, and gave her some of the most intimate and precious companionship of her life. She delighted in being the lone woman among them.

According to his secretary Theodora Bosanquet, Henry James had been in a slump, depressed, had "lost his spring" for the preface to The Golden Bowl, *on which he was working without enthusiasm. But on 14 November she recorded: "Mr. James recommenced work—after a week's break—breaking ground on a new fiction which opens splendidly. Mrs. Wharton is staying with him" (quoted in Horne, 469). Edith Wharton and Henry James nourished each other both artistically and personally.*

Bahlmann's reply to Wharton's plea for understanding when she fled New York must have contained reassurance and sympathy.

Queen's Acre Windsor
Nov. 17th [1908]

Dear Tonni—

Your sweet letter of the 6th has just reached me here, & I must write at once to say how glad I am to get it, & how touched by what you say.—Of course I knew you wd understand—but if I could have had an hour with you before leaving, I should have felt so much happier!— But I was right to come, I *had* to come. I have pulled myself together already, & am sleeping better, & feeling like a normal being. There come turning-points when one has to go sharply round the corner without looking behind, & this was one.

I am glad you have gotten well over the throes of preparing for the tenants, & also that the servants are placed. The Whartons were so queer about Bagley, & by their indecision I suppose they have lost the chance of getting her good kitchen-maid with her.

I had three very pleasant days in London, with a whole group of friends—Mr. James, Mr. Howard Sturgis, Mr. Gaillard Lapsley, Mr. Berry, who came over with me to stay a few days on his way to Egypt, & Mr. Jacques Blanche, the painter, whom I saw great deal last winter in Paris. We all lunched & dined together, & on the 12th Mr. James, Mr. Berry & I motored down to Rye, taking in Canterbury. The weather was like summer, warm & bright, & I never saw the country lovelier. We have had a succession of such days since, & indeed it has been like Lenox in Sept. ever since I arrived.

On the 13th we motored Mr. Berry over to Dover, & saw him off; & then I stayed on at Rye for three delightful days. Yesterday Mr. James & I motored over here, through the lovely Kent & Sussex landscape, making a detour to see Bodiam Castle, & another to see George Meredith at Box Hill. What was my surprise when Meredith, on hearing my name, sat up-right in his chair (you know he has locomotor ataxia) & holding out both hands, exclaimed: "Why, my dear child, is it you—is it really *you?* I've read every line you've written, & I've always wanted to see you! I'm just flying through France in your motor at this minute."[1]

As our visit was unannounced & I knew this was spontaneous, I was really "emue" [touched] & proud! I wd rather have had it from him than from any one living.

I am here with Mr. Sturgis for a week, in this pleasant peaceful house, & then I go up to London to stay with Lady St Helier till Dec. 4th. After that I don't know what I shall do, but London is so full, owing to Parliament, that I may stay there till Teddy comes. Invitations are showering in, & there are always endless opportunities to see pleasant people.

At any rate, Munroe is always the safest address.

I return the "charity" list. Please raise Reynolds to $30 for his holiday. —

I think I asked you to give F. Thayer $25 a month, as usual. — I shall send her ~~next~~ this week some ms wh. she will send to you for revision, & you will hand to Mr. ~~Scribner~~ Burlingame, please. —

It was very stupid of Macmillan to send those books, as he knew I was here. Will you ask Teddy to bring them back, or rather — No! Send them back to

The Messrs Macmillan

St Martin's Street

London W.C.

& I will get them to give me 6 copies here instead.

I must stop now, as I have several letters to write, & then I am going with Mr. Sturgis to see the King open a new Hall at Eton.[2]

Give my love to Mrs. Winthrop when you see her.

Yr affte

E.W.

Why do you say you have a foreboding of "something worse" than my being away this winter? If you mean that we may stay for the summer, I hope, in that case, you won't object to coming out to see me? — You don't know how, meanwhile, I miss your devoted hand for notes & letters!

1. George Meredith (1828–1909) was an English novelist and poet and a friend of such diverse writers as Thomas Hardy, Dante Gabriel Rossetti, and Leslie Stephen. Edith was proud of this encounter and told the story in several letters to friends.

2. This was Memorial Hall, dedicated to the memory of the Eton men who had died in South Africa.

Here we see Wharton completely immersed in the London literary and social scene. Not only did she attend the king and queen's opening of Memorial

Hall, but she also met men and women of letters, politicians, and nobility with equal zest and appreciation. Arthur James, Lord Balfour was a former prime minister; the same office would later be held by Winston Churchill, then thirty-three and recently married to the niece of Wharton's host, Lady St. Helier. Wharton also mentions a new acquaintance, John Hugh Smith, who would become, and remain, a close friend. Henry James wrote to Hugh Smith: "Ah, my dear young man, you have made friends with Edith Wharton. I congratulate you. You may find her difficult, but you will find nothing stupid in her and nothing small" (Lubbock, 56).

52 Portland Place W

Dec. 4th [1908]

Dear Tonni—I was just going to send you a report of my doings when your letter of Nov. 23rd came.—I fancy you are au courant of what I have been doing since, as I asked Teddy to send you one or two letters in which I described some of the things that I thought wd amuse you— This is a wonderful life, so crowded & interesting & congenial; & the bright weather we have had till quite lately has made it seem actually like the season!

Lady St. Helier's kindness is really inexhaustible. She keeps open house, & racks her brain to find people who may interest & amuse me. And then every one is so hospitable that one hasn't a minute—or a mouthful—alone!

I had a delightful Sunday at Cliveden, where I met all manner of interesting people, including the great Mr. Balfour, who is quite charming, & so simple & "cosy." The place, you know, belongs now to the young Waldorf Astors.[1]

Since then the week has been a steady rush. Mr. James came up to spend a night with Lady St. H., & we dined with the Macmillans [Edith's English publisher and his wife], where we met Lady Ritchie (Thackeray's daughter) & some other "literaries." Then we had a pleasant dinner here: Winston Churchill, "Lulu" Harcourt (one of the Cabinet Ministers), Ld & Lady Middleton, the Duchess of St. Albans, & the

J. M. Barries, & Sir Schoenberg McDonnell, whom I knew before & especially like.² We also had a delightful luncheon while Mr. James was here, with the Duchess of Sutherland, Edmund Gosse, Sir Alfred Lyall, Ld Carlisle, &c—And so it goes.—~~Tomorrow~~ Today I lunch with with Lady Bective, who is quite charming, & tomorrow with Lady Pollock.³ Tomorrow afternoon Mr. James comes up to town again, & I motor him down to Windsor, where we spend Sunday with Mr. Sturgis. On Monday we all come up to drive with the Barries & see his play, "What Every Woman Knows." On Tuesday I lunch with Mr. Gosse at the House of Lords, & we have a big dinner here.⁴ On Wed. I dine with a clever young friend, Mr. John Hugh Smith, who is on the whole the most intelligent being I have met here; on Thursday I go to spend the day with Ld & Lady Burghclere at their place in the country; on Saturday to Ld & Lady Elcho for Sunday.⁵—Yesterday the Duchess of Sutherland arranged to have me meet Herbert Trench, the poet whose poems I admire so much, & whom I greatly wanted to see.⁶ He is charming, & with Mr. Gosse, Mr. Thurston Temple (the novelist) & my young friend J. H. Smith, makes up the most *luminous* group I have found here.—Last night George Alexander sent us stalls for his play ("A Builder of Bridges" by Sutro) & Mr. Mallick dined here & went with us.—We are also to try to go to Wimbledon to see Ld Munley if we can manage it before I leave.—

With all this I am sleeping better & better, & consequently feeling better by day. The fog has been thick for the last three days, but it does not rain, & I get a good walk every morning.—I am sorry to hear what you say of Fanny T. & Mrs. Morse.—Alas for such poor little morbid miseries! And how they point to the wasted emotions in women's lives.

I'm *very* sorry about Ella's cold. If she wants to go off for a week I'll pay for it—with her mother if necessary. Explain to Teddy & it will be all right.—I am glad to report Mitou & Nicette in the best of health!—

I don't know when I shall go to Paris. Not as long as pleasant things turn up here.—

I wonder if you wd mind sending this letter to Miss Norton. I know it will amuse her to hear of all I have been doing, & I am frightfully pen weary with endless notes & letters, & *no Bahlmann!!*

Yr affte E.W.

I left the "engagement list" thinking you might use it as a Xmas present. I don't want it, so do as you please with it.

I reflect that I wrote to Miss Norton a day or two ago—but do send this to Mr. Winthrop, because I wanted to write him today, & my arm is too stiff. Tear off this last half sheet before sending to him.

1. William Waldorf Astor II (1879–1952) and his American wife, Nancy Langhorne Astor (1879–1964).

2. The playwright James Barrie (1860–1937) was the creator of Peter Pan.

3. Lady Bective was so charming that Howard Sturgis began using the word "bective" to denominate charming people. Lord and Lady Pollock were friends with Henry James and Sally Norton, among other of Wharton's friends.

4. The author and critic Edmund Gosse (1849–1928) was librarian of the House of Lords.

5. Both Lord and Lady Burghclere were writers, he of plays, she on historical subjects. Lord Hugo and Lady Mary Elcho entertained all the aristocracy at their stately Gloucestershire home, Stanway. Wharton and Lady Elcho (later Lady Wemyss) would become close friends.

6. The playwright and poet Frederick Herbert Trench (1865–1923) would shortly become artistic director of the Haymarket Theater.

Dijon
Dec. 24 [1908]

Dear Tonni,

We are off—Mr. Sturgis & his cousin Mr. Haynes-Smith—for a brief dash to Hyères & back, to use up the week before I get possession of the rue de Varenne. I left England (& Mr. James) with Mr. Sturgis on the 20th, going to Harry's for two nights in Paris. Then we three started for Dijon, spending yesterday here, in delicious sunshine, seeing all the beauties of this wonderful old place. Today we are going to lunch with the Comtesse Arthur de Vogüé at their château of Commarin, near here, & then we motor on to Lyons.[1] Tomorrow we go to Avignon, &

the next day to Hyères, or rather Costebelle to wish the Bourgets merry Xmas. Then we shall return by Nimes & Autun to Paris. I am feeling much stronger than in England. There I was sleeping very well, & feeling soothed & peaceful, but, as I always do in that heavy climate, rather "saggy" & inert, whereas in France I feel light & active. So now my cure is complete, I hope!

My last days in England were crowded & pleasant. I think I wrote you from Stanway, where I spent three delightful days with Lady Elcho & a pleasant party. The house is a perfect example of an unchanged Elizabethan country house, & the park lovely, with exquisite views over the Cotswolds. I motored back to Windsor by way of Gloucester & Fairford, & then went to London again for a last brief visit to Lady St. Helier, where the gaiety at once began again, & kept up until I left. I think I saw everybody worth seeing in London in the course of my various visits to Portland Place!—

There were great times when we met the angels on arriving in Paris. They were wild with joy, well, fat & happy. Now they are off with me, of course, & having a glorious time. This reminds me: will you get from Richards a bottle of Mitou's mysterious "bladder medicine," & ask Teddy to bring it out? His bottle got broken before he had taken a sip!—

I hope you are going to have a good Christmas, & wish I could have sent you a little personal present—but the Custom House makes even a book impossible.

Your last letter reached me just as I was leaving Paris, & I appreciate it, & understand *perfectly,* & promise not to worry about you again. So there!

Yr affte E.W.

1. Marie Adele Hermengilde de Contades, wife of Arthur, Comte de Vogüé. The comtesse's father-in-law, Eugene Melchior, whom Wharton had met in 1895, was a noted author and Academician, and a friend of Wharton's friends Paul and Minnie Bourget. The Château de Commarin is an enormous moated castle that has been continuously occupied by the de Vogüé family for twenty-six generations.

My Dear Governess

Avignon

Dec. 26 [1908]

Dear Tonni,

Your beautiful Heart followed me here (as I know it does every-where!), & overtook me this morning. I refer in this instance to the lemon verbena heart, wh filled the room with a delicious mystical fra-grance before it was even out of its wrappings. Never did I smell any-thing so sweet! Thank you a thousand times. I am grateful for the Ro-man present, wh. I look forward to seeing before many months; but I'm sure it can't be more exquisite than this.

I wrote you from Dijon so this is only a word of thanks, & an answer to yr question about the books & the print. Please tell Reynolds to mail the books to me (registered) to 58 Rue de Varenne, or if there are too many, to send in one parcel by the American Express Co. In the latter case he might send them to you, & you could send by the Am Ex. Co. from N.Y.—Ask Teddy to bring me the ancestral engraving.—

We had a delightful luncheon at the Château de Commarin, near Dijon, with my friends the Arthur de Voguës; the owners of the hôtel de Voguë, of guide-book fame, at Dijon. Commarin is a beautiful old moated château, full of treasures & untouched by the Revolution. Thence we motored to Lyons, & yesterday came here—in a deluge, alas! But it is clear again, though not as beautiful as the first day you & I saw Avignon long ago. Do you remember?

Affly Yrs

E.W.

I hope I have already told you that you did right in sending the French books to Lenoxdale—& thank you so much for covering them. I'm de-lighted that Ella is better.

If you get this too late to send the engraving by Teddy, send by express, please.

More than three years elapse between the last letter and the next. Anna Bahl-mann came to Paris in the fall of 1909, and in November she and Wharton toured Germany. Later in the winter, Bahlmann was pressed into service as companion to Teddy Wharton's sister Nancy, who was in France. Edith Wharton's emotionally intense years continued as she battled with Teddy's family over his health and the proper treatment for him. She endured Teddy's rapid mood swings, his wild behavior punctuated with fits of tears and remorse, and meanwhile attempted to conduct an affair with the mercurial and elusive Morton Fullerton. Toward the end of 1909, Teddy confessed to having gambled with his wife's money, effectively embezzling $50,000. He resigned from managing her affairs and replaced the money with funds he had just received as a legacy from his mother's estate, but this would begin an ongoing argument over whether he should be able to regain control of his wife's finances. To Teddy, his usefulness as a husband, indeed his manhood, was at stake.

The Whartons decided to sell their New York home and buy an apartment in the rue de Varenne, across the street from where they had been renting. Teddy agreed to try a sanatorium on Lake Constance, in Switzerland, in June of 1910. But he was unhappy there, and in July Bahlmann was dispatched to visit him and try to persuade him to stay, which he did for a short while longer. The following month Bahlmann sailed to New York to close up the Whartons' house. Their move would leave her homeless.

What was she to do? She had always lived in New York. Bahlmann knew that Edith Wharton needed her secretarial skills and Teddy Wharton needed her company and reassurance. Yet a move to Paris would mean leaving friends and community, losing the income and pleasure she derived from teaching, and putting an ocean between herself and her family. Her former pupil Pauline Robinson expressed the dislocation: "It gives me a pang to think that I shall never see again the books, and all your things, in their right places — it is such a wrench to change one's life. . . . I can assure you Anna [Pauline's sister] and I would sadly miss our talks with you. They have helped us — and your stories have been responsible for much of my happiness" (27 August 1910). In the end Anna Bahlmann followed Edith Wharton and remained in her service for the rest of Anna's life.

In Paris, Walter Berry moved in to 53 rue de Varenne for several months, perhaps simply because he needed a place to stay, perhaps in order to ameliorate Teddy Wharton's erratic, potentially dangerous behavior toward his

My Dear Governess

wife. Other treatments were tried, but to no avail. By summer 1911 the couple retreated to The Mount in an attempt to find a situation that would make Teddy happy. But his behavior was so capricious and untenable that Edith began a paper trail to document his instability.

In these days before xerography, Bahlmann copied important handwritten letters so that Wharton could retain a copy. After a particularly heated and thorough conversation with Teddy about financial matters in which he declared that he no longer wished to be in charge of them, Edith resolved to document their financial relationship and wrote letters of understanding to him and to his brother William explaining exactly what the couple had agreed to. When, just hours later, an agitated Teddy became vituperative, accusing his wife of humiliating him, Edith again wrote to William describing this reversal and Teddy's refusal to abide by the agreement just made. These are painful letters, rational and controlled portraits of Teddy's desperate mental condition and Edith's attempt to be fair and yet to protect herself without unnecessarily agitating Teddy or his family. The copies we have of these letters exist in Anna Bahlmann's calm and clear handwriting.[1]

Despite the turmoil in her personal life, Wharton was quite productive in the ensuing years. In 1911–12 she published the short story collection Tales of Men and Ghosts; *a half-dozen short stories in magazines; several poems; and* Ethan Frome, *which she had written initially in French as a linguistic exercise.* The Reef *would be published in November 1912, and* The Custom of the Country *would begin serialization in January 1913.*

1. The letters can be seen at the Beinecke Library, YCAL Wharton, and they can be read in *LEW,* 245–51.

53, Rue de Varenne. Tel.
706–13
[1912?][1]

Dear Tonni—

I didn't want to tell you of Docky's death till you had your other little friend in your arms to comfort you.—White will tell you it was the most perfect doggie-death ever seen.

He romped, barked & bustled through his last day, & had a good supper, & stole some of Nicette's. Then his heart suddenly & painlessly failed, & he dropped asleep & *stopped* in his sleep. He is buried in a nice quiet garden at Chantilly.

I hope you will find your rooms more comfortable. I have put a gas stove in the *bathroom* so that it can be warmed instantly in the morning, but I wish the fire kept up there during the day. Please let this order be carried out by the servants.

Affy

E.W.

1. This is a personalized Paris pneumatic slip, which ordinarily would have been sent through pneumatic tubes under the city. However, it does not bear any official stamps and is addressed simply to Miss Bahlmann, with no address, so it seems plausible that it was left for Anna when she was traveling.

In February 1912, Bahlmann was visiting Wiesbaden when she was called back to the rue de Varenne: "Mr. Wharton is having one of his quiet spells & frequently asking for me, & I shall be only too glad if I can relieve his wife, at least for a time" (card to William Bahlmann, 17 February 1912). Later Wharton spent a month motoring to and around Spain with her friend the Comtesse Rosa de Fitz-James. Bahlmann remained in the rue de Varenne, sharing, with Nancy Wharton and White, the care of Teddy.

Hotel Ritz, Paseo del
Prado Madrid
Sunday April 14 [1912]

Dear Tonni,

I have actually done some work for you, & shall send it back from Biarritz tomorrow.

I have changed my plans & decided to go back to Hendaye by train with Mme de Fitz-James & then motor with her to Biarritz. I shall probably stay at Biarritz a few days, as I want a rest after all I've been doing &

My Dear Governess

seeing, & I also want to go on a little with The Reef. Yesterday we went to Toledo, & had a long glorious day there. It is wonderful, but the general effect is perhaps a little less out-of-the-world than the incredible Avila. However, it's all interesting, & I mean to come back next year & see it all. As for the climate of Madrid, it seems made for me. I never felt so well anywhere. It seems to carry me on wings, & if I were free I shd stay here another month just for the sake of my work.

We have had only one rainy day since we left. Now the weather is glorious again, & luckily cooler. —

Tell Teddy the horses, mules, & mokes are *never* yelled at or beaten.[1] The dogs also are numerous & cheerful. —

Thank you for your letter, & for enclosing my mail. I'm so glad dear Tucker is well. Do give her plenty of Bois-rides!
Affly Yrs

E.W.

I gave up motoring back because the roads are so bumpy that I was afraid I shd be rather tired, & also because the Auto Club here told me I had [better?] not try to go to Saragossa, which is what I chiefly wanted. The roads beat N.Y. State, & the streets of Madrid resemble Park Ave when we first lived there. Spaniards must feel quite at home in the U.S.

1. "Mokes" presumably referred to donkeys, but in the mid-nineteenth century the slang term was also applied to Negroes.

In early May, Teddy Wharton returned to the United States and Edith Wharton proceeded with legal action. The Whartons were granted a French divorce in March 1913, and while it would have been a relief, it could not have been easy. On 12 June 1913 she wrote to her friend Eunice Maynard, after thanking her for her supportive letter: "My chief sensation now is one of utter weariness. I suppose I shall come to life again before long, but at present I'm rather numb." A second disruption, also painful, came when her brother Harry disavowed her irrevocably, probably at the instigation of his new wife, whom Edith Wharton had never met. She thus found herself with no home in America and bereft of two of her closest family members.

Nevertheless she worked, and she found other friends with whom to travel. Morton Fullerton had left Europe and, more recently, so had Anna Bahlmann, who was at this time in Plymouth, Massachusetts, proofreading galleys of The Custom of the Country. *Wharton went to Germany with the art historian Bernard Berenson (1865–1959) and also, presumably, with Gross, who was by then in her sixties. Her comment in the next letter about not wanting to make the long trip home from Vienna "alone" is a tiny hint that her servants, sometimes including Anna Bahlmann, are not really people, not able to keep her adequate company.*

The house in Epping, England, of which she speaks is Coopersale, a country home near Hill Hall, the home of her friend Mary Hunter; Wharton is considering purchasing the house and settling in England.

Hotel Esplanade Berlin

Aug. 26 [1913]

Dear Tonni,

I was so pleased to hear from Fanny Thayer today that you were really in Plymouth at last!—It was too bad that you had to be in N.Y. so long in the heat. But I hope the good Plymouth breezes have blown away that unpleasant memory.

We have had a very delightful week. Weimar is charming & the Garten Haus [of Goethe] gave me a thrill—& so did the very lovely Tieffurt Park & the dear little Schloss! At Dresden, at the Bellevue Hotel, with its perfect garden, we had three good days; & then we came here. We had the luck to arrive at the moment of the re-opening of the opera, & we have already heard Der Rosenkavalier (ravishing, & *so* well done), & Rheingold. Tonight we have Walküre, & the next night Siegfied & Götterdämmerung, & after that Strauss's last opera, Ariadne. In between they give (tomorrow) Faust (Part 1) at the Deutsches Theater—so you can picture our week!—

Next Monday I am going back to Paris, on my way to Le Touquet, where I want to spend a few days with Bessy.[1] Dr. Berenson goes back to

Italy, via Austria, & I shd. go as far as Vienna with him if I didn't dread the long trip back alone. As it is, I shall stop two days at Badenweiler to let Gross go & see her niece & the new baby at Mulhausen close by. After that, I think I may go to England to buy my place near Epping. This little trip has been pleasant, but wandering summers are not for me. — You can do just as you like about sailing on the 1st or 11th. Don't bother a bit about the price, but come just when you want. If I find it impracticable to go to England with Tucker, I'll wait till your return. There is no hurry about that.

Please thank Fanny T. for her letter. I am so glad to hear that Mrs. Morse is rather better. — I have just cabled Scribner — as I feel less tired — that I will try to revise the remaining chapters of the "Custom" (for the book) from the magazine proofs I have here, & send them this week. So you'll understand if they don't get you to do this part.
Yrs affly,

E.W. (over)

Of course you will have to do the last two chapters, as there will be no time to send me proofs of these.

1. Elizabeth Frelinghuysen Davis Lodge, widow of Edith's friend George Cabot (Bay) Lodge. Widowed with three young children after only nine years of marriage, Bessy was lonely.

Hotel Esplanade Berlin
Aug 29 [1913]

Dear Tonni,

I am glad to get your first Plymouth letter, but so sorry the heat has followed you there. I hope it is long since over. Here the temperature is perfect — & Berlin the wonder-city of Europe!

After rashly cabling Scribner the other day that I wd after all revise the last chapters for the book, I decided, on re-reading my unrevised duplicate galleys, that it was much wiser to let you do it from the magazine version; & I cabled them to disregard my first cable. — But I have just rec'd duplicate galleys of the last two chapters, & these are still so fresh in my mind that I have revised them & hurried them off to Scribner by this post, with a line to say that they are to be used for the book *if not too late.* The rest I leave to you.

When you give your list[1]

1. The paper is torn here and the rest of the letter is missing.

Two important friends of Edith Wharton's are introduced here, and both would become frequent visitors and traveling companions. Percy Lubbock (1879–1965), whom Wharton had met at Howard Sturgis's home in 1906, was a literary critic who would be best known for his The Craft of Fiction *in 1921 and, later,* Portrait of Edith Wharton *(1947), which some critics argue is an unnecessarily malicious representation of its subject. Lubbock would be a good friend to Wharton during and after the war, but they would become somewhat estranged by his 1926 marriage to a woman whom Wharton did not like.*

Robert Norton (c. 1866–1946) was an Englishman, a diplomat who retired early to pursue his love of painting. He would remain a friend of Wharton's, traveling with her and editing, with her and their mutual friend Gaillard Lapsley, the collection Eternal Passion in English Poetry, *which appeared after Wharton's death.*

53 Rue de Varenne
Oct 12 [1913]

Dear Tonni,

Your letter of the 3d came yesterday, & I am very glad you have decided to stay on. Take as many more weeks (or months even) as you want, for Fannie Thayer must need some one really sensible & helpful more than ever before, & I am so glad for you both that you can be together. *Do* try to get her to Lakewood for ten days at least & go with her & make her comfortable.

I shd like to make my contribution $100, so please [ask] H[erman]

E[dgar] for another $50.—I've just had a big unexpected dividend from Macmillan—& I'm sure the Custom will be a gold-mine! So allons-y![1]

Give my love to F.T., & tell her she'll be able to do much more for Mrs. Morse later if she will take care of herself now.

All well here. I have had Percy Lubbock & next week Mrs. Hunter & Robert Norton are coming.

Tucker looks like a white rose, & plays like a kitten!—Lovely weather.

Yr Affte

E.W.

1. Wharton's October royalties for *The Custom of the Country* amounted to four hundred pounds sterling and were deposited into her account some time after 17 October 1913 (Towheed, 150).

We do not know what difficulties Wharton's typist, Fanny Thayer, was facing. These letters give just a tiny glimpse of the way unmarried, middle-class women had to cobble together a living by being companions, governesses, and secretaries, much as Lily Bart had tried, unsuccessfully, in Wharton's novel The House of Mirth.

Wharton traveled to New York in December 1913 for the wedding of her beloved niece Beatrix Jones and Max Farrand. Trix had met Farrand when she was designing some of the grounds for Princeton University, where he taught history and was at work on his classic study The Framing of the Constitution *(1913). Trix was as strong and determined as her mother and aunt, and when Farrand's sister-in-law took a private peek at her working, she is said to have exclaimed: "If that lady really wants Max, she'll get him!" (Brown, 102). Trix might have been daunted by her own parents' experience of marriage, or by her Aunt Edith's recent divorce, but by all accounts hers was a very happy marriage.*

This letter corrects the common assumption that Edith attended the wedding.

Ritz-Carlton Hotel,
Madison Avenue & Forty
Sixth Street New York
Dec 23rd [1913]

Dear Tonni,

Here I am in the whirlpool, bobbing about like a bewildered bit of straw! But anyhow (with all the Unberufens in the dictionary, be it said!) I seem to be better, & my cold, after a last furious kick in the steamer, has apparently stayed behind in Hoboken.

We had a *perfect* trip, as smooth as this blotting pad, but the old ship just wouldn't move—she stayed on one wave, & we arrived two days late even for *her!* My explanation is that she is to be taken off after this trip, & put on the Boston line, & she just couldn't bear it!!—

I found a lot of fashionable acquaintances on board; all surprised & grieved that I didn't play bridge & dance the tango (including Mrs. Wm Goddard (aetat 70), & I had a glorious time reading about Prehistoric Man, & wondering why the race had retrogressed so fast in the last 40,000 years.

Walter met me at the dock & we were up at the hotel in no time, in a beautiful Looey suite—& Gross slid through the Custom House like a letter in the post. Imagine my distress at finding that Minnie had been very ill for the last 10 days with influenza & abscess in the ear, & that Trix had been married almost at her bedside (Minnie just managed to get into an armchair for the ceremony) with no one present but John Cadwalader & the servants![1] She (Minnie) is now improving rapidly, & I am lunching there today to meet the bride & groom (just back from Lakewood)—but for a week before the wedding she was having a much worse case of influenza than mine, & 3 days before, they told her it was utterly impossible for her to go out. Luckily they had time to put off the breakfast & the company—but you can fancy how harassing & distressing it all was.

I hear nothing but pleasant things of Farrand, & everyone says that Trix is in a state of bliss. Tant mieux!—

The weather is heavenly—as warm as Oct.—& N.Y. certainly has improved "au physique" more than I had thought possible. — I hope you are all getting on well & peacefully là bas, & I was so glad to get your good cable about Charlie.

I wanted so much to write to Bessy by this post, but I am submerged these first days, & still, of course, rather tired, as I had a bad return of bronchitis on the ship — so will you please send her this letter with my love, & ask her to share it with you — & thank her for her Xmas card, rec'd yesterday.

With best love & 1914 "vous"[2]

Yrs Ever,

E.W.

I've just had such a good visit from dear old Bagley, & have been trying to telephone F. Thayer, but not successfully yet. I am dining out every night, & shall be glad of my quiet week on the France when the time comes, I fancy. I sail on Jan. 7th. Everybody here wearing aigrettes, including *Bagley!!*[3]

1. John Lambert Cadwalader, a cousin of Minnie's, acted as financial adviser and unofficial guardian to Minnie and Trix after the divorce from Wharton's brother, Frederic Jones. Upright, stern, and a well-respected lawyer, he was instrumental in helping Trix to discover and achieve her career as a landscape designer. At his death just a few months after the wedding, he made one of his largest bequests, $20,000, to Trix.

2. A play on the French *vous,* you, and *voeux,* wishes.

3. According to Katherine Joslin, an *aigrette* was the tufted crest of an egret, worn on hats. See her discussion of hats, 73–76.

In 1913 Anna Bahlmann contracted with Scribner's to translate a novella by the German author Gottfried Keller, Romeo und Julia auf dem Dorfe *as* A Village Romeo and Juliet. *It provided her with her own project and money earned from someone other than Wharton. Bahlmann was unaware that the Scribner's editor appealed to Wharton to "limber up" the language a little, which she did, quietly. But Anna Bahlmann was proud to have her name as translator of this tale of forbidden love between two poor young vil-*

lagers. She was allowed a half-dozen copies of the book to be sent to friends;
that she had one of them sent to Morton Fullerton suggests a warm relation
between them. His letter of praise to her reveals much about his character and
style: "I congratulate you with real joy on your having attached so beautifully
your name to so beautiful a thing. I congratulate you and thank you, for I
should never have known A Village Romeo and Juliet *but for you. I drank it*
with ecstasy, & then came the feeling of gratitude to you for having thought to
hand me the crystal cup, bubbling over with sunlight and all the divine illu-
sions of our first loves" (29 March 1914). The letter continues, equally fulsome.

On 29 March 1914 Anna Bahlmann sailed from Marseilles to Algiers with
Wharton, chauffeur Charles Cook, Wharton's new maid Elise Devinck, and
friends Gaillard Lapsley (who made it only as far as Algiers before turning
back with the grippe) and Percy Lubbock.[1] *They traveled from Algiers to*
the oasis Ben Saada, where they saw "a sort of epitome of it all—the cara-
vans of camels, the nomads, the wonderful white figures in the silent sun-
baked streets, the brilliant violet-&-rose-&-orange women washing in the
'oued,' the Ouled-Naïls dancing ventriloquently on a white roof-terrace in
the moonlight, their hand fluttering like tied birds . . ." (EW to Morton
Fullerton, 9 April 1914, LEW, 315–16). They saw the desert, went northeast to
Timgad and Constantine, then on to Tebessa and Tunis, Kabylia, "interest-
ing on account of the beautiful & extraordinarily picturesque Berbers" (EW
to BB, 16 April 1914, LEW, 318). It was also during this trip that Wharton
was awakened in the night by a man bending over her in bed, intent per-
haps on robbery, perhaps something more dangerous. It terrified her, but she
carried on with the trip without complaint.

While in Algiers they encountered Georges Rodier, a friend of Henry
James. Rodier would keep up a correspondence with Bahlmann during the
War and reference memories of meeting her at the Casbah.

Anna Bahlmann left North Africa and returned to Paris ahead of the
other travelers.

1. I use the spelling of Elise's family name as transcribed by Lee (800 n. 4)
rather than "Duvlenk," as transcribed by Lewis.

Majestic-Hotel Tunis
Monday April 29th [1914]

Dear Tonni,

I hope you had a fairly smooth crossing, or that, if you didn't, the memory of Dougga [Tunisia] partly consoled you for what one has to pay to see this enchanting country. — We have had three uneventful days since you left. One afternoon we motored to Zaghouan, which is lovely, the next I went to take tea with Mme de Chabaunes at Utique — not exciting — & yesterday we went back to Kairouan & had a delicious afternoon there seeing again quietly what we had had to gobble in haste before.

Our friend Hassan, smaller & grimier than ever, joined us before we had taken six steps from the door of our hotel, & acted as our guide, to the great amusement of the whole [grown-up?] population of Kairouan, to whom he is evidently very well known.

Tonight we sail for Naples, dropping Rodier en route at Palermo, and within the week we shall probably be in Rome. At Naples I expect a barrel-full of letters, for I've had none here for eight days!

I enclose some nonsense for you to type — you can judge by the date whether you had better send it to Rome or Florence, but I should think Rome would be safe. I don't expect to get to Florence before the 10th or 12th.

How Tucker must have celebrated your return! I hope you have treated her to many taxi trips. Do go & see Minnie Bourget & tell her all about our journey. — Bessy you will see of course.[1]

Give my love to Gross & tell her all goes well.

Yours affly,

E.W.

Don't register the copy you return.

1. Bahlmann was probably giving lessons to one or more of Bessy Lodge's children.

Anna Bahlmann was called to Manassas, Virginia, to care for her old friend Louise Schultz in her final illness. Evidently it was a difficult situation, made more so by family pressures and by the extreme heat of a Virginia summer. Despite Wharton's desire to remove Bahlmann from the situation, Bahlmann stayed on until the end, 8 August 1914. Her loyalty to her friend earned her a small legacy, and it also meant that by the time she was available to leave the United States, Europe was at war and she was unable to return to Paris.

Wharton was just back from a three-week trip through Spain with Walter Berry. She had rented Stocks, the English country house of the novelist Mrs. Humphrey Ward in the little town of Tring, for the summer and fall and she was on the verge of making the move there, having closed up her apartment on the rue de Varenne and sent the servants ahead to England.[1] This letter, written three days after Austria-Hungary declared war on Serbia and just one day before Germany declared war on Russia, suggests in its mundane discussion of travel arrangements that the gravity of the situation in Europe had yet to make itself felt in a personal way.

1. Mary Augusta Arnold Ward (1851–1920) was as erudite as Wharton, if more moralistic, and a successful novelist and public intellectual.

Hotel de Crillon Paris
July 31 [1914]

Dear Tonni,

Both your letters to Stocks were forwarded promptly, & your account of the situation wrings my heart — & more, much more, on your account than on anyone else's. I am so thankful you got the nice niece to come & take control, & I do hope that by this time your poor patient heroic friend is released, & out of reach of tormenting daughters-in-law & all the last base miseries. I wish you could have helped her across the breach — but of course in the circumstances, you couldn't.

I want to get you as soon as possible out of the air of sadness & sordidness you are plunged in. Don't you think you'd better come over to Tring as soon as you can? I'm sure the country quiet there will do you

My Dear Governess

good. I go the day after tomorrow, & expect Minnie & a number of other people.

My trip was delightful to the end, but we got back to a very depressing state of things here. This morning there seems a *slight* hope of avoiding war—more than that can't be said.

Cook's wife is very ill, & poor Gross, here alone, had a nightmarish time getting her to the Am. Hospital. Apparently it is "alcoholic paralysis"! A pleasant discovery for a bridegroom!

Tucker, well & springy & merry, & as white as a snow-ball, sends best love.

As I do—

Yrs affly,

E.W.

6

"This sudden incredible catastrophe"

AUGUST 1914 TO APRIL 1916

Events of 1914 marked the beginning of the end of the more than forty years of companionship between Edith Wharton and Anna Bahlmann. As early as 1911 Wharton was indicating in letters to others that she found Bahlmann's company sometimes trying, sometimes a little boring. By now Wharton had many friends whose humor, intellect, and social standing more closely matched her own. It's no wonder that, with less of Wharton's conversation and few other friends or pupils with whom to discuss what she read, Bahlmann's imagination may have begun to stiffen along with her arthritic knees. And for Wharton, with the responsibility of Teddy's well-being gone, her need for Bahlmann's presence diminished. She even used the occasion of a visit to the marketplace on their recent trip to Algiers to make fun of Bahlmann in a letter to Gaillard Lapsley. Wharton recounted to him Bahlmann's misunderstanding of a string of ambergris beads that Wharton had purchased from a prostitute at one of the souks. She reports the conversation thus:

> These chaplets are said to make the negresses irresistible to the Arabs.
>
> *A.* Oh — is it a kind of charm?

Me. No — it's simply that they smell so awfully good.

A.   (puzzled, but still seeking.) Oh — I thought it was like something that has been blessed by the Pope. (Percy's hilarity has to be choked off.) (23 April 1914, *LEW,* 320–21).

Anna Bahlmann's confirmed innocence about sexual matters was the source of Wharton's somewhat malicious humor.

Nevertheless, the women remained closely connected. Wharton continued her concern for Bahlmann and still employed her secretarial skills, so that there ensued a little argument about whether Bahlmann, while in America, should continue to receive her salary. The war was escalating in Europe, and Wharton was raising funds for its victims. Bahlmann, having received the small legacy from Mrs. Schultz, and being unable to return to Paris, felt she could and should be independent, and so she refused to draw on Wharton's account. She settled in New York at the Martha Washington Hotel, read proofs of Wharton's long story "Bunner Sisters," and knitted bandages and raised funds for war charities.[1] Wharton chided her about the money (as she comfortably might; "Bunner Sisters" alone earned her $2,000, compared with Bahlmann's monthly salary of $150) and wrote news of the war and of the latest dog, Tucker.

The following letter was written on the day Germany declared war on France; the next day Germany invaded Belgium.[2]

1. Bahlmann had a suggestion to make about the story, and found it wiser to tell the editor Robert Bridges rather than Wharton herself: "I wonder if you could suggest to Mrs. Wharton that no German ever refers to this country as 'the States' — (Galley 7 — chapter III.) The English and Canadians use that expression, while a German always speaks of this country as 'America': now & then, but rarely, as 'the United States'" (21 November 1914).

2. Most of my information about the chronology of the war comes from the Web site www.firstworldwar.com (Duffy). See also March and Halsey.

Dear Tonni,

Here we are blocked in Paris! We were to leave yesterday morning, when suddenly mobilization began & we are here till goodness knows when. Many others are in the same plight, & as hotels & restaurants are rapidly closing, owing to the enrolment of every valid man in France, we are laying in provisions for camping in the rue de Varenne.

Still, it is likely that foreigners will be able to leave in two or three weeks, when the mobilization is complete. But, if I get away myself, I shall not be allowed to take my motors, & they may be requisitioned at any moment.

I managed to get White over yesterday (without any luggage) to England, to take things in hand at Stocks, where I have the servants & all my clothes, except what I had on the motor trip.[1] If I find we can't get to England, I shall dismiss all my servants & hand the house back to Mrs. Ward!

Minnie Jones is here, also blocked, & many other people I know. It is extremely exciting & interesting, & the general feeling among French people is: "Oh, let's fight & have it over."—England's lukewarmness alone makes the situation alarming. If she doesn't act energetically today, no one can say what awful disaster may follow, & it is incredible that even the Little Englanders shouldn't see it.

Walter is looking after me, & lots of French men I know are here—Mr. Taigny, the Margeries, St. André, Rodier, & of course Fullerton.[2]—Everybody comes in every day, & of course there is only one subject of conversation. There has never been a war like it—& may never be again, for it may do away with the cursed armaments.

Don't worry, we'll [sic] all well, including little Tucker.
Yrs affly,

E.W.

1. It is interesting to note that Alfred White, long the personal servant to Teddy Wharton, should have chosen to remain with Edith rather than return to America with Teddy.

2. Olivier Taigny (1863–1941) was a diplomat whom Edith had met at Rosa de Fitz-James's salon. Pierre de Margerie (1861–1942) was secretary general of the Ministry of Foreign Affairs in France and was the one to receive Germany's declaration of war. R. W. B. Lewis describes Alfred de Saint-André as "a man with no visible achievements, no vocation, and for that matter no very large income," but good company and a connoisseur of out-of-the-way restaurants (*EWAB*, 196–97).

The Battle of the Frontiers, comprising offensive attacks on five fronts, began with the successful French invasion of Mulhaus on 7 August, sparking great celebration in France. Next came the French invasion of Lorraine on 14 August. The Battle of Mons, begun on 23 August, was the last Battle of the Frontiers and the first offensive by the British.

Although most of her staff was in England, Edith Wharton had Catherine Gross and Elise Devinck, her housekeeper and personal maid, reopen her Paris apartment until they could travel. She was one of an estimated 7,500 Americans marooned in Paris, but she neither complained nor sat still. She cabled Scribner's *to determine whether the editors would like her impressions of the first days of war, and she organized the first of the numerous war charities that she would oversee in the years to come. This was an* ouvroir, *a workroom, for women who had lost their livelihoods when the mobilization closed down businesses and took their husbands, fathers, and brothers away to war. The women were in critical need of work to earn their living, and Wharton's ouvroir supplied them with a very small salary as well as lunch. Most of the sewing went to the French Red Cross and other charities. The stories of German atrocities for the most part proved to be exaggerations (Price, 15, 16, 25, 31–32).*

53, Rue de Varenne

Aug. 15 [1914]

Dear Tonni,

I haven't written before because I felt that my letter would only rot in a mail bag at Havre; but now that Britannia rules the wave, heaven bless her, I hasten to send a signal over it.

As you will have guessed, I was caught here by this sudden incredible catastrophe, & my only regret is that I am saddled with Stocks, as this is the heart of the universe at present, & I'd so much rather stay here. But my luggage & household are all over there, & I shall try to get off in about a week, when the rush is over. Unluckily they are so strict at the English Custom House that it seems useless to try & take Tucker, & as the only alternative is to leave her here with Gross (who would have her friend Eugène's wife with her) I shan't go till it seems really sure that the Allies have the Teuton Savages right in their hold. I'm not going to leave my Gross to the chance of a siege—but just now it doesn't look much as if William II were going to get as near Paris as his dear parent.[1] It is too horrible, isn't it, to think that Goethe & Nietzsche belonged to this race who have put themselves outside the ban of civilization?[2]

Well—when I found I was caught here I moved over to 53, & we got a little cook, & took in Minnie & her maid, who were also in Paris. They went to England the day before yesterday, & poor Bessy Lodge & her children are also there, imprisoned with the dread In-laws. What an ending to her happy year!

Nearly all my friends are with their regiments, & the over-ages, such as Rodier, St. André, &c &c, are working all day at the Croix Rouge. I am also busy making muslin compresses for the Croix Rouge, & finding poor women to make shirts & pyjamas for them. I am trying to get up a little work-room for poor girls in this quarter, as they are all out of work—but no one has any money to give just yet! Luckily Herman was able to cable mine out to me, so I have had the pleasure of helping a little.

Lots of Americans are in Paris. Walter is here, very busy helping stranded compatriots, & new people turn up every day. The French people are admirable, & have developed unguessed qualities of coolness, courage & patience. The War Office gives out hardly any news, & no one thinks of complaining. They have announced today that there will be *no news* for the next day or two, so it is thought that a great battle is expected. It is very curious living under martial law, having to have every telegram visée at the Police Station, not being able to leave Paris in one's auto, having to speak French over the telephone, &c &c. There are German spies everywhere, & the other day I saw a crowd before the Astoria, & was told that a wireless plant had been found on the roof, & the manager, a German, shot immediately. There have been many other executions since, but little is said about them. It is *a fact* that German towns, a week ago, were placarded with the announcement that the French Senate had rejected the war vote, that Poincaré had been assassinated & that Paris was in full commune?![3] Travellers coming back from Germany have seen these notices, & German prisoners have said they had been told so. Here, on the contrary, the press admits that there is no news from Germany. Nothing can exceed the discretion, prudence & moderation of government, press & people. At this moment the French are indeed proving themselves to be the torch-bearing nation! It is thrilling to be among them, & see their great qualities put to the test so triumphantly.

I am so glad you had got away from Manassas & were on your way to Fanny Thayer when you wrote. I hope you have stayed there longer than a week. You say nothing about poor Mrs. Schultz, so I suppose there is no change. Your letter from N.Y. came yesterday, by the way— only 12 days on the way.

We are all well, & Tucker sends you a big hug.

Yr affte E.W.

1. Kaiser Wilhelm II (1859–1941) was the son of Wilhelm I (1797–1888), who had invaded Paris during the Franco-Prussian War in 1870–71.

2. According to Carol Singley, Wharton was "briefly captivated by Friedrich Nietzsche's celebration of the irrational and his radical critique of Christianity,"

and he was of help in "solving a spiritual crisis brought on by a passionate extra-marital affair" with Morton Fullerton (Singley, 17).

3. Raymond Poincaré (1860–1934) had been prime minister of France before being elected president of the republic in 1913, a position he still held when the war began. "Full commune" refers to 1871, when Paris was occupied by Prussia after a four-month siege. After the Prussians left the city, a popular government of the city took shape as the Paris Commune.

53, Rue de Varenne
Aug 24 [1914]

Dear Tonni,

You'll see from the enclosed that I am well & busy! My work-room has started off with a rush, & I now have over 5000 fcs in hand, & we are employing 30 women, getting orders for lingerie, &c — & all is going so well that I can contentedly leave for England on Thursday next. — So hereafter, address Stocks, Tring ("Herts" not necessary.)

You'll excuse my [not] writing more, as the work-room has used up all my time & strength. All well, & all send love.

Your affte,

E.W.

Attached by a straight pin to the letter is a letter to the editor of the New York Herald, *written by Wharton, headlined: "Help Is Appealed for, and Inquiries Are Made." Dated 21 August, the letter describes the workroom Wharton organized at 34 rue de Vaneau and lists the major donations she had received, many from her friends, totaling more than 3,000 French francs. It is a thank-you to donors and a plea for further donations of money and dressmaking materials to help her continue to employ—and feed—thirty Frenchwomen. Although Wharton claimed that the workroom had used up all her strength, it was only the first of many larger wartime charities she would found and manage.*

By the time of the next letter, both Russia and Japan had entered the war, and Russia was engaged against the Germans in the Battle of Tennenberg.

The Germans captured the Belgian city of Dinant on 23 August, and Belgian refugees were teeming into Paris. Wharton had relocated to England and was staying with her friend Howard Sturgis in Windsor.

Queen's Acre, Windsor
Aug. 29 [1914]

Dear Tonni,

Here I am safe in England with Gross & little Mrs. Tucker! I came over two days ago, going to Boulogne by motor. Walter came with me, & was to have crossed over to England, but when we reached Boulogne the news was so bad that he jumped into the motor & hurried back at once to Paris, to his sister [Nathalie Alden], who had just arrived from Vichy. I hope he is bringing her over today—if indeed it is still a possible thing to do!

This awful horror of destruction has come on us all in the last few days so suddenly that one is dazed.—I was weak enough to let Elise take a later train to Boulogne, & stop over to see her sister, & I don't yet know whether she has arrived, as I went to Rye the first night, & then came over here yesterday. White stayed in London yesterday to meet Elise, & I hope she is safely at Stocks by now. I am going there this afternoon with Minnie, whom I pick up in London on the way.

It is useless to suggest your coming back now. We must wait to see what turn things take. Here, all is outwardly serene, but they are at last beginning to understand that Germany is close to them.—

Well—perhaps the next few days will bring better news!—Little Mrs. Tucker sends a hug. She is well & jolly, & not a little proud of being on British soil, among the heroes of the battle of Mons, a number of whom came back with us the other day from Boulogne.

Your affte E.W.
Gross is well.

The French government left Paris and moved to Bordeaux, based on the advice of the French Army commander in chief, Joseph Joffre (1870–1931), whom Wharton knew.

Stocks, Tring

Sept 4th [1914]

Dear Tonni,

Your letter of Aug. 16th from Manassas, has just been returned to me from Paris. — I am so glad poor Mrs. Schultz died quickly & unconsciously, & that now you can close the door on that great sadness. You must be so happy for her that she has done with life. —

I rejoice that you received a little legacy, & that you mean to use it in getting some rest, & giving a good holiday to Fannie. May this plan have been carried out!

You will want to know about our trip. I have an idea I wrote you a line from Rye, but am not sure, as I was so unutterably tired when I reached England, & had so many notes to write, that my memory is blurred.

Anyhow, Gross & I left Paris in the motor on Aug 27, with Tucker. Walter came with me, & meant to come to England, but decided at Boulogne that he had better go straight back for his sister — but yes, I'm sure now I told you this. — Well, it was lucky he did, for I have just heard from Nathalie that they could get no place in any train, & so Cook motored them (her & her friend) to Dieppe on Sunday. I suppose he then went back to Paris, but I haven't heard yet, as letters come so slowly. Walter is in Paris, & means to stay. I quite understand his wanting to, & I wish I were there too! If I had ever dreamed of the developments of the last week I should never have left my work there. But when I left Paris it seemed that it wd be perfectly possible to go back whenever one wanted, & I didn't feel I was of much practical use there at that moment.

Well — it is lovely here, & I have Percy Lubbock with me, & other people are coming — but I am inconsolable at the thought of this awful calamity. There are persistent rumours that Russian troops have been pouring through England for 8 days past, on their way to join the Allies,

& people likely to know believe this. It seems the only hope!—I am heart-broken. My whole life was France, & all that France *was*.—But we must go on hoping.

I don't like to advise you to come just yet. Let us wait & see what the next month brings. I hope H. Edgar has given you regularly your $150 a month. If not, please write at once & ask for it.—He has luckily been able to send me my money as usual, so I am all right, & am going to take in some convalescent soldiers here.[1] Yours affly, E.W.

1. Wharton moved to London before she could arrange to take in convalescent soldiers.

The first Battle of the Marne, which would successfully halt the German advance for a while, was being fought, and the First Battle of Masurian Lakes began as well the day that Wharton wrote; Russia would ultimately lose the latter to Germany. Much of Belgium had been captured, and the city of Louvain had been devastated. Wharton was suffering from the dissonance between the peaceful beauty of her pastoral English surroundings and the chaos of war on the Continent, and she was longing to be closer to Paris.

Stocks
Sept 9 [1914]

Dear Tonni—At last the blackness has broken, & one can draw breath! So much hangs on the next few days that one daren't draw it aloud—but, any how, even the lapse of time is getting to be a bigger & bigger advantage every moment for the Allies—& one the Germans can least afford to let them have.

I have arranged to take the Wards' town house, 25 Grosvenor Place, S.W. for the rest of the season, & am moving up tomorrow while they come here. The weather is so lovely, & this place so perfect, that in some ways London will be depressing, but not so much so as to sit here, unable to write, & seeing, between me & these serene lawns & gardens, the perpetual vision of horror beyond the channel.

My Dear Governess

In London I shall have many friends, the nearer news, & be nearer Paris, to which I mean to go back as soon as it is possible to make the trip without risk of being stranded on the way. And then I think I may be of real use among the Belgian refugees, & that will be a comfort.

I hear from Paris every few days, & know that my work-room is open, & thriving, & that reassures me. — Percy Lubbock has very kindly stayed on, & will be with me till I leave tomorrow. Mr. James feels, as I do, that the country is unendurable, & he is coming up to London very soon — which will also be a comfort.

I do hope you were able to coax Fanny T. away for a while. — Won't you write to Mary Bagley, give her my love, & tell her about me? I will write soon, but I am so overwhelmed with letters from people asking how & where I am, that my pen falters! —

Yours affly, E.W.

Tucker lies at my side (in the garden) on her pink mat, wondering where luncheon is. Mrs. Berenson & Mr. Scott are motoring down to lunch with us.[1]

1. Geoffrey Scott (1883–1929) was a protégé of Bernard Berenson's, a renowned conversationalist, and said to be devastatingly handsome as well. Berenson's wife, Mary, was in love with him. Scott had recently published his first major work, *The Architecture of Humanism*. Late in the war he would move into Wharton's apartment and serve as her secretary.

25 Grosvenor Place S.W.
Sept 12th [1914]

Dear Tonni,

It is discouraging to find, from your letters of Aug. 23 & 31, just received, that you have heard nothing from me later than my cable of Aug 6th. I have written regularly & fully, & have received all your letters; but apparently the French out-going mails have been much more disorganized than the others. Perhaps later you will get all my letters in a bunch.

Now that it is once more possible to send half-rate cables, I have rushed one off to tell you that Tucker is safely & cheerfully here with me—but meanwhile you may have had a letter from me announcing her safe arrival in Great Britain.

I am so sorry you were not able to get Fanny T. away for a holiday. It is too bad to hug one's misery in that way—it so fatally attracts more!—My congratulations on the legacy—& may it prove more than $800! As executors' estimates are always conservative, it probably will! But I see no reason for "blowing" it all in at once with such ostentation. I don't know why you should stop my small remittance, & I hope you will at once revoke your instructions to H. Edgar. I am getting my money easily & regularly, & there has been no reduction in the amount.

It is too early yet to advise you what to do. We must await the result of the big battle going on now. My own plans are still uncertain. I moved up to the Ward's town house the day before yesterday, but as soon as I can go to Paris fairly easily I shall probably do so. There is nothing to be done here at present, as the immense influx of stricken Belgians has overwhelmed the Relief Committee & amateur helpers are not wanted.—Oh, if you knew the horrors perpetrated you would not fear anything Russia can do—you would only pray with all civilized people that the German Empire may be exterminated. I didn't believe the stories at first—but now they are too well authenticated. Belgian children arrived in Paris before I left with their hands cut off. Mme Forain, in one of the the hospitals in the north, has in her care a man with his eyes put out & his ears cut off. Lady Gladstone, whose husband is chairman of the Belgian Relief Committee, told R. Norton she had seen a Belgian woman with her ears cut off. Mrs. Cooper Hewitt had under her care in her Paris hospital a girl violated by six men under her parents' eyes. The mutilations of soldiers are innumerable. It is a vast sadic orgy, which no judicial people could believe in at first, but which, now the wounded & refugees are pouring in, is written up in awful letters before us.

You ask news of my friends. St. André & Rodier are in Paris, working hard at the Croix Rouge, Bélugou ditto.[1] Walter is there also, doing work on an international committee organized by Hanotaux to investigate & export the German violations of the right of nations.[2] He is probably also helping our Ambassador in various ways.

My Dear Governess

I don't know where Mme de Fitz-James is, but am trying to find out. Jean du Breuil was last week with his regiment waiting to be sent to the front.[3] John Hugh-Smith has volunteered, & is with his regiment in Yorkshire. He comes to town tomorrow on leave, & I shall see him.

England seemed hardly alive to the war when I reached here, but that glorious retreat from Mons has roused her, & she is putting forth her strength.

I am glad to be in town, & see how wise I was not to try to stay alone in the country at such a time. Mr. James is coming to stay with me next week, & later I shall have Percy Lubbock again, & Geoffrey Scott. — The Berensons are at Arundel, & I am motoring down to lunch with them tomorrow.

I also go to Windsor often, & see people as much as I choose to, for every one is here, or passing through.

I do hope this letter will hit the mark!

Address here till "avis contraire."

Yours affly,

E.W.

I keep Gross busy, & she is very plucky, & worrying much less than in the beginning. She wrote you also, & hopes you got her letter. She is so happy to have Tucker here. I wish so much you were here to complete the group. This house is delightfully situated, overlooking the whole extent of Buckingham Palace Gardens, & full of air & light.

It occurs to me that the French P.O. *may* have suppressed my letters on account of your name, so I shall hereafter enclose to H. Edgar.

---

1. Wharton had known Léon Bélugou (1865–1934) since at least 1908. He was a friend of Morton Fullerton's, an engineer, journalist, and teacher. He assisted Wharton by finding a lawyer to handle her divorce and thereafter became a close and trusted friend (Lee, 297–99).

2. Gabriel Hanotaux (1853–1944), French historian and statesman.

3. Jean du Breuil de Saint-Germain (1873–1915) had traveled with Edith Wharton and Rosa de Fitz-James in Spain in 1912. He was part of Mme de Fitz-James's salon, and he was in love with the widow Bessy Lodge. Their chance for happi-

ness was cut short by his death in action at Arras. Edith Wharton eulogized him as having "always loved and sought justice" (Wegener, 204).

Wharton returned to Paris to discover that the directress of her ouvroir had closed the shop and absconded with all the funds, nearly $2,000. She soon reopened, and then expanded the organization, and in November, with a small international group of friends, founded her second charity, the American Hostels for Refugees (Price, 23–29).

53 Rue de Varenne
Oct 9 [1914]

Dearest Tonni,

I was glad to get your letter of Sept 24 from Plymouth. It came fairly quickly, & I hope now the mails will steadily improve. (It is more than can be said for my hand-writing, for I knit all day long, which does not conduce to an elegant calligraphy.)

I am literally *steeped* in the work of the ouvroir, which thrives & grows, & is now organized on really business like lines. It takes a lot of doing to run an atelier de couture for 50 women if you take to it late in life, but everybody is so kind & interested that there isn't a dull minute. I get there at 10 a.m., & from then till dinner I am busy every minute. I have two delightful girls to help me, one of whom, my "directrice," who is a skilled dress-maker, gets there at 8:30 & works till after 7. Mme Desbruissons has lent us a cutter, Elise cuts out every afternoon, & M Boccon Gibod works like a slave for us, & gives us free of charge the services of his "caissière"—for our accounts are already rather complicated![1]— We have skilled dress-makers & lingères, & also poor refugees from the ravaged towns, type-writers & stenographers who know as much about sewing as I do—which makes the atelier hard to run; but universal bonne volonté, & the intelligence of my assistants, help us over all difficulties. Gross runs around in the motor delivering orders & trying to buy wool (almost impossible), & Tucker *sometimes* keeps shop, but not often, as she does not like the chairs.

My Dear Governess

Excuse this short & egoistic letter, but I eat, sleep, talk, think, only ouvroir; & so with every one here. Each is attached to his little patch of work. Vandoyer has lost his brother, Mme Metman hers, Mme Scheikevitch hers—les devils se multiplient! But everyone is brave & steady & quiet, & the savages are going to be beaten—

I'm so glad you're *not* one of them!! Stay where you are for the present, knit me mittens & belly bands. You'll always find some one to bring them to Europe, & we can't have too many. Your affte EW

1. Wharton's friend André Boccon-Gibod was the attorney who secured her divorce from Teddy Wharton. He served as legal counsel to Wharton's charities during the war.

While Wharton was exhilarated and exhausted by her labor on behalf of the victims of war, Bahlmann, stuck in New York, felt displaced without any real work to do. Wharton declined to send for her because, as she told her niece Beatrix, "She's too ineradicably 'Boche'!" (26 October 1914).[1] *Bahlmann was naturally—as was Edith—devastated by the sight of her beloved German civilization turning monstrous and destructive. Bahlmann exercised her outrage by writing a passionate essay called "A Belated Remedy: An Unavailing Cry." Her argument was that Germany was overpopulated, that the country didn't have enough work to provide a living wage for all its families. The blame should fall to German women, she argued. While "motherhood claims our deepest reverence," nevertheless, if "in man philoprogenitiveness is unbounded, it becomes woman's duty to lead him to cultivate reasonable restraint" (5). In other words, if women would prevent men from making so many babies (and this at a time when contraception was still taboo), the babies would not have to become* Kanonenfutter, *cannon fodder. The logic of her argument is almost pitiably naïve and shows us the degree to which Bahlmann's intellectual faculties were failing. Still, she kept looking for ways to help with Wharton's relief efforts.*

1. "Boche" was a disparaging French term for a German.

53 Rue de Varenne
Oct 12th [1914]

Dear Tonni,

Your letter of Sept 29 has just come—not such a long time, as things go! Just about what we allow from Paris to London.

I am glad you have found something to do for the Belgians. If we all slaved night & day for them it would be but a drop of water for their agony. As for me, if I could stop working an hour a day I should never have the heart to look forward. But my work-room provides a steady grind which is sure now to last all winter. Orders come in very regularly, & we have about $1000 in the bank, so we are feeling cheerful, & the 50 are working away with a will. Zézette Du Bos, a charming girl, Mlle de Bormans, manage the "intelligence office" dept & the "manutention," Mlle Landormy runs the two big ateliers with a masterly hand, & I fill up the gaps.[1] I don't know if I told you when I last wrote that M. Boccon Gibod is one of our most devoted helpers, besides being a generous contributor. His caissière does our book-keeping, & he runs errands for us all day long.

Every afternoon at 5.30 White or Armand appears with a thermos full of tea, & we all picnic on my desk—for the work begins at 10 & lasts till 6.

The day before yesterday (Sat. p.m.) Walter & I motored down to see the Gays, who have stuck faithfully to the Bréau, though the fighting was so near them. We spent the night there, & on Sunday motored to La Ferté-Gaucher, Montmirail & Meaux, & back to Paris. To do this required a strong "pull" at the Place de Paris, & the most elaborate passes. We went over the ground where much heavy fighting went on a few weeks ago, but strange to say saw no sign of it but several blown-up bridges & smashed motor lorries. The villages had escaped. It is very difficult to get motor permits on account of the spies, & it is only because I have an acquaintance on General Galliénié's [sic] staff that I was able to.[2]

I am very cross with you for refusing to accept your usual remittance. I am very well off, & goodness knows I shall need no dresses & give no dinners this winter—so don't be a goose, but ask H. Edgar to begin your usual stipend again as soon as this reaches you. I should like you to take a little flat somewhere near Fanny Thayer, unpack your furniture & make yourself comfortable for the winter, for as things look at present I don't think it advisable for you to come here.

I am all right ~~here~~, but your name *is* bad, & one doesn't really know yet that there won't be a return on Paris. So do settle down in New York comfortably for the winter.—Do a lot of knitting & send it out to me when you get the chance *by some one*—I don't believe parcels are delivered by express or post. Belly bands & socks (if you can make them?) are invaluable. You can surely hear of people coming now & then who would bring a few things gladly.—Of course hand-knitted sweaters are best of all, but they are very long to do, & expensive. Buy yourself $30 of wool for me, & go ahead anyhow! Ask H. Edgar to pay you for it.

I am sorry indeed that Fanny Thayer would not go away with you. Poor thing! It's rather late to become a militant suffragette. She must be the only one left in the world.[3]

We are all well, & Gross has some hope of hearing of her people through the Geneva Red Cross. Tucker sends you a hug.
Yrs Affty,

E.W.

Please send me from Scribner 2 copies of Mr. Brownell's new book, & have it charged to my account.[4] Books come easily.

Rodier is working at a hospital in Brittany & I sent him some money to buy tobacco for some Tunisian soldiers, & one of them sent me a "thank you" in Arabic!

1. Zézette du Bos was the wife of Wharton's friend and translator Charles Du Bos.

2. General Joseph Gallieni (1849–1916) had made his career in the French colonial empire. Except for his age—almost exactly Anna Bahlmann's age—he might have been made supreme commander of the French Army during the war. His strategy was considered crucial to the successful defense of Paris.

3. One of Edith Wharton's few remarks about woman suffrage, this shows how out of touch she was with the political climate of her own country. Women

would earn the right to vote in just five years, after seventy-two years of political action.

4. Edith Wharton's editor and friend William Crary Brownell had just published *Criticism*. In a tribute to Brownell after his death, Wharton wrote: "In all his writings he showed his essential quality: enthusiasm guided by acumen. He could not have been so great a critic had he not had so generous a nature" ("William C. Brownell," in Wegener, 209).

> Ouvroir de Mme
> Wharton
> Au Petit St. Thomas
> 25, Rue de L'Université
> Oct. 17, 1914

Dear Tonni,

I seize a rather rare morning off to send you more news—though it's always the same news, & will be while this outstretched struggle lasts.

We have all given up talking of the war. East & west, there's nothing left to say, & the bulletins get more laconic every day. Yesterday I was at our Chancery talking with the Ambassador when the afternoon communiqué came in. He put it directly into my hand, & it was only the same meager sliver that was served up later in all the papers.

So I've really nothing to tell you except that we're all well, that the ouvroir continues to flourish & grow bigger, & that I spend all my days there.

Few people, of my friends at least, have come back to Paris. Most of them are awaiting events in the north east, I fancy! But I couldn't rot in the country, & I'd rather be here than anywhere.—Last Sat. Walter & I motored down to the Gays at Le Bréau. They hadn't seen a soul for a month, & they are not even allowed to motor to Melun (see next paper) so strict are the military regulations in their district. [inserted at the top of the page: "I got my permit from the military governor of Paris."] One can't wonder, seeing that the millions of "Kub" advertisements we have been seeing all over France for the last six months (with a cow underneath the mysterious word) have turned out to be plans of the principal French farms with map of the environs! They were every-where about Melun, which is an important railway centre. Of course it was the old dodge of looking at the picture at a certain angle, & seeing the map come out.[1]

Well—we spent the night there, & then motored out the next day to the battle grounds of La Ferté Gaucher & Montmirail. Hardly any traces of war except three blown up bridges & a few holes in the Château of Montmirail. It seems it is like that now, unless the Germans willfully burn & destroy. Nobody fights in the houses, as they used to, & consequently the villages are unscratched unless they are deliberately destroyed. The country looked as calm & sweet as when I came there from Spain. Not a hay stack was burned, & the ploughing was going on. The roads were undamaged, & only a few skeletons of motors lay in the ditches. If only it had been like that in Belgium!

The cook boy, Roger, goes off tomorrow to join the 1915 class. But of course he won't have any fighting for months, we'll hope never.—I may have told you all this in my last letter, for I forget when I write to people. If I did, excuse the monotony of the tale. St. André, Fullerton, & Walter are almost the only people I see. The Gays stayed with me two nights this week, & are now in England—& so is Walter for a few days—Best love, E.W.

1. This is likely to have been rumor rather than fact.

It was finally safe for Anna Bahlmann to return to Paris, but she did so at the cost of a family Christmas in Missouri. She wrote to her niece, Anna Bahlmann Parker:

Dearest Annchen,

Your letter brought the tears to my eyes, & I can only repeat that I am terribly disappointed at not going to see you this winter. It is a sat-isfaction, at least, to see that you understand the situation & feel that I must go. . . . Please thank all the members of the family who contrib-

uted toward the ten dollars. I shall take it with me & convert it into warm caps & shawls for the refugees; & you may rest assured that no Christmas present could have pleased me better. . . . I'm sorry that I am too tired to write you as fully as I want to, but you will read between the lines how much love this letter carries you. (9 December 1914)

Once Bahlmann arrived in Paris, she took on an almost crushing burden of work. Wharton was at the peak of her executive powers and probably needed two or three energetic assistants. Bahlmann, now nearly sixty-six, simply couldn't keep up with the frenzy of Wharton's activities, and the relationship grew strained. Edith tried to get Anna to have her hearing tested, but Anna refused to make the appointment. Edith railed (privately, to friends) at the space Anna took up in her apartment, which left her less room to accommodate guests, and after a while she began to complain that Anna did not record names of donors properly, took too long at dictation, and showed other signs of waning powers. Edith Wharton, about whom Anna Bahlmann had once said "her kindness & her powers of organization are directed in twenty directions, so that while her body rests, her mind does the work of ten people" (to Sarah Norton, 30 November 1906), was functioning at superhuman levels, and she wanted those around her to do the same.

But for Bahlmann it was impossible, as one can see in her letter to her brother William, excerpted here.

April 7th [1915]
My dear Captain,

The letter you finished on March 2nd found me chasing from the prefecture to the commissioner of police, in consequence of a new regulation for aliens, namely: the permit to stay in France which I procured on arriving, had now to be furnished with my photograph, which in turn had to be inspected & stamped by a series of police officials, & as the notice was given out only a week before the expiration (March 21st) of the term set, you may imagine the scurrying on the part of all foreigners, the interminable waiting, etc. etc. The French habit of "shutting up shop" from 12 till 2 in order that luncheon may be enjoyed, added an-

other complication. When that was over I expected to pay off some of my letter debts, when there came the news of the Ypres children, an account of which was in the Paris Herald I sent you. The Belgian Prime Minister told Mrs. Wharton about the children, & she used her name & influence to good purpose. Her letter was copied by several French papers, &, as usual, the very poor responded most generously, relatively. Our success has been overwhelming, more than 10,000 fcs having been received, much of this in 1, 2 & 5 franc pieces. It came near being the death of me, however, for in the last ten days I have opened over a thousand bundles, put their contents on a list & sent receipts to the donors; sorted the worn clothes from new garments & food supplies, & it was no joke for my rheumatic knee. But of course I was glad to help in that way, since it was out of the question for Mrs. Wharton to neglect her daily work at her Ouvroir & at the American Hostels. The things for the children are being sent to Ypres in installments & the money is being used to house them in barns & convents or any buildings with roofs left, under the care of some Sisters of Charity. Well, as I handled a good deal of dirty paper, I suppose I got a germ, for I have had an atrocious cold, with hacking cough, have been shut up in my room four days, but have now turned the corner & expect to go downstairs tomorrow.

Could Wharton, who relied on servants and others to handle bureaucratic problems and manual labor, have understood the strain placed on Bahlmann? It's hard to know. As Anna's letter suggests, Wharton was embarking on her third major charitable endeavor, the Children of Flanders Rescue Committee, which would house, feed, and educate hundreds of children and care for elderly refugees. She wrote a story for Scribner's about the war, "Coming Home," and began to collect writing and art work from noted friends for a book that could be sold as a fund-raiser. She also toured the war zones.

Postcard of Cassel—
Porte de Bergues
Cassel
21 juin lundi [Monday,
21 June 1915]

Merveilleux voyage, temp radieux. A Berck vu Léon et Mme Wender, tous deux bien contents de ma visite. Demain soir Dunkerque. Serons de retour vendredi pour diner. Pensées affectueuses, E.W. [Marvelous trip, weather radiant. At Berck saw Léon {Bélugou} and Mrs. Wender, both happy with my visit. Tomorrow evening Dunkerque. We will return Friday for supper. Affectionate thoughts]

While Wharton's postcard makes it sound—perhaps for the benefit of censors—as if she is on vacation, actually she was carrying supplies to and touring the front, gathering material for the essays about the war and the look of France that she was writing for Scribner's *and which would be collected in* Fighting France *(1915). Cassel was the headquarters of the British army, from which they conducted the northern part of the war on the Western Front. Wharton was traveling with Walter Berry, and the day this was written she toured the ruins of Poperinghe and then Ypres, Belgium, about which she wrote: "We had seen other ruined towns, but none like this. . . . Ypres has been bombarded to death, and the outer walls of its houses are still standing, so that it presents the distant semblance of a living city, while near by it is seen to be a disemboweled corpse. Every window-pane is smashed, nearly every building unroofed, and some house-fronts are sliced clean off, with the different stories exposed, as if for the stage-setting of a farce. In these exposed interiors the poor little household gods shiver and blink like owls surprised in a hollow tree" (FF, 152–53). About Cassel itself she wrote: "It is one of the most detestable things about war that everything connected with it, except the death and ruin that result, is such a heightening of life, so visually stimulating and absorbing. 'It was gay and terrible,' is the phrase forever recurring in 'War and Peace'; and the gaiety of war was everywhere in Cassel, trans-*

forming the lifeless little town into a romantic stage-setting full of the flash of
arms and the virile animation of young faces" (FF, 146).[1]

In June, Anna Bahlmann was diagnosed with breast cancer; an opera-
tion in July revealed that the cancer had spread. Nevertheless, she went back
to work within a month of her surgery and remained in Paris until the fall.
Wharton urged her then to return to the United States to avoid having her
rheumatism aggravated by the cold damp Paris winter. It is probable that
Wharton was, by that time, also glad to be able to replace Bahlmann's services
as secretary, having expressed in letters to friends her frustration at how slowly
Anna worked and how many mistakes she was making in recording dona-
tions. Wharton expected nothing less than total devotion and competence in
all the people who surrounded her, but in truth, very few could keep up with
her activity. And Bahlmann did not have the benefit of the occasional vaca-
tion, which Wharton enjoys on the western coast of France when she writes
this card.

1. Count Lev Nikolaevich (Leo) Tolstoy (1828–1910), *War and Peace* (1863–69).

> Postcard of Saint-
> Thegonnec (Finistère).
> Le Calvaire, XVI° siècle
> Brest
> Thursday 16 [September
> 1915]

Such a lovely trip yesterday from Trestraou here with a wonderful old
grey haunted castle at the end of the day. We went all through the country of the "Calvaires," of which this is one of the most famous. Today we
go to the Pointe de Raz, Douarnenez, &c, & spend the next two days at
Quimper. Good weather & such a blessed rest!

> Yours, E.W.

Anna Bahlmann returned to the United States in mid-November 1915. Be-
fore leaving she wrote a codicil to her will, explaining that her ship might be

torpedoed on the voyage and she wished to be sure that the last of the legacy from Mrs. Schultz would be accounted for in her estate. In witness to the codicil were the fine, clear hand of the butler Alfred White (who sailed with her) and the shakier hand of the chauffeur Charles Cook. Her ship arrived without incident.

Safely in New York, Bahlmann did some work for Wharton and gave a talk in Brooklyn about Wharton's war charities, sending the proceeds to France. Wharton's project for a gift book to be sold to benefit her war charities, The Book of the Homeless, *was coming to fruition, and she had started a fund to buy coal for those in need. Here Wharton enjoys another vacation in the south of France.*

> Postcard of La Cote
> d'Azur Hyères
> H. Costebelle Dec. 2
> [1915]

I'm down here basking for two or three weeks next door to the Bourgets'. It's lovelier than ever, & I wish you were here with me. Ms [Messieurs] Gide & Bélugou motored down with me & spent several days, & Mr. Norton joins me the day after tomorrow.[1]

Not a word from you or White yet, but I hope for a letter soon. — I never enjoyed sunshine & flowers so much. I should like to stay all winter. Much love. E.W.

1. The French author André Gide (1869–1951) was a new friend of Wharton's who was helping with her charities. She once described him as a "mass of quivering susceptibilities" (*EWAZ*, 102).

> Postal card, no picture
> Paris
> Dec 29 [1915]

The delightful Xmas box arrived duly by White, & Nicette & I send you all our thanks & appreciation of everything, especially the turkey & the "clips." I wish I cd write a real letter, but the gov't has taken the

Petit St. Thomas building, & is turning me out in 2 days, & I can't send more than this. I am so interested & delighted in the idea of your giving "talks" & the beautiful result of the one in Brooklyn. It is going to the Enfants de Flandres. All well here, Mr. Norton staying with me & M. Rodier coming next week. Best love, E.W.

Anna Bahlmann went to see her friends the Tuckers in Virginia, where she gave another talk to raise funds for Wharton's war charities. Then, in February 1916, she made the long train journey to Missouri to stay with her niece Anna Bahlmann Parker and family. This letter from Bahlmann to her former pupil Pauline Robinson, here in its entirety, reveals her state of mind as well as the circumstances of her family life, so different from her life with Edith Wharton.

Kansas City, Missouri
Feb. 6 [1916]

My dearest Pauline,

You may like to know that I am settled here, after a longer sojourn at Norfolk than I had expected. My friends, the Tuckers worked hard to get me an audience for my "talk" on the relief work in Paris, with the result that we were offered a school-building, one man lent us the seats, the printers printed the tickets, gratis, & the Belgian consul bought 15 of them; & when everything was ready those confounded suffragists chose the very day & hour for a monster meeting; & as Norfolk is honey-combed with women's clubs, we had to postpone our affair. The rector had advised our asking 25¢ a ticket, as everybody, after Christmas, feels so poor. Well, the place was packed, we had all the F.F.V.'s [first families of Virginia], & I was able to send Mrs. Wharton $36. Of course you've seen what a success "The Book of the Homeless" has been. Did you read its touching preface & Gen. Joffre's letter?

Well, I finally started for the West, knitting mufflers through the long Pullman days & pondering on the strange ways, the barbarous & the superfine, I encountered. For instance, the train-porter brings you every day a new oiled-paper bag to put your hat in & keep it from the dust; the dressing-rooms have piles of sterilized individual drinking-cups, but the food in the dining-cars is uneatable. Three generations met me at the station when I arrived ten days ago. I found my niece & one of the children suffering from ptomaine poison, & the former now has bronchitis, while I have added a new stunt to my repertory & am enjoying what the doctor calls intercostals neuralgia. But that, too, will pass & when I am well enough to go out, & people begin to call, I shall find out what prospects there are for another "talk." My niece's three-story house has a "yard" on all four sides, with a park across the way & a trolley-line between, & is really pretty & practical; & if there were some doors between the hall, the two parlors & the dining-room, it would be quite charming. But Americans like living on a tea-tray & never feel the want of privacy. There are two bathrooms & eight bedrooms: mine is large & cheerful, & my niece has filled it with all sorts of contrivances for comfort, even to an electric reading-lamp by the bed. The people here are proud of their natural gas (*not* the human kind) which is supplied to the houses by pipe-lines & does the cooking without ashes or dirt. But just at present, owing to a break in the main line & the frozen ground, the gas is unreliable & meals "might unsartin." As for servants, no one but millionaires can have them, & my niece, like her neighbours, has a young girl from the country (I beg her pardon, "a young lady") who is studying stenography, etc. at the High School, & who, in return for her room & board, washes the dishes & puts the food on the table, all the rest of the work being done by the mistress of the house.

If it didn't hurt so to take a long breath, I should enjoy a good laugh at the weather. In Norfolk it was so warm that the violets were coming out, & it rained all the time; here we are fixed on zero, & it rains every day, each down-pour adding a new sheet of sleet to the pavement; &, as usual, the oldest inhabitant cannot remember such a wet winter! I'm sure if I travelled to the moon, I should carry rain to those waterless wastes.

All this time I'm wondering how you are, & my thoughts make their faithful rounds to all my old friends. I fear you are having the usual "downs-&-ups" in temperature. How are your mother & dear Anna & Herr Baby, & your father & Beverley? And do you still hear from Paul? Do write me some day when time & inclination agree, & meanwhile please give my love to all your family & all my wishes for their health. Ever your affectionate old friend,

Anna Bahlmann.

P.S. Don't you think the outlook in Europe is very black? At Norfolk I saw several groups of Germans, on shore leave for the day from the ships that are interned there, & it angered me to see their stature & superb bearing, as compared with the slouching Americans of the streets.

It was the last full letter from Anna Bahlmann that anyone saved. Anna Catherine Bahlmann died suddenly and unexpectedly on 15 April, after falling unconscious several hours earlier. Her niece cabled Minnie Jones, who in turn cabled Edith Wharton. This was Wharton's reply.

HEART BROKEN PLEASE SEND FAMILY PROFOUND SYMPATHY
WHARTON

The next day Wharton wrote to her sister-in-law.

Golf Hôtel Beauvallon
s/Mer
April 17, 1916

Dear Minnie,

I was really stunned by the news of Anna's death, coming so suddenly, & so soon after Egerton's. Not that I "wish her back"—heaven forbid! There was only suffering ahead, & she had no illusions about it, & this is the very end she prayed, but dared not hope, for. Only I wish she had stayed here, & I could have been with her to the end. Kansas City could never have seemed as much like home to her as the rue de V., where she was—I won't say "comfortable," for that she resolutely refused to be—but at least used to things, & properly waited on. Poor little unquiet bewildered & tender soul! I wish I could have done more for her this last hard year. . . .

It was a season of death. The war had claimed many friends and children of friends, including Jean du Breuil, who had been in love with Bessy Lodge, and Robert d'Humières, who had been in the process of translating The Custom of the Country *into French when he was called up. Wharton's footman, Henri, was also killed. Closer to her heart were two dear old friends, victims of age rather than war. Henry James died in England in late February 1916, followed in March by Egerton Winthrop.*

Even before the war, great craters of human loss had marked the landscape of Edith Wharton's life, from the death of her beloved father when she was eighteen to the shocking disloyalty and rejection by her oldest brother, Frederic, when he chose to divorce Minnie and persuaded their mother to take his side against Wharton in the long financial struggle that ensued. Lucretia all but broke off relations with her only daughter and died unreconciled to Wharton, who had devoted her first thirty years to caring for her mother. Next Wharton's brother Harry, a longtime bachelor and ally in the argument against Freddy's remarriage, himself settled down with a disreputable woman who was successful in her mission to alienate him from Wharton in the hope of keeping all of the family money for herself. This estrangement from her favorite brother pained Wharton deeply. Add to these losses her choice for lover of a man incapable of fidelity and unworthy of her trust and, perhaps most disturbing, her husband Teddy's devastating decline into an unknowable stranger, and we can understand Edith Wharton's perception late in life of isolation and settled loneliness. It is no wonder she wrote harshly of her mother in her memoir and downplayed her reliance on Anna Bahlmann.

At the time of Anna's death, however, Wharton wrote to her friend Lizzie Cameron, "I am completely crushed by this last blow. It is an unhoped-for blessing that that my poor little Anna should have died so quickly & painlessly, & I can't regret her death, but—I do so grieve for her having been away from me" (quoted in Price, 90–91). She wrote to Bahlmann's niece as well.

Golf Hôtel Beauvallon
s/Mer
April 17th [1916]

Dear Mrs. Parker,

The cable announcing Anna's death came last night, & you can imagine the shock it gave me. I was so reassured by your letter that I was looking forward to the possibility of seeing her here again as soon as it was safe for her to cross; & only last week I wrote her a long letter, telling her all my gratitude for the share I know she must have had in obtaining for the Hostels a generous gift from the Kansas City Relief Fund.

You know, to some degree at least, what Anna has been to me for so many years, what a friend & helper & companion, & you will understand how it adds to my sorrow that she should not have been with me when the end came. Yet I am glad for her sake, & for yours & your father's, that you were all together for the last months of her life, after so many years of separation; & her letters show me how happy she was in this reunion, & how much your affection & your devoted care were appreciated by her. I let her go reluctantly, & only because of her insistence, & because I thought she might be right in thinking that the Paris winter climate aggravated her rheumatism; & I was much worried at the idea of her undertaking so long a journey. But, alas, I think for a long time the end had been inevitable, & I can only be thankful that it came suddenly, since I know she foresaw & dreaded much suffering in the months to come.

I shall never have a friend like her, so devoted, so unselfish, so upright, so sensitive & fine in every thought & feeling. — I send you all my deepest sympathy, dear Mrs. Parker.

Yrs very sincerely,

Edith Wharton

If it does not interfere with any arrangements of yours, I should like to put up a simple marble headstone, & of course bear any expenses connected with her illness, the funeral &c. She accepted so little from me during her life that I should like to do this.

Although her will indicated a wish to be cremated, Bahlmann was buried in Warrensburg, Missouri. Her tombstone, designed by Wharton's niece Beatrix Farrand, reads: "Anna Bahlmann. Born March 5th 1849. Died April 15th 1916. In loving remembrance of her Goodness, her Patience, and her Courage. This stone is placed here by her friend and pupil, Edith Wharton."[1]

Anna Bahlmann left two boxes of books at Minnie Jones's house, a silver patch box and one brooch in Edith Wharton's safe, a few hundred dollars in her bank account, and several folders of letters, most of them from Edith Wharton. Her former pupil Beverley Robinson settled her estate, being co-executor with her friend Fanny Thayer.

Edith Wharton lived on in Paris and the south of France for twenty-one years. She wrote many more novels, stories, and poems, and an autobiography in which she mentioned Anna Bahlmann by name only once, but referred to her as "my dear governess."

1. Correspondence with Beatrix Farrand, who designed Anna's tombstone, indicates that the final sentence of the epitaph was suggested by Wharton because she thought it would please Bahlmann's family, who were proud of Anna's long association with the famous author. Wharton herself preferred to leave it off, and she left the delicate negotiation in Beatrix's capable hands, with the result that, at the family's request, Anna's name remained linked to Edith's even in the grave.

BIBLIOGRAPHY

Auchincloss, Louis. *Edith Wharton: A Woman in Her Time.* New York: Viking, 1971.

Bahlmann, Anna Catherine. "A Belated Remedy: An Unavailing Cry." MS. YCAL Bahlmann.

———. Clothing ledger. MS. YCAL Bahlmann.

———. "Cousins." MS. YCAL Bahlmann.

———. Financial ledger. MS. YCAL Bahlmann.

———. Letter to Myra Abbott. 26 June 1882. MS. YCAL Bahlmann.

———. Letters to Lydia Abbott Bahlmann. 18 October 1874, 25 July 1875. MS. Transcriptions supplied by Laura Shoffner.

———. Letters to William F. Bahlmann, various dates. MS. YCAL Bahlmann.

———. Letter to Robert Bridges. 21 November 1914. MS. Archive of Charles Scribner's Sons. Manuscripts Division, Department of Rare Books and Special Collections, Princeton University Library (hereafter Scribner's Princeton).

———. Letter to William C. Brownell. 31 January 1910. MS. Scribner's Princeton.

———. Letter to Sarah Norton. 30 November 1906. MS. YCAL Wharton.

———. Postcard to Charles Parker, Jr. Undated, MS. YCAL Bahlmann.

———. Letter to Beverley R. Robinson. 21 August 1894. MS. Robinson Family Papers, NYHS (hereafter Robinson NYHS).

———. Letter to Pauline Robinson. 6 February 1916. MS. Robinson NYHS.

———. Report card for Anna Robinson, 1896–97. MS. Robinson NYHS.

Bahlmann, William F. "Autobiography of William Frederick Bahlmann." N.d. MS. YCAL Bahlmann.

Bell, Millicent. *Edith Wharton and Henry James: The Story of Their Friendship.* New York: Braziller, 1965.

Benstock, Shari. *No Gifts from Chance.* New York: Scribner's, 1994.

Berenson, Mary. Letter to Bernard Berenson. 23 July 1915. MS. The Berenson Archive, The Harvard University Center for Italian Renaissance Studies, Villa I Tatti.

"Bernhardt as Gismonda." *New York Times,* 16 November 1894. Online.

Berry, Walter. Postcard to Edith Wharton. 1923. MS. YCAL Wharton.

Brandon, Ruth. *Governess: The Lives and Times of the Real Jane Eyres.* New York: Walker, 2008.

Brettell, Caroline. "Elsie Clews Parsons." Barn at Stonover Farm, Lenox, Massachusetts. 10 August 2010. Lecture.

Brown, Jane. *Beatrix: The Gardening Life of Beatrix Jones Farrand, 1872–1959.* New York: Viking, 1995.

Chanler, Mrs. Winthrop [Margaret Terry]. *Autumn in the Valley.* Boston: Little Brown, 1936.

———. *Roman Spring.* Boston: Little Brown, 1934.

Conant, Alan Jasper, et al. *The Commonwealth of Missouri: A Centennial Record.* Bryan Brand, 1877. Online (Google Books).

"Dancing at Delmonico's." *New York Times,* 6 January 1891. Online.

Duffy, Michael, ed. The First World War. Online (www.firstworldwar.com).

Dwight, Eleanor. *Edith Wharton: An Extraordinary Life.* New York: Abrams, 1994.

Edel, Leon. *Henry James: The Master, 1901–1916.* New York: Avon, 1972.

Editor, Charles Scribner's Sons. Letter to Edith Wharton. 10 Oct 1913. MS. Scribner's Princeton.

Fullerton, William Morton. Letter to Anna Bahlmann. 29 March 1914. MS. YCAL Bahlmann.

Garrison, Stephen. *Edith Wharton: A Descriptive Bibliography.* Pittsburgh: University of Pittsburgh Press, 1990.

Goldman-Price, Irene. "Young Edith Jones: Sources and Texts of Early Poems by Edith Wharton." *Resources for American Literary Study* 34 (2011): 95–106.

Goodman, Susan. *Edith Wharton's Inner Circle.* Austin: University of Texas Press, 1994.

Gouverneur, Marian. *As I Remember: Recollections of American Society during the Nineteenth Century.* New York: Appleton, 1911.

Halsey, Francis Whiting. *The Literary Digest History of the World War.* Vol. 1. New York: Funk and Wagnalls, 1920.

Harden, Edgar F. *An Edith Wharton Chronology.* Basingstoke, Hampshire, England: Palgrave Macmillan, 2005.

Homberger, Eric. *Mrs. Astor's New York: Money and Social Power in a Gilded Age.* New Haven: Yale University Press, 2002.

Horne, Philip, ed. *Henry James: A Life in Letters.* London: Penguin, 1999.

Hughes, Kathryn. *The Victorian Governess.* London: Hambledon, 1993.

Jay, Cynthia. "Laura Chanler's education." E-mail to the author, 20 September 2010.

Jones, Lucretia. Letter to Pauline Robinson. 13 January 1897. MS. Robinson NYHS.

Jones, Mary Cadwalader. *Lantern Slides.* Boston: Merrymount (privately printed), 1937.

Joslin, Katherine. *Edith Wharton and the Making of Fashion.* Durham: University of New Hampshire Press, 2009.

Keller, Gottfried. *A Village Romeo and Juliet.* Trans. A. C. Bahlmann. New York: Scribner's, 1914.

King, Greg. *A Season of Splendor: The Court of Mrs. Astor in Gilded Age New York.* New York: Wiley, 2009.

King, Moses. *King's Handbook of New York City, 1892.* 1892. Rpt. New York: Barnes and Noble, n.d.

Lee, Hermione. *Edith Wharton.* New York: Knopf, 2007.

Lehr, Elizabeth Drexel. *"King" Lehr and the Gilded Age.* New York: Blue Ribbon, 1935.

Lewis, R. W. B. *Edith Wharton: A Biography.* New York: Harper, 1975.

Lubbock, Percy. *Portrait of Edith Wharton.* New York: Appleton-Century, 1947.

March, Francis A., with Richard Beamish. *History of the World War.* Philadelphia: United Publishers of the United States and Canada, 1919.

Marshall, Scott. *The Mount: Home of Edith Wharton.* Lenox, Mass.: Edith Wharton Restoration, 1997.

McClelland, Averil Evans. *The Education of Women in the United States.* New York: Garland, 1992.

Nadel, Stanley. *Little Germany: Ethnicity, Religion, and Class in New York City, 1845–80.* Urbana: University of Illinois Press, 1990.

"Portraits Much Admired." *New York Times,* 3 November 1894. Online.

Powers, Lyall, ed. *Henry James and Edith Wharton Letters, 1900–1915.* New York: Scribner's 1990.

"Pre-Raphaelite Pictures." *New York Times,* 8 January 1893. Online.

Price, Alan. *The End of the Age of Innocence: Edith Wharton and the First World War.* New York: St. Martin's, 1996.

Puknat, E. M., and S. B. Puknat. "Edith Wharton and Gottfried Keller." *Comparative Literature* 21 (1969): 245–54.

Ramsden, George. *Edith Wharton's Library.* Settrington, England: Stone Trough, 1999.

"Record of Amusements." *New York Times,* 14 March 1880. Online.

Robinson, Pauline L. Letters to Anna Bahlmann. Various dates. MS. YCAL Bahlmann.

———. Letters to Anna Foster Robinson and Beverley R. Robinson. Various dates. MS. Robinson NYHS.

Rutherfurd, Margaret S. C. Letter to Anna Bahlmann. 1–9 July 1873. MS. YCAL Bahlmann.

Sedgwick, John. *In My Blood: Six Generations of Madness and Desire in an American Family.* New York: Harper's, 2007.

Singley, Carol. *Edith Wharton: Matters of Mind and Spirit.* Cambridge: Cambridge University Press, 1995.

Skaggs, Merrill M. "Viola Roseboro: A Prototype for Cather's *My Mortal Enemy.*" *Mississippi Quarterly* 54 (2000–2001): 5–21.

Sloane, Florence Adele, and Louis Auchincloss, eds. *Maverick in Mauve: The Diary of a Romantic Age.* New York: Doubleday, 1983.

Stuyvesant, Mary Pierrepont. Letter to Margaret S. C. Rutherfurd. 30 August 1873. MS. Rutherfurd Family Papers, NYHS (hereafter Rutherfurd NYHS).

Stuyvesant, Rutherfurd. Letter to Margaret S. C. Rutherfurd. 19 and 29 August 1873. MS. Rutherfurd NYHS.

Tankard, Judith B. *Beatrix Farrand: Private Gardens, Public Landscapes.* New York: Monacelli, 2009.

Towheed, Shafquat. *The Correspondence of Edith Wharton and Macmillan, 1901–30.* Basingstoke, Hampshire, England: Palgrave Macmillan, 2007.

Tuttleton, James, Kristin O. Lauer, and Margaret P. Murray, eds. *Edith Wharton: The Contemporary Reviews.* Cambridge: Cambridge University Press, 1992.

Van Rensselaer, Mrs. John King, with Frederic van de Water. *The Social Ladder.* New York: Holt, 1924.

Wegener, Frederick, ed. *Edith Wharton: The Uncollected Critical Writings.* Princeton: Princeton University Press, 1996.

Wharton, Edith. *A Backward Glance.* New York: Scribner's, 1934.

———, ed. *Book of the Homeless.* New York: Scribner's, 1916.

———. *The Cruise of the Vanadis.* Jonas Dovydenas, photographer. New York: Rizzoli, 2004.

———. *The Decoration of Houses.* With Ogden Codman, Jr. New York: Scribner's, 1897.

———. Diary, 1924. MS. YCAL Wharton.

———. *Fast and Loose.* 1877. Charlottesville: University Press of Virginia, 1993.

———. *Fighting France.* New York: Scribner's, 1915.

———. "La Folle du Logis." 1926. In *Selected Poems,* 98–101.

———. "The Fulness of Life." *Scribner's Magazine* 14 (1893): 699–704.

———. *George Eliot.* 1902. In Wegener, *Edith Wharton,* 71–78.

———. "Gifts." In *Selected Poems,* 149.

———. *Italian Backgrounds.* 1905. Rpt. Hopewell, N.J.: Ecco, 1993.

————. Letters to Anna Bahlmann. Various dates. MS. YCAL Bahlmann.

————. Letter to Margaret Terry Chanler. 25 September 1902 or 1903. MS. YCAL Wharton.

————. Letter to Beatrix Farrand. 26 October 1914. MS. YCAL Wharton.

————. Letter to Mary Cadwalader Jones. 11 December 1914. MS. YCAL Wharton.

————. Letter to Eunice Maynard. 12 June 1913. YCAL Wharton.

————. Letter to Sarah Norton. 9 August 1903. YCAL Wharton.

————. *The Letters of Edith Wharton.* Ed. R. W. B. Lewis and Nancy Lewis. New York: Scribner's, 1988.

————. *Life and I.* In *Wharton: Novellas and Other Writings.* New York: Library of America, 1990. 1071–96.

————. "A Little Girl's New York." *Harper's Monthly Magazine,* March 1938, 356–64.

————. *A Motor Flight through France.* New York: Scribner's, 1908.

————. "Mrs. Manstey's View." *Scribner's Magazine* 10 (1891): 117–22.

————. *Selected Poems.* Ed. Louis Auchincloss. New York: Library of America, 2005.

————. "That Good May Come." *Scribner's Magazine* 15 (1894): 629–42.

Wharton, Edward R. Letter to Sarah Norton. 26 February 1907. YCAL Wharton.

————. Letter to Anna Bahlmann. 27 August 1908. YCAL Bahlmann.

Woody, Thomas. *A History of Women's Education in the United States.* New York: Science Press, 1929.

Wright, Sarah Bird. *Edith Wharton A to Z: The Essential Guide to the Life and Work.* New York: Facts on File, 1988.

————. *Edith Wharton's Travel Writing: The Making of a Connoisseur.* New York: St. Martin's, 1997.

ACKNOWLEDGMENTS

This project would have been impossible without the family of Anna Bahlmann, particularly the writer Laura Abbot Lyon Shoffner and Dr. Brent M. Parker, who preserved the letters and documents and who have been most generous in tracking down family history and in encouraging a full exploration of the story of Bahlmann's life.

Many people and institutions have assisted me with this project, and I am grateful for their help. I list them here in the order in which I encountered them. Chris Coover of Christie's was the first to allow me access to the material. The Beinecke Rare Book and Manuscript Library at Yale University supported my research with the Donald C. Gallup Fellowship in American Literature and all the resources and assistance that went with the fellowship. Beinecke curator Louise Bernard gave encouragement and practical assistance in finding funding and an outlet for publication. Archivist Michael Forstrom catalogued the material thoroughly and quickly so that I could work with it. Curator Kevin Repp helped to translate several passages in German, as did Christa and Jeffrey Sammons; Leah Jehan helped me with copying and other services; Eva Guggemos solved some knotty research problems; and the rest of the public service staff was uniformly helpful and friendly. Cynthia Russett, Larned Professor of History at Yale, shared thoughts on women's education. I thank my editor at Yale University Press, Ileene Smith, whose insistence on high-quality work made this a much better book. Her assistant, John Palmer, walked me through the publication process, and Dan Heaton's elegant copyediting enhanced the book. Others at the press promoted this project, and for their silent assistance I am grateful. Felicia Eth served as consultant and agent in the process of seeking a publisher.

The Edith Wharton Society awarded me a fellowship to travel to archives. Members of the Society, many of whom have been friends for decades, encouraged me by listening, writing on my behalf, reading and commenting on the manuscript in various iterations, and affording me opportunities to share my research. Donna Campbell, Hildegard Hoeller, Margaret Murray, Elsa Nettels, Julie Olin-Ammentorp, Melissa Pennell, Carole Shaffer-Koros, Carol Singley, and Gary Totten were particularly helpful. Special thanks go to Fred Wegener, who graciously read and commented on the entire manuscript. The staff at The Mount, Edith Wharton's house museum in Lenox, Massachusetts, welcomed me and provided many courtesies including access to Wharton's library. Susan Wissler, executive director, first alerted me to the letters and has offered encouragement through the entire process. Molly McFall and Ninke Dorhout, librarians, Anne Schuyler, house manager, and researcher Sarah Kogan were particularly helpful. The novelist Jennie Fields shared her imagination of Edith Wharton and Anna Bahlmann as well as offering practical and moral support during the writing process. Thanks to Laura Bush for her support of all things Wharton.

I visited numerous archives which accorded me cordial assistance, including the Firestone Library at Princeton University, the Lilly Library at Indiana University, the Redwood Library in Newport, the New-York Historical Society, the New York Public Library, and the Morgan Library. Archivists at Winterthur, the Environmental Design Archives at UC Berkeley, the National Portrait Gallery, the John Jay Homestead, and the University of Virginia assisted me via e-mail. I appreciate assistance from the Lenox Public Library and the Pittsfield Athenaeum. Other writers and historians who gave of their time and expertise include Cornelia Brooke Gilder, Judith Tankard, and Connie Wooldridge. John Arthur helped put me in touch with Cynthia Jay, who shared family history and insights, and Keren Weiner assisted me with genealogical research. I am grateful to Julia Masnik at Watkins Loomis for securing the necessary permissions.

Many colleagues and friends gave time and a ready ear while I was working on this project (and forgave me when I did not have enough time for them), among them Richard Dutton, Richard Kopley, and Bruce Smith; Deborah, Deb, Bev, Kathy, Jerry, Elizabeth, Dave, Karen, and Joy. No one assisted me more than my cherished husband and companion, himself a talented scholar, Alan Price. The book is the better for all of their help; any remaining weaknesses are, of course, my own.

Acknowledgments

CREDITS AND PERMISSIONS

The previously unpublished letters of Edith Wharton to Anna Bahlmann, various excerpts from other letters and works by Edith Wharton, and all images of Wharton are published here with the permission of the estate of Edith Wharton and the Watkins/Loomis Agency. An excerpt of a letter dated 23 July 1915 from Mary Berenson to Bernhard Berenson is published with the permission of The Berenson Archive, the Harvard University Center for Italian Renaissance Studies, Villa I Tatti, courtesy of the President and Fellows of Harvard College. Letters from Anna Bahlmann to William C. Brownell dated 13 February 1909 and 31 January 1910, from Anna Bahlmann to Charles Scribner's Sons dated 18 January 1909, from Anna Bahlmann to Robert Bridges dated 21 November 1914, and from Robert Bridges to Edith Wharton dated 10 October 1913 courtesy Archives of Charles Scribner's Sons, Manuscripts Division, Department of Rare Books and Special Collections, Princeton University Library. Letters from Mary P. Stuyvesant and Rutherfurd Stuyvesant to Margaret S. C. Rutherfurd dated August 1873 courtesy Stuyvesant Rutherfurd Papers, MS 605, New-York Historical Society. Letters from Pauline Robinson to Anna Foster Robinson and Beverley R. Robinson and letters from Anna Bahlmann to Pauline and Beverley Robinson courtesy Robinson Family Papers, New-York Historical Society. Drawing by Beatrix Farrand of Anna Bahlmann's headstone courtesy Beatrix Farrand Collection (1955–2) of the Environmental Design Archives, University of California, Berkeley. The portrait of Edith Newbold Jones Wharton by Edward Harrison May, courtesy National Portrait Gallery, Smithsonian Institution. The photograph of Edith and Edward Wharton with their dogs, courtesy Clifton Waller Barrett Library of American Literature, Special Collections, University of Virginia Library. The photographs of Edith Wharton in the snow and of Pen craig Cottage, courtesy of Lilly Library, Indiana University, Bloomington. The photograph of the William Bahlmann family courtesy of Laura Abbot Lyon Shoffner and Brent M. Parker. Anna Bahlmann's passport application comes from the National Archives by way of Ancestry.com.

INDEX

Bahlmann, Anna Catherine (cont.) lates Keller for Scribners, 241–42; travel to Europe, 188–89, 196–99, 213–20 passim; travel to North Africa, 242–43; will of, 269–70, 276; work during war, 248, 261, 262–63, 266–67, 270, 271–72

Bahlmann, Anna Louise. *See* Parker, Anna Bahlmann

Bahlmann, Lydia Abbot, 9, 10; letters to, 26, 85

Bahlmann, William, 8, 9, 10, 16; letter to, 266–67

Bain, Alexander, 150, 151n4

Balfour, Arthur James, 227

Barrie, James M., 228

Baylies, Mrs. Edmund. *See* Van Rensselaer, Louise

Beaumont, Francis, 29, 30n7

Bective, Lady, 228, 229n3

Bellay, Joachim du, 162

Bellini, Giovanni, 113

Belmont, Raymond, 42, 44n2

Bélugou, Léon, 258, 259n1, 268, 270

Berenson, Bernard, 236–37, 259

Berenson, Mary, 257, 259

Bernhardt, Sarah, 141

Berry, Walter, 143, 144, 151, 176, 179, 223, 224, 225, 244; first meets E.W., 61; moves into 53 r. de Varenne, 232; supports E. W.'s writing, 7–8, 171, 173; during the war, 249, 251–52, 254, 258, 262, 264, 265, 268

Berty, Adolphe, 151, 152

Bjornson, Bjornstjerne: *Der Handschur*, 127

Blanche, Jacques Émile, 211, 212n2, 225

Boccon-Gibod, André, 260, 261n1

Bosanquet, Theodora, 224

Botticelli, Sandro, 66

Boucher, François, 66, 108, 109

Bourget, Paul and Minnie, 118, 119, 142, 144, 184, 210, 243; travel with Whartons, 145, 181, 184–85, 191–92

Bouton, J. W., 92

Brassey, Anna, 42, 44n3

Breuil, Jean du, de Saint-Germain, 259; death of, 274

Bridges, Robert, 248

Brownell, William Crary, 171, 180, 192; *Criticism*, 263, 264n4

Browning, Robert, 51; "May and Death," 39

Brown-Séquard, Dr. Charles-Édouard, 66, 67n5

Brunetière, Ferdinand, 106, 107n1

Bryan, Michael, *Bryan's Dictionary of Painters and Engravers*, 109, 111n4

Bulwer-Lytton, Edward George: *What Will He Do With It?*, 43, 44n5

Bulwer-Lytton, Edward Robert, 39, 40n3, 54, 56

Burden, Mrs. Joseph (*née* Harriet Griswold), 214, 215

Burghclere, Lord and Lady, 228, 229n5

Burlingame, Edward L., 84n3, 97, 98, 118, 149, 174

Byron, George Gordon, Lord, 51

Cadwalader, John, 240, 241n1

Canfield, Augustus Cass, 194–95

Carvalho, Madame Miolan, 59, 60n1

Cather, Willa, 161n2

Centennial International Exhibition of 1876, 34, 35n2

Century Magazine: E. W. published in, 83, 84n3, 190

Chanler, Margaret Terry (Daisy), 2, 4; seeks governess for daughter, 190

Index

Jameson, Anna Brownell, 88, 89n1
Jay, Eleanor (Mrs. Arthur Iselin), 75n1, 167, 168, 169
Jay, Julia, 74, 75n1; illness and death of, 167, 168
Jay, Mrs. William (*née* Lucy Oelrichs), 18, 135, 164, 168
Jay, William, 74–75, 174
Jeune, Lady. *See* St. Helier, Lady
Joffre, General Joseph, 255, 271
Jones, Beatrix (Mrs. Max Farrand), 13, 18, 26, 29, 34, 36, 148, 151; designs A. C. B.'s tombstone, 276; designs gardens at The Mount, 189; and divorce of her parents, 158; and inheritance, 188, 241n1; marriage of, 239–40; and work, 162, 163n4, 164
Jones, Frederic Rhinelander, 25, 29, 54, 61; buys Pen craig, 179; divorce of, 156–57, 159–60, 188, 189, 274
Jones, George Frederic, 25 and passim; death of, 58, 274; supports E. W.'s writing, 6–7, 36
Jones, Henry Stevens (Harry), 21, 25, 64, 112, 208–9, and passim; and brother Fred's divorce, 158, 160; rift with E. W., 235–36, 274; supports E. W.'s writing, 6–7; travels with Whartons, 192, 193
Jones, Lucretia, 25, 122–23, 125, 139, 188, and passim; and A. C. B., 13, 17, 74, 101; breaks with E. W., 21, 158, 274; death of, 188; and Fred's divorce, 158, 160; in Paris with newlywed Whartons, 66, 68; supports E. W.'s writing, 6; and T. Wharton, 64
Jones, Mary Cadwalader (Minnie), 7, 25–26, 39, 61, 148, 195; and A. C. B., 18; book on the fan, 150, 151n2; and

daughter's marriage, 240; at death of A. C. B., 273, 276; divorce from Fred, 157–58, 159–60, 274; education of, 2–3; proofreads for E. W., 172; and the war, 249, 251

Kean, Katherine Winthrop (Mrs. Hamilton Fish), 18, 24n6
Keller, Gottfried: *A Village Romeo and Juliet,* 241–42
Kneeland, Adele, 166, 167n2
Kugler, Franz, 55, 56n3

La Farge, Margie, 122
Lancret, Nicholas, 109
Land's End, 101, 105, 118; possible sale of, 119; Whartons homesick for, 133, 142, 167; Whartons set up, 106, 109–10
Lapsley, Gaillard, 223, 224–25, 238, 242
Lavisse, Ernest & M. A. Rambaud: *Histoire Générale du IV Siècle à nos Jours,* 136, 138
lawn tennis, 32
Lee, Vernon, 123, 124, 140
Lefroy, Edward Craycroft, 179, 180n1
Le Maître, Jules, 106, 107n1
Le Nôtre, André, 115, 116n1
Lippincott's Magazine: E. W. published in, 173
Lodge, Elizabeth Frelinghuysen Davis (Bessie), 236, 237n1, 241, 243, 251; and Jean du Breuil, 259–60, 274
Lodge, George Cabot (Bay), 197
Longfellow, Henry Wadsworth, 45, 83–84; "The Masque of Pandora," 28–29
Lorenzetti, Ambrogio: "Good and Bad Government," 94